TRAITS OF A HEALTHY FAMILY

Fifteen Traits
Commonly Found in Healthy Families
By Those Who Work with Them

Dolores Curran

WINSTON PRESS

Cover design: Studio One

Library of Congress Catalog Card Number: 82-70489

ISBN: 0-86683-643-8

Printed in the United States of America.

5   4   3   2

Winston Press, Inc.
430 Oak Grove
Minneapolis, Minnesota 55403

TRAITS OF A HEALTHY FAMILY

Dedication

I dedicate this book to all families everywhere and to the goodness that exists within them. Without that goodness this book could not have been written.

I particularly dedicate this book to the family I know best and love most, my own. Their goodness, humor, and support buoyed me up when the typewriter let me down. While we don't claim to be the world's, or even the neighborhood's, healthiest family, it is in my husband, Jim, and my children, Teresa, Patrick, and Daniel, that I am most able to realize what being a family really means. To them I pen a public "Thank you" and an unabashed "I love you." Because I do.

Acknowledgments

My most obvious debt and gratitude goes to the 551 survey respondents who took the time to share with me their insights on what constitutes a healthy family. To them, most of whom I have never met, I owe a sincere thanks for devoting an hour of a busy professional day with children, parents, and families in order that other families might benefit.

I thank, too, those families with whom I have worked who answered my questions with patience, often protesting at the same time that they were no healthier than any other family. They will find their responses to my probing and their suggestions peppered throughout the book.

Equal indebtedness is due the many researchers and family authorities whose words are found in the pages of this book. While it is impossible to thank them all personally, I thank them here on behalf of all of us who work with families and all of us who live in families for their professional research and invaluable insights into family living.

Specifically and with great gratitude, I thank my friends and advisors who helped me to design and to interpret my survey and who shared professional insights from their specific field of family association: Deborah Bublitz, M.D., F.A.A.P.; James Curran, Ph.D.; Henry L. Fischer, Ph.D.; Barbara Flieger, R.N.; Gordon Flieger, M.S.; Charles H. Fraser, M.D., F.A.A.P.; Ann LeMoine, R.N., C.P.N.P.; Lois Shugart, M.A., M. Div. Finally, I thank my editor, Lois Welshons, for her sensitive and professional assistance in producing this book.

Contents

An Invitation to Families.....*ix*

1. Once Upon a Family.....*1*

2. The Search for Family Strengths.....*17*

3. Communicating.....*31*
   Trait 1: The healthy family communicates and listens.
   Trait 13: The healthy family fosters table time and conversation.

4. Affirming and Supporting.....*59*
   Trait 2: The healthy family affirms and supports one another.

5. Respecting Others.....*79*
   Trait 3: The healthy family teaches respect for others.

6. Trusting.....*99*
   Trait 4: The healthy family develops a sense of trust.

7. Sharing Time.....*117*
   Trait 5: The healthy family has a sense of play and humor.
   Trait 9: The healthy family has a balance of interaction among members.
   Trait 14: The healthy family shares leisure time.

8. Fostering Responsibility.....*165*
   Trait 6: The healthy family exhibits a sense of shared responsibility.

9. Teaching Morals.....*185*
   Trait 7: The healthy family teaches a sense of right and wrong.

10. Enjoying Traditions.....*199*
    Trait 8: The healthy family has a strong sense of family in which rituals and traditions abound.

11. Sharing Religion.....*217*
    Trait 10: The healthy family has a shared religious core.

12. Respecting Privacy.....*231*
    Trait 11: The healthy family respects the privacy of one another.

13. Valuing Service.....*243*
    Trait 12: The healthy family values service to others.

14. Getting Help.....*257*
    Trait 15: The healthy family admits to and seeks help with problems.

A Final Word.....*267*

Notes.....*269*

Sources.....*277*

Index.....*281*

An Invitation to Families

"What's good about families?" a newspaper reporter asked me. "All we ever hear about is what's wrong with them. Can families be good today?"

Yes, they can and they are. I meet and work with them every week in seminars, classes, and conferences. They have a strength and goodness that shines through their lives, but they share a common parental pitfall—they focus on disappointments and weaknesses rather than joys and strengths. They can tell me in a minute what's wrong with them, but they aren't sure what's right with them.

Rather than another look at the problems of today's family, this book is a look at family strengths. Rather than a challenge to ferret out weaknesses, this is an invitation to readers to focus upon their own family's health by becoming aware of the traits commonly found in the healthy family and studying the hallmarks of these traits.

Although I have read much about the legendary perfect family in our society, I have yet to meet one in my work. I suspect such a family doesn't exist. It certainly doesn't in our home. But, as parents, we constantly pit ourselves against that fantasy family and come out wanting. When we do that, we're neither honest nor fair to ourselves because we set up an impossible model to imitate. Failure is built into such a scheme. Families are families, after all, with warts and beauty marks unique to themselves.

I have never worked with a family that exhibits all fifteen of the traits that are presented in this book, including mine. I doubt if I ever will. Readers who consider themselves failures if they miss three out of fifteen on a test are apt to end up reading this book with a red pencil and a sinking heart. I hope they are few.

Rather, I hope readers model the man who told me after a talk on these traits that he felt pretty good about his family. "Four out of fifteen isn't all bad," he said.

I laughed and agreed with him, but the woman behind him gasped. Actually, I have more hope for him than for her. A sense of humor is one of the healthy traits. Gasping isn't.

1
Once Upon a Family

Your family is what you've got. . . . It's your limits and your possibilities. Sometimes you'll get so far away from it you'll think you're outside its influence forever, then before you figure out what's happening, it will be right beside you, pulling the strings. Some people get crushed by their families. Others are saved by them.

—Peter Collier

I sat in the courtroom with about twenty other prospective jurors and listened to the defense attorney question one of our number who'd just been called. First he established that she was the mother of four children, the youngest twelve years old. Then he began to probe.

"Now, Mrs. Johnson, with three children either in their teenage years or past them, I'm sure you've experienced minor scrapes with the police or other authorities."

She shook her head no.

He paused in surprise. "None of your children has ever had a little run-in with the law?"

"No."

"Not a traffic ticket or a warning? Not petty vandalism? A party dispersal? Nothing?"

"No, not that we know of anyway," she said, offering a nervous little laugh.

"Well, Mrs. Johnson," the defense attorney said slowly, speaking in staccato, "I never thought I would find you, but here you are—the perfect parent. With the perfect children." He shook his head, strode along the jury box, and continued to question her with a mixture of disbelief and irony. "I find it hard to believe that you reared three teenagers in today's society without any problems at all. What did you do? Lock them up?"

Some of us tittered, but the rest began to get nervous. Our eyes met. Mrs. Johnson had seemed to be a strong and confident woman in the jurors' room, but now as we watched, she was being reduced to apologies for rearing children who had never been in trouble with the law. The skillful attorney hammered away on the theme of her perfect family for several more minutes and then abruptly dismissed her.

We sensed the lawyer's purpose. He was trying to intimidate the rest of us before we even reached the stand. His twenty-year-old client faced a serious reckless driving charge, and the attorney didn't want parents of youth with clean driving records on the jury. So he was putting forth his basic premise early—that it's normal for young people to have problems with the police; that just like toilet training and acne, it's a part of growing up. Conversely, if a family *doesn't* have such experiences, it's abnormal—in a satirical sense, perfect.

The attorney's clever manipulation was of particular interest to me because for several years my work has been directed toward answering the question, What is a good family? And how can others be made better?

I came into my work on the family in a roundabout way fifteen years ago through parenting education in my church. Basically a writer and not a family specialist, I began writing parent-church material designed to give parents more confidence in establishing a rich home faith environment.

At that time, interest in the family on a national scale was almost nil. Outside of social work efforts, early childhood education, and a few church study groups, family education was unheard of. Materials were scant, and the prevailing attitude—still found in some rural areas—was that parents who attended any kind of parenting or family course must be having difficulty at home. They weren't good parents. Or their marriage was in trouble. This attitude was understandable because the few community courses available did indeed stem from a pathological or problem base: alcoholism, divorce, depression, poverty. Virtually no programs were designed for ordinary families, families who didn't have major problems but did want to foster a rich family life.

In our church we began to offer those ordinary families something called parent sacramental preparation, a series of lessons to help parents take on the responsibility for certain religious milestones in their children's lives. Very quickly we discovered that these parents wanted more than religious help. They wanted family help. They yearned to know how to be better families. But in order to achieve better family life, they had to know first how good they were. They needed something that we'd neglected to offer families in our culture—

criteria against which they could judge themselves and their efforts in producing a healthy family life.

Gradually we began to provide communication courses and other family living courses. It's interesting to note that the most popular widespread attempt to meet family communication needs—Thomas Gordon's *Parent Effectiveness Training* (P.E.T.)—circulated first through churches. Later, P.E.T. and its numerous imitators became popular in the general community but only after the nation became aware that families in our society were changing and that our total culture was responsible for meeting their changing needs.

For many years, we'd focused on the weaknesses and hurts of the family. Now, in a measure of maturity, we're beginning to focus on the strengths of the family—strengths that can be isolated and examined, and, more important, used as criteria for families that want to be healthier.

What constitutes a healthy family as opposed to a merely passable one? At last this question is getting attention from family professionals. If, as Tolstoy submitted, "All happy families resemble one another; each unhappy family is unhappy in its own fashion," then we should be able to isolate the traits that healthy families have in common. Knowing what these traits are should be immensely useful to those of us who have families and to those of us who work with them.

Further, isolating and naming these traits might help us to answer the question, What is a healthy family anyway? Mrs. Johnson, the prospective juror, allowed herself to become confused when the lawyer defined the healthy family as one with a clean police record. Yet she knew she didn't have a perfect family. The rest of us in the courtroom knew we didn't have perfect families either, but the doubt was planted.

To parents, it often appears that professionals in the various institutions of our lives—school, court, church, health, government, sports—have different, often self-serving definitions of the healthy family.

Police officers identify a healthy family by its absence of criminal activity. Teachers define it by school attendance and the willingness of parents to support educational goals. Church leaders look for faithful attendance at services and weekly support envelopes. Doctors and public health officials require the absence of major physical and mental health problems. Coaches pronounce a family healthy if it volunteers eagerly and never misses a game. All these criteria present parents with a plethora of confusing standards.

And we're no longer guided by the old norms about what a family should be. The functions of the traditional family have either disappeared or become secondary and we haven't yet integrated new norms and rules for the new family functions.

We live in an evolutionary time for the family. Although we're beginning to get a clear picture of today's family, we're still very influenced and often confused by our old ideas of family functions. Let's take a careful look at our traditional notions of what a family is.

Historically, the family had five major functions. The first was *to achieve economic survival.* This function called for a father-breadwinner, who went out into a hostile world to earn food and shelter for his family. Since this was a full-time occupation, it required a "helpmate," who was the mother-breadmaker, the tender nurturer of spouse and children, and the primary, if not sole, caregiver in the family. It also called for many children for economic reasons. The more children a family had, the richer the parents, the bigger the homestead, the more old-age security there would be. There were no teenage years. One was either a child or an adult. At thirteen, the child was considered worthy of an adult's wage. If living at home, he or she turned all wages over to the parents. The family was an economic unit.

A second function of the family was *to provide protection.* Family members needed one another as a protection from hostile forces outside the cave, the manor, or the igloo. They banded together to face the elements, to fight off intruders and illness, and to feed and protect their helpless, who could not protect themselves. The highly touted extended family of the past was not nearly so common as popular literature would like us to believe, but where it did exist, it usually arose from a need for mutual protection. Families emigrated together because they didn't want to face hostile cultures alone. They gathered under ethnic blankets and formed ghettos for the same reason. They marched together across the prairies to open our country, not because they couldn't exist without one another emotionally but because they needed the physical presence of one another for protection.

A third major function of the family was *to pass on the religious faith,* whatever it might be.

Historically, up to the eighteenth century, the family was the primary medium for passing on the religious story, doctrine, and traditions. (Only those destined for ordination or the sons of the very rich and powerful were enrolled in any kind of formal religious schooling.) And the family took on this role quite comfortably. The stories they passed from generation to generation were religious legends and beliefs that gave them the security of belonging not only to their own immediate family but to an historical family as well, with heroes, values, strengths, weaknesses, and hope. Significant events such as births, marriages, and deaths were ritualized religiously as entire villages turned out for fasts and feasts. Faith was an integral part of daily family life.

Fourth, the family served *to educate its young.* Boys worked alongside their fathers at a trade or on the farm while girls learned homemaking and parenting skills from their mothers. Most children who learned to read before the advent of nineteenth century free public schools learned from their mother and from religious books. The two books considered necessities in the early American family's library were the Bible and *The Pilgrim's Progress,* which served as texts for both the religious and educative functions of the family. Throughout history, if children learned to read and write at all, it was through the family, unless it was a rich and noble family that could afford tutors. Considering these first four functions of the family, it's easy to grasp the paired symbolism of the gun and the Bible as tools of family life in young America. The gun produced the game and protected the family while the Bible produced faith and staved off ignorance.

A final major function of the family was *to confer status.* In the old country, you were your family name, and it was very difficult to change that status. If your father was a respected blacksmith, you were expected to become the same. If your father was the town drunk, you didn't have much chance of becoming a teacher or a priest. An untarnished family name was a valuable legacy in a society that wasn't mobile.

This built-in, stratified society drove many people to emigrate to America where they could begin a life without the restrictions imposed by their family name. A generation or two later, it drove many of the grandchildren of the Pilgrims and the Puritans west for the same reason—so they could become their own persons unburdened by the weight of the family name or so they could establish new prestige by acquiring riches and land that their name did not give them. This searching has set in motion a mobility that has never really ceased in our country.

These, then, were the major functions of the family for a thousand or more years. There were other functions, of course, but they were secondary. If a family met these five, it was considered healthy, or good.

Certain norms of behavior followed these functions. A good family was one in which the father was an authoritarian breadwinner, the mother a good housekeeper and loving mother, and the children willing workers. It was a family that ganged together—on the surface, at least—to protect its own. It didn't "wash its dirty linen in public." Although the internal family life might have been in shambles, it gave the impression of being a close-knit family to outsiders. The good family was a church-going family as well. It supported its schools, and there was never scandal linked to its name.

We found it easy in days past to define a good family. In my childhood, I knew what a good family was just from hearing my parents talk. "He comes from a good family" usually meant "from one like ours." The term "good family" was used in praise, for instance when someone would say about a local marriage, "Isn't it wonderful? They both come from good families." And the phrase "good family" was spoken in sorrow when a young person deviated in some way from the work or faith values of the family. Then someone was sure to comment sadly, "Isn't it too bad? He comes from such a good family."

In the family, as in design, form follows function. Because success and failure are tied directly into function, the only acceptable reason for a family breakdown was a failure to meet one of its functions. If a man was a ne'er-do-well who could not support or protect his family, it was acceptable for his wife to take the children and go home to her parents or brothers. If a woman was a negligent mother or a horrendous housekeeper, it was acceptable for her husband to put her aside for another. If the children refused to contribute to work on the farm, it was acceptable to put them out. Every family had its black sheep, and parents were not considered unloving if they refused to support children beyond the age of twelve or so.

If either parent left the church or embraced a new religious belief, separation was socially accepted, and even encouraged, in the believing community. If scandal tainted the family name—if a man embezzled or a woman was sexually promiscuous—society understood the need for the family to separate itself from the one who caused the scandal.

Family fragmentation, then, was not unknown. There was alienation and separation, even divorce. The difference between family fragmentation then and now arises from cause. The acceptable causes of fragmentation in the past were directly linked with the acknowledged functions of the family.

When one of the functions broke down, society had to step in and fill the need. It had to feed the widows and orphans or care for the children neglected by a father. It had to protect the defenseless, indoctrinate the godless, and educate the ignorant. Because this burden usually fell upon the local community in general and upon the church community, these societies became arbiters of values. A man who didn't support his family was considered immoral. A woman who didn't care about cooking was not quite as Christian as one whose place in society was assured by the lightness of her cakes. Cleanliness was next to godliness, with the work ethic sandwiched in between.

A good family, then, was one that was self-sufficient, didn't ask for help from others, supported its institutions, was never tainted with failure, starved before it went on welfare, and met all the criteria of good families as determined by community and church.

People paid little attention to what went on *inside* a family—whether there was good communication, emotional support, or trusting relationships. People were only concerned about whether a family met the more obvious, visible family standards set by society. Today there are many people among us who sincerely believe that if we return to those old functions, we will somehow return to a good family once again, a family that is close, loving, and problem-free. They forget that living according to those functions never did guarantee a family like that.

Respected family specialist Dr. Ashley Montagu suggests that this longing for the old family functions is a collective turning upon the family by all those who feel their domestic hopes to be unrewarded and their expectations betrayed. "This reaction," he writes, "indicates that the problem may lie not so much with the family itself as with the excessive demands that Americans have made upon it—in the form of myths and misconceptions which, in fantasy but not in fact, have converted the home into a shrine and the family into a band of angels. Foremost among these myths is what may be called the 'legend of the Waltons': The nostalgic saga of the ideal 'extended' family embracing three or more generations in its magic circle—a Norman Rockwell vision of a golden age from which we have sinfully fallen away to our present stage of nuclear fission."[1]

Somewhere along the trails of history, these five functions of the family began to change and ultimateiy disappear. The family today has experienced and suffered the fallout from this major sociological change. Let's take a look at these historical functions in light of the modern western family.

Economically, we simply don't need each other to survive anymore. A man can get along without a woman in today's fast-food, laundromatic, easy-sex society. A woman doesn't have to be attached to a man for food, shelter, and respectability as she once did. The spinster aunt of old who lived with her brother or cousin is an anachronism replaced by the modern career woman who makes a deliberate decision for the single life. In contrast to the past, today the single woman generally enjoys a more affluent life-style than the married woman. This is because of the great financial demands that children make on working parents.

Children are no longer economic assets but costly luxuries. A 1981 report from Cornell University shows that the direct and indirect expenses involved in raising a child can easily top $100,000 by the time the offspring reaches age eighteen and then proceeds to graduate from a four-year, public university. This is the estimate for an urban family with a moderate standard of living. If the youth chooses an expensive private college instead, an additional $40-50,000 may be added on.[2] A couple with the national average of 1.8 children faces a $125,000 responsibility prorated over a minimum of eighteen years for a middle-class life-style. That's $7,000 a year for the first child with each additional child costing $3,500 or more, considering ongoing inflation. A far cry from the days when a child was considered an economic asset! Parents today are expected to furnish ever more in the way of tuitions, camps, lessons, braces, contact lenses, and the like while asking ever less in the way of old-age security for themselves. Parents worry whether there will be enough time between the last college tuition and retirement to rebuild a sound financial base for old-age needs.

Paradoxically, children don't need parents as much as they once did for economic survival. Teenagers who live apart from their parents and have jobs of their own while attending high school are a growing reality in our society. "Hitting the road"—a phenomenon of the sixties in which youth as young as thirteen took off on their own and found peer support along the way— has become an option for many. Young people can easily find a network of supportive peers whether it's in the drug culture or the cult society. Armed services, part-time jobs, and religious groups all provide outlets for young people, who were formerly tied to the family for survival.

The *protective* function of the family has to a large extent been relegated to welfare and police agencies. The family is no longer the primary protective unit in our society. In fact, so dependent has the family become upon government to furnish all kinds of protective services that school systems have been forced to assume responsibility for immunization of children. After a few thousand deaths by polio during the past several years in our country, some state legislatures ordered schools to refuse to allow children to attend without valid immunization records. (Incredibly, some parents fought this requirement because it emanated from government rules. We've come a long way from the family who protected its own from illness as well as from hostile forces.)

The *religious* function has been turned over to the professional church, although some churches are making a valiant attempt to return it to the home, with the church serving as a support system. Their attempt is meeting with mixed success. Parents were taught too well to believe that the Sunday school, the parochial school, the Christian educator, or Sister would not be able to pass on the story better than they could. They fear that if they, the parents, take on the primary religious stewardship in the family, the children's faith will suffer. I've been active in my own Roman Catholic church in this area of family during the past decade and can attest that while the church is striving courageously to reeducate parents to their primacy as religious nourishers, parents are just as tenaciously resisting the return of this function to the home.

The family's *educative* function has been transferred to the schools. Any residual parental teaching in the home has been further eroded by television. Parents support the education system simply by paying taxes and supervising homework, some resisting even that.

We no longer confer *status* in our society through the family name unless it's in such rare and famous families as the Rockefellers or Kennedys. Today our status comes from our jobs, our incomes, and our addresses. Professions such as medicine command higher status than those such as teaching, primarily because of income differential. Generally speaking, the higher the income, the more status we confer on a person and his family. This is a distinct value change from the era when the family name was more important than the family income.

When it became obvious in the first part of this century that long-recognized family functions were changing, there were dire predictions that the family as a unit would disappear. Those unfulfilled predictions should be of some solace to us today whenever we hear similar predictions. A former Secretary of Health, Education, and Welfare, Patricia Harris, commented that when Cain slew Abel, Adam probably turned to Eve and said, "The future of the family is in jeopardy."

In 1934, a commission appointed by the government to study the family, the Hoover-Ogburn Commission, found that indeed the original reasons for people to become and remain a family no longer existed, and therefore, the family would disappear. That didn't happen, as we who were born around that time can witness. Rather, the family, as a constantly changing, fluid unit, simply developed new functions which, we are belatedly and painfully recognizing, are foundational to family life today.

What are these new functions? In a word, *relational.* We marry so we can love and be loved, not feed and be fed. We join together in a search for intimacy, not protection. We have children so that we can give and be given to, care and be cared about, and share the joys of connecting with posterity, not for old-age bread and bed. Abraham Maslow once observed that we are the first generation in the history of peoples sufficiently beyond sustenance to be able to focus on the quality of our relationships.

It shouldn't surprise us that our family breakdowns and ruptures are once again directly related to our family's function. If our deepest relational needs aren't being met, we will search for them elsewhere. If our spouse doesn't see us as a person but solely as a wage-earner or sex object, we will search for our personhood elsewhere, perhaps in another spouse, perhaps in work, or even in alcohol. If we are lonely in marriage, alienated in daily family life, or unable to communicate with those nearest and dearest to us, we will search for alternatives. These alternatives come in the form of separation, divorce, infidelity, workaholism, volunteerism, chemical dependency, teen alienation, depression, and even suicide.

We're in the midst of a despairing society today, one that considers the family in general as a failure. It looks at the divorce rate and pronounces that the good old family of yore has disappeared. It points to homosexuality, unmarried cohabitants, and women who prefer careers to children as evidence of decadence, hedonism, and immorality.

There are two schools of thought regarding what can save the family. One school says that in order to have strong families, we must adopt again the functions of the earlier family. If Dad once again becomes the sole breadwinner, if Mom is content to be the at-home nurturer, and if the children do their chores, then we will return to the order and solidarity of the traditionally good family. The other school of thought holds that we cannot meet today's needs with yesterday's structures. Instead we must develop new solutions. If a married couple is not communicating and experiencing intimacy, merely asking the husband to make more money or the wife to become a full-time mother isn't going to help because the intimacy hunger will remain.

It's difficult for different generations to comprehend these two such different systems. I recall a time when friends of mine, married for twenty years, announced their impending divorce. My mother, who was seventy years old, shook her head and said, "I don't understand why they're divorcing. He's always been a steady worker, and she's such a good mother."

It would have been futile for me to say, "But they haven't grown together" or "They don't share the same values." She wouldn't have understood what I was saying. We were viewing the divorce from two different value systems, hers tied into the old formula for the good family, mine tied into the search for ways and means of developing healthy relationships in the family of today. Her system ascribed a morality to fixed family functions while mine acknowledged the family as a living organism whose functions could change.

Later, when I served on the White House Conference on Families in 1980, I realized how emotional the forces are on both sides of these value systems, almost destructive in the sense that they have become politically divisive and therefore are not likely to seek nor find any common solutions. In fact, at some of the state conferences held prior to the national one, the family was set back a good many years because the two factions destroyed public confidence in one another.

We were more fortunate in my state of Colorado. Participants of many ages and attitudes managed to come together, set aside differences, and work together toward helping today's families rather than simply judging them and finding them worthy or unworthy of support. While I conducted a session on using the local church as a family resource center, I observed with joy as people from a great diversity of denominations and agencies shared ideas on how to support the family in a variety of ways: how to help the family to better communicate, how to relieve the trapped feelings young mothers experience, how to utilize older couples who feel somewhat useless once the children are gone, how to develop healthier sexuality in the family, how to affirm children and spouses, how to share day care, how to help husbands understand the phenomenal changes in their wives and how to help women lead their husbands into such an understanding, and how to teach parents to let go of their grown children. The session, originally scheduled for an hour, had to be cut off at the end of two hours, and all of the 200 participants went away with new ideas for helping their families meet relational needs that are different from any experienced in earlier cultures. I was exhilarated to see how positively people react to ideas that emanate from a preventative, or wellness, stance in the family.

Nostalgia for the old days exacts its price. I once heard Urie Bronfenbrenner, professor of psychology, human development, and family studies at Cornell University, say he wished we could discuss the family without nostalgia because only then can we learn something about its terrible weaknesses and great strengths. When we suffer from nostalgia, we fall into the danger of selective memory. All of the families of the past were not good families, and all of the families of the present are not hurting families. Each is a family in its own time with its own needs and strengths.

Old attitudes die hard, nevertheless. When John Hinckley attempted to assassinate President Reagan on March 30, 1981, the commentators announced in a tone of wonder and mystification that little was known about Hinckley except that "he comes from a good family." What did they mean by good family? That he had two parents at home, that they were religious, that they were affluent, that they owned their own home, and that they were respected in the community—all the old visible traits of what we used to call the good family?

But we know that families aren't good simply because of these characteristics. Yes, on the outside, a family can be successful in an American sense of the word. Its members can be achievers and possess lots of property. They can be church-goers, with the parents' marriage intact. Sadly, the family members can be miserable inside that family. In writing of the unfairness of making easy judgments about families today, single-parent columnist Antoinette Bosco said, "I don't believe I ever heard anyone remark that a child was having a problem because he or she was the product of a two-parent family, regardless of the disorder that does exist in many such homes. Such criticisms would upset the image of stability we like to ascribe to families by virtues of their structures."[3]

She's right. We can no longer depend on traditional structures as criteria of family health today. Nor can we focus on family problems alone. As a nation, we have focused so long on weaknesses in today's families that we've ignored their strengths. A mother said to me at a workshop a few years ago, "We don't have any real problems, so we can't get any real help, right?" Exaggerated perhaps, but she was right. Most lists of adult education offerings are full of workshops for the divorced, the alienated, the people with problems. We've tended to serve the family from a position of weakness rather than from a base of strength.

Why? According to sociologist Theodore Caplow of the University of Virginia, we Americans cling tenaciously to the idea that the American family is about to collapse even though, Caplow holds, that simply isn't so. Caplow says that the decay of the American family is a myth. After interviewing 6,000 respondents, he thinks that Americans have more, not less, solid relations with family members than a generation ago and that we are able to communicate better with spouses than our parents could with one another. The reason we are so

willing to accept the idea of the disintegrating family, which is fostered
by the media, is that it makes us feel better about our individual successes and failures. It helps us carry an enormous load of guilt if we
believe that everybody else is producing miserable, disobedient, and
lawless children.[4]

Writers and publishers capitalize on our guilt and anxiety. Recently I
stood before the family section of a large, franchised bookstore and
copied down the depressing titles, apparently titles that sell. Here are a
few selections for modern parents: *Families Under Siege; Raise Your
Kid Right: Candid Advice to Parents on How to Say No; How to Live
with Your Teenager: A Survivor's Handbook for Parents; Raising Siblings: A Sane and Sensible Approach to Raising Brothers and Sisters
without Raising the Roof; How to Be Happy Though Married;
Redirecting Children's Misbehavior; Adolescence Is Not an Illness;
Parenthood without Hassles; Keeping Kids Out of Trouble; How to
Help Children with Common Problems; How to Fight Fair with Your
Kids . . . and Win; Coping with Children's Misbehavior; Discipline
without Tears;* and *Surviving Family Life.*

One wonders why people would have children at all in such a
pessimistic, despairing environment. Many aren't. I was asked to
develop a talk on family life for the women's resource center of our
local college. "Our students asked for this," the dean explained.
"They've heard the rhetoric on both sides—the Betty Friedan stance
that children ruin a woman's chance for happiness and the Phyllis
Schlafly stance that in order to be happy a woman has to have
children. What they want is a sober look without political biases.
What are the myths and realities of family life today?"

Not just women students are confused, either. Young men are asking questions about their role as husbands and fathers. What is expected of them? Can they learn to be a spouse and to parent in ways
different from their own parents so that they can meet the intimacy
needs in today's families? It's an exciting, yet fearful adventure for
them. They want a chance at being a good family before our culture
assigns them to the rubble pile of fragmented marriages and broken
relationships.

Ashley Montagu explains this desire for family that exists in spite of
the many negative warnings we hear. "The very stresses and threats of
modern life outside the home—out there in what is variously termed

the lonely crowd, the asphalt jungle, the neon wilderness and the air-conditioned nightmare—may have the paradoxical effect of enhancing the attractiveness of family life as a site of enduring relationships and an island of stability in a madly gyrating world."[5]

We are experiencing a new family in our midst. Contrary to going back to the good old traditional family structure, we're seeing a new brand of family emerge with a variety of designs. Only 15 percent of our nation's families typify the traditional structure of working father with mother and children at home. Where young adults of the past placed financial and job success as their top priority, today's young people put family success at the top in survey after survey. According to a January, 1980, Harris survey, 96 percent of Americans listed "having a good family life" at the top of the list of goals they have for themselves.

In the fifteenth annual American Freshman survey conducted in 1980 by the American Council on Education and the University of California, Los Angeles, researchers found that 63 percent of the 300,000 college freshmen surveyed selected raising a family as an important life goal. But—and here's what bears watching—in the same study, 93.3 percent marked that women should have job equality while only 26.6 percent marked that women's activities are best suited for the home. All this merely indicates the irrationality of looking in the past for solutions needed in the present.[6]

Popular psychologist Eda LeShan summed it up when she said, "Our expectations are higher than ever before. We don't want to live with anyone unless there is love—not some silly idea of romantic love, but the sort of love that nourishes the soul and enables people to grow. We seek the kind of love in which people want more for each other than for themselves and want most of all to enhance their own lives by helping someone else become all that he or she can be."[7]

It's a beautiful goal, but is it possible? Yes, it is. I know it is because I work with families who typify this kind of love, growth, and support. Generally, they are quiet, unobtrusive families who don't get a lot of honors and publicity. They expect problems and deal with them in a caring way. They don't embrace one psychology to the exclusion of all others. They work together to find solutions, applying common sense and trying new methods in order to meet new needs. What stands out in these families is their sense of optimism and their willingness to listen, communicate, support, share, and affirm.

It was about these families that author Evelyn Kaye spoke when she wrote, "Parenthood is always uncertain, perplexing, and inconclusive. There are no Pulitzer prizes for teaching your children that it is wrong to lie, steal, or cheat. There are no televised awards ceremonies for helping children recognize that discussion and awareness can solve problems more successfully than violence and fighting."[8]

These parents and their families have much to offer the rest of us. By studying them closely and pinpointing their strengths, we can use them to evaluate our own family health. They supply us with criteria by which we can scrutinize ourselves. They give us a list of strengths rather than a list of problems. Their contribution is invaluable. We know our problems—we're unsure of our strengths.

2
The Search for Family Strengths

Our family is not yet so good as to be degenerating.
—Kurt Ewald

When I embarked upon this project of discovering what traits, or qualities, healthy families share in common, I didn't intend to write a book. I had been commissioned by my church to write a paper on "Family—a Church Challenge for the Eighties."[1] As I did research for my paper, I noticed a common thread running through the writings of such respected family professionals as Urie Bronfenbrenner, Robert Coles, Virginia Satir, Jerry M. Lewis, Ken Keniston, T. Berry Brazelton, Edward Shorter, Rhona and Robert Rapoport, and others. The common thread was their call for someone or some group to recognize and publicize the strengths of the good families of today in order to help other families to be better. Intrigued, I began to compile a list of desired family traits mentioned most frequently by these professionals. Ultimately I developed a talk for parents in which I discussed a number of these characteristics.

This talk rapidly became my most popular one. I was invited to do a seminar on it at the annual ecumenical convocation at Stanford and later at seminars in Canada, Hawaii, and Germany as well as in major cities across our mainland. All of this told me that there is great interest in the strengths of the family. Families asked many questions: What are these family strengths? How do we perceive them? How many do we have in our family? How can we use them to compensate for any weaknesses?

When I began to plan a book on the subject, I decided to test the validity of the experts' observations, so I conducted some of my own research. When I began, I was aware of the work of two groups studying the healthy family. The first group was Dr. Jerry M. Lewis and his team at the Timberlawn Psychiatric Center in Dallas, who studied families from a family system approach.[2] They brought in volunteer families, gave them problems to solve, videotaped the interaction during these problem-solving sessions, interviewed them later, and studied the results in detail. From this work, Dr. Lewis and his team have given us invaluable insights into some of what goes on within healthy families.

A second team studying happy families consisted of three members of the faculty of the Department of Human Development and the Family at the University of Nebraska, Nick Stinnett, Barbara Chesser, and John DeFrain.[3] They conducted a National Study of Family Strengths in which they contacted empirically 350 families who met four established criteria. Two criteria called for subjective self-assessment: Each couple had to consider themselves happily married, and they had to be satisfied with the parent-child relationships in the family. Two criteria were based on structural factors: Each marriage had to be a first marriage, and the family had to be intact. These researchers came up with six traits that were shared by the families they studied. I am indebted to both teams for their valuable research and quote them occasionally throughout this book.

However, this book is very different from the empirical approach of science. Rather than gathering more hard data on the family, I was looking for an overall evaluation based on the experience and intuition of professionals, a "sense" or "feel" for families that they would not be able to share on a scientific instrument calling for proof and evidence.

With this as my goal, then, I did not go to families themselves in order to identify traits. I think families have too little objectivity and too little experience in self-assessment to be able to judge themselves alongside others. Most of us have close experience with only two or three families at the most—our family of origin, our family of con-struction, and, perhaps, another close family or two in our lives. I've found that many healthy families with whom I work, in fact, protest being called healthy. They don't so designate themselves. The profes-sionals who work with them do.

A licensed marriage and family therapist from California warned me in a comment she made on her survey response about the danger of studying only the families themselves, rather than consulting the peo-ple who work with families. "I hope you are careful in your sampling and send these surveys only to family specialists," she wrote. "If not, it's my sense that your data will be erroneously skewed. Many of these items are stereotypes and are popularly believed but have no support in the professional literature. There's the tendency, if you aren't careful, to identify pseudomutual families—those who look good to others—as healthy. They participate a lot in community, civic, school, and religious organizations and the neighbors like them, but little honest interaction happens between and among members. These are believed by family therapists to be the most difficult to work with therapeutically."

I went directly to the professionals—the teachers, doctors, principals, pastoral ministers, directors of religious education, boy scout directors, YMCA leaders, Big Brothers, 4-H leaders, family counselors, and other persons in similar positions who work closely with lots of families. These people were my basic source of information and insights.

I knew from years of working with families through institutions that if you want to know where the good families are, ask those people who work with them. They can single them out very quickly. I am not devaluing the need for empirical research on family, which we badly need. But we need to listen to the subjective wisdom of those who work with flesh-and-blood families as well as those who work with statistics. They have keen insights born out of years of experience in working day after day with a variety of families. When I asked the professionals if they thought the healthy families they encountered shared any traits in common, they answered with an emphatic yes.

A responding pediatrician put it this way: "At first, certain families stand out. After a few years, you realize certain characteristics stand out. And then, many families later, you connect the two and watch for those traits in good families. They're usually there."

The professionals I consulted worked in five institutional areas of our culture that touch families closely:
1. Education: principals, counselors, teachers
2. Church: pastoral staffs, counselors, educators
3. Health: pediatricians, school nurses, family physicians, pediatric nurse practitioners
4. Family counseling: counselors, therapists, mental health personnel, and social workers
5. Voluntary organizations: directors, leaders, coaches.

I wanted to identify the traits of a healthy family for two reasons: first, to give families some kind of positive criteria with which to evaluate themselves; and second, to force institutions to scrutinize their own policies and behavior in regard to how they either encourage or cripple those family strengths.

Concretely, I set out to discover answers to the following questions:
1. What strengths, or traits of health, do professionals agree are

found in healthy families? 2. On what family traits do they disagree? 3. Does the family get different messages about good family living from different institutions in their lives? For example, does the church have a different definition of healthy family than, say, family counselors or youth league directors?

I invited a few respected professionals in each of the five fields mentioned earlier to come up with a list of possible traits of a healthy family. Together we isolated fifty-six possible traits. Using this list of traits, I devised a simple instrument, which I sent to 500 professionals in the five categories.

Following is the entire survey. I suggest readers take a moment to prioritize fifteen traits of the healthy family as they define it. I realize many do not work with families professionally and therefore have primarily their own families upon which to make a judgment, but prioritizing the instrument might give readers a bit more insight into the responses of the professionals, who work with multiple and diverse families.

Dear Family Specialist,

I am gathering material for a book on the traits of the healthy family and would very much value your professional insights on this topic. I am attempting to discover if there are qualities commonly found in the healthy family (as defined by you in your professional sphere) so that families who are striving to be healthier can evaluate their strengths and weaknesses and build from there.

I would appreciate your taking the time to check fifteen of the traits listed below. While many or all of the traits can be considered positive, which do you most commonly perceive as evident in the healthy family? Your name and address are optional but please identify your profession. I hope to compare the prioritization of traits by professionals who work with parents as well.

Please return by _____ if at all possible. Thank you in advance for your cooperation.

Sincerely,
Dolores Curran

Please check fifteen (15) traits you most commonly find in healthy families which you encounter in your work.

1. _____ communicates and listens

2. _____ is affirming and supportive of one another
3. _____ has a balance of interaction among members
4. _____ develops trust
5. _____ has a sense of play and humor
6. _____ respects the privacy of one another
7. _____ fosters family table time and conversation
8. _____ fosters individual dining habits
9. _____ exhibits a sense of shared responsibility
10. _____ shares leisure time together
11. _____ encourages individual use of leisure time
12. _____ has a strong sense of family; treasures family traditions
13. _____ honors its elders
14. _____ looks forward to the adolescent years
15. _____ able to let go of grown children
16. _____ prays together
17. _____ has a shared religious core
18. _____ permits religious flexibility among members
19. _____ is not religion oriented
20. _____ admits to and seeks help with problems
21. _____ feels problems are private responsibility of family
22. _____ allows members to be part of their peer culture
23. _____ shares the same values
24. _____ accepts and encourages individual values
25. _____ values the work ethic
26. _____ values college
27. _____ values high income
28. _____ values work satisfaction
29. _____ values service to others
30. _____ is consumer-oriented; finds gratification in goods
31. _____ is cause- or movement-oriented
32. _____ values rural or small-town mores
33. _____ values metropolitan mores
34. _____ values risk and courage, public acting out of principles
35. _____ values going along and keeping peace
36. _____ teaches a sense of right and wrong
37. _____ teaches respect for others
38. _____ operates from a base of parental rules
39. _____ operates from a base of mutually negotiated rules
40. _____ operates from a base of few or no rules
41. _____ establishes roots in one community
42. _____ is mobile, living in many communities

43. _____ is known and respected in the neighborhood
44. _____ treasures privacy over community affairs
45. _____ is active in community affairs
46. _____ is heavily involved in "little league" type activities
47. _____ volunteers freely for school/church type activities
48. _____ has control of family time and calendar
49. _____ is a heavily-viewing television family
50. _____ is a moderately-viewing television family
51. _____ views relatively little television
52. _____ is financially secure
53. _____ has two parents living at home
54. _____ has a wife/mother who does not work outside the home
55. _____ has three or fewer children
56. _____ owns its own home

Additional comments are welcomed. Please use the space provided on the back of this form.

Name _____

Address _____

Professional Title _____

No envelope is needed to return this form. Fold so my return address on the other side of this form shows, staple or fold shut, and mail.

I deliberately avoided asking respondents to prioritize the traits in order of importance, one through fifteen, because in many cases they cannot be compared or weighted. I only wanted to find out what traits they most commonly find in the families they consider good, and so I asked them to simply check fifteen of them.

Much to the amusement of my husband, who a few years ago went through the arduous task of trying to get back the necessary percentage of research response required for his doctoral dissertation, I had a 110 percent return on my survey. People were apparently intrigued by the exercise, and they photocopied the instrument and passed it around to colleagues. It was used as the program at meetings of at least three professional groups: one a gathering of pediatric nurse practitioners, another a family counseling workshop, and the third a national convention of pastoral team members. My results are based on 551 returns, all of them from professionals who work with families in one of the earlier-mentioned five fields.

Who were the 551 professionals I surveyed? Because of my work with the family over the years, I was able to contact professionals in all parts of the country whose work and judgment I respect. Although greater numbers of professionals in education and church work responded than the other three groups, no group numbered fewer than fifty respondents and responses were evaluated on a percentage basis. For example, while 37 percent of my church-related respondents checked "prays together" as a trait commonly found in healthy families, only 21 percent of educators, 20 percent of voluntary organization personnel, 16 percent of family counselors, and 7 percent of health-related personnel responding chose it as such a trait. If, as in a few cases, a higher percentage of health personnel chose a certain trait over that of educators, I made note of that in order to bring it to readers' attention.

While not scientifically selected, my respondents span professional, geographical, and religious boundaries. I did not attempt to study inner city, or poverty level, families. The general consensus of my advisory team seconded the consensus of national authorities on the family: Family income has little relevancy to health in a family unless that income is insufficient; in that case, all other family problems are aggravated and the focus becomes needs rather than strengths. (Ken Keniston has written masterfully on this subject in the Carnegie Council on Children report called *All Our Children: The American Family Under Pressure.*)[4]

My respondents, then, work mainly with lower-middle-, middle-, and upper-middle-income families who live in urban, suburban, and rural areas. Most work with Anglo-American families, although I had significant response from those working with Hispanics in the Southwest and those working with the interesting racial mix that makes up Hawaii.

Here are the fifteen traits commonly perceived in the healthy family by those people who work with families. (The trait listed first was selected the *most* often by respondents, the trait listed second received the *next* most votes, and so on.)

The healthy family . . .

1. communicates and listens.
2. affirms and supports one another.

3. teaches respect for others.
4. develops a sense of trust.
5. has a sense of play and humor.
6. exhibits a sense of shared responsibility.
7. teaches a sense of right and wrong.
8. has a strong sense of family in which rituals and traditions abound.
9. has a balance of interaction among members.
10. has a shared religious core.
11. respects the privacy of one another.
12. values service to others.
13. fosters family table time and conversation.
14. shares leisure time.
15. admits to and seeks help with problems

Most of the comments written on the returned surveys were about my limiting the number of traits to fifteen. "Give me thirty," pleaded one school principal, and many others echoed his plea.

Why fifteen? Because I had to stop somewhere. Ten traits didn't seem enough, and I didn't want to overwhelm readers of my book with too many traits. Several respondents indicated that certain items naturally belong together, and I have paired some of those traits in upcoming chapters—specifically, traits having to do with communication and family table time and also those traits that revolve around the use of family time.

Another common comment had to do with the subjects of love and sex, neither of which appear on the survey. I struggled with whether to include these items, but my advisory group cautioned against doing so because they're difficult to judge from outside of a marriage. Doctors, teachers, ministers, coaches, and counselors have little way of judging whether or not there is love or satisfying sex within a marriage. All of my advisors offered personal instances in which families with whom they were working were presumed to be loving when, in fact, later revelations indicated there had been little or none present at the time. "We simply can't judge love," said a pastoral counselor. "Only individuals themselves can judge that."

So I omitted love and sex from the list. For our purposes, we're presuming that the marriage in a healthy family is built on a foundation of love with a satisfying physical manifestation of that love, but this is a presumption. Whether or not a family can be healthy without love and/or sex remains to be tested by another instrument.

So what did I discover, once the surveys were tabulated? Mainly that there was much more unanimity than I had anticipated there would be. The idea that the family is getting diverse messages from the different social institutions wasn't borne out in this research.

In the only variance that touched upon the top fifteen traits, health professionals put a significantly lower value on the sharing of leisure time together in the healthy family. While between 45 and 50 percent of other respondents checked "shares leisure time" as a healthy trait, only 26 percent of health-related respondents checked it. How to interpret this? I don't know. Might it be that medical people don't see shared leisure time as important to the healthy families they experience in their work, or is this a case of their personal lives becoming enmeshed with their objective prioritizing? In other words, could it be that doctors, who are so limited in the amount of time they can spend with their own families, place a lower value on shared leisure time for this very reason?

Finally, I want to acknowledge those traits that were mentioned so rarely by professionals that families can stop worrying about them. In a total of 551 responses, the following traits were mentioned fewer than five times as being significant in the health of a family:
— is consumer oriented; finds gratification in goods
— values rural or small-town mores
— values metropolitan mores
— is mobile, living in many communities
— values going along and keeping peace
— feels problems are private responsibility of family
— treasures privacy over community involvement
— fosters individual dining habits
— is not religion oriented
— values high income.

Other traits seldom selected included those traits dealing with educational levels, owning homes, and the size of families. These variables seem to have little to do with the health of a family. The important family traits can be found in small or large families, in rural or urban America, in families with high school or college educations, in families who own or rent, and in mobile or rooted families. From my experience with many families across the country, I suspected that this was the case, so I was especially gratified to have the professionals verify my perceptions.

I must share with readers my disappointment in discovering one physical family trait that apparently does affect the health of the family—the trait of being a single-parent family. Though I'd been hoping that this would not be so, too many professionals who work with families marked the item "has two parents living at home" as a trait of family health to let it go unnoticed.

Because single parents seem already to have so much working against them, and because many single-parent families with whom I work seem as healthy as many two-parent families, I admit I was hoping to discover that the number of parents in the home didn't matter. But the professionals who answered my survey mirror the research in this area.

As depressing as this information may be, I hope that readers who are part of a single-parent family will not become discouraged. Rather, I hope such readers will focus on their particular family strengths as they read this book. For example, single-parent families often have a strong balance of interaction among members; that is, they are less likely to have coalitions of children against parents or teens against younger siblings than are often found in two-parent families. A single-parent family can certainly use this plus to offset some of the problems incurred by having an absent parent. I remember watching a wonderful scene in which a fifteen-year-old big brother helped his seven-year-old brother learn to ride a bike. The big brother was patient, loving, and reassuring. I wonder if he'd have behaved like that if the father had been readily available to take on this normal privilege of parenting.

Children in single-parent families are noticeably more responsible, often stepping in to do chores and help solve family problems. Many prepare dinner for their working mothers, get on with their homework without prodding, and take care of those personal needs that are assigned to parents in the two-parent family.

The single-parent family is not without healthy family characteristics. If it can focus on its strengths rather than its rather dreary statistics, it can produce warm and loving relationships. Many of us in family work have seen that happen.

After tabulating the traits prioritized by my professional respondents, I tackled the question so often asked by families, "How do we know if we have this trait? How do we know if we're communicating well or not?" It is here that I drew upon my work with families over the past fifteen years. I have conducted hundreds of seminars, workshops, and classes on various phases of parenting. My weekly column, "Talks with Parents," appears in fifty-eight newspapers and draws considerable mail from the estimated 4½ million readers. From my close exposure to families and their daily lives, I was able to formulate some of the hallmarks that indicate the presence or absence of a particular trait. While these certainly are not the only hallmarks, they are the ones I've found to be the most obvious and should be helpful to families in evaluating their own health.

At times I went to particular families and asked some questions: How do you deal with teenage privacy? Do you routinely schedule activities in your family that interrupt the dinner hour? If not, what do you do when a youngster wants to play in a sport that takes place at the same time as family dinner time? How are chores allocated? How do you know when a family fight ends? And so on. Many of these families were those with whom I have worked and who embody a good number of healthy traits. A few were indicated to me by principals, pastors, and pediatricians as families worth studying. The insights I gleaned from these families plus the many other families with whom I have worked over the years make up the body of the book.

I've written this book, obviously, for people in families who want some help in evaluating their own family life in order to make it better. But my research and suggestions in the chapters that follow are not for families only. I invite social and political institutions to examine themselves thoroughly. If there are fifteen commonly accepted characteristics of the healthy family, what is the responsibility of an institution toward respecting and fostering these traits, *especially if they conflict with some of the goals of the institution*?

At the White House Conference on Families National Research Forum on Family Issues, Dr. Urie Bronfenbrenner of Cornell stressed, "The future of the family lies in the relations between families and other institutions. That's where the attention must be."[5]

Let's give it our attention, then. I invite the staffs of various institutions—all those people involved in church ministry to the family:

teachers, administrators, school board members, and educators; physicians, public health agencies, nurses, hospitals and clinics; psychologists, therapists, mental health workers, family and marriage counselors, social workers; Boy and Girl Scout, 4-H, Campfire, and youth league leaders, coaches, and all other recreation leaders—to take a penetrating look at each of these fifteen traits and then to focus on the question, How can we as an institution better help the families we serve to develop and strengthen this trait? And examine also the corollary question, How do we as an institution regularly weaken this trait because of our policies and goals?

If, for example, the healthy family respects individual differences, do we weaken this trait by implying that some differences are more acceptable than others? What about a boy who doesn't care about playing summer baseball? Are we going to make him feel less acceptable for this, or are we going to support his decision, even if we need him on our roster to justify our budget and goals?

If one of the healthy family traits is developing a sense of right and wrong, what happens if an institution's sense of right and wrong differs from that of the family? Let's say, for example, that a family has a value that strongly opposes abortion but that when a daughter becomes pregnant, the family counseling institution insists that the daughter have an abortion in order to receive any other aid. What about the attitude of some schools and churches that parental support of their goals should be automatic and total? Yet, one of the healthy family traits is that parents are supportive of one another and their children. How do institutions help families resolve this conflict of support when children are clearly unhappy in school or church?

If healthy families share some of their leisure time, what happens when an institution insists upon parental involvement which consistently interferes with the amount of leisure time a family has to share? Churches, Scouts, and other such groups are especially prone to do this. Many a family that has wanted to spend a rare weekend away together has been made to feel guilty for doing so because of a church function or a Saturday ballgame.

Families have been trying far too long to reconcile these differences by themselves. The time has come for the institutions to look at themselves with the same careful eye they have used for families. Urie Bronfenbrenner says, "In this country, we have been taught that most of the problems experienced by families have their origin within the family and therefore ought to be solved by the individual family member primarily concerned. . . . We as a nation need to be reeducated about the necessary and sufficient conditions for making human beings human. We need to be reeducated not as parents, but as workers, neighbors, and friends; as members of the organizations, committees, boards; and, especially, the informal networks that control our social institutions and thereby determine the conditions of life for our families and their children."[6]

Parents constantly say that they can't rear good families in bad environments. Who is more responsible for the environment in which we try to rear families than our institutions? We need to reverse our institutions' perpetual appeal for family support and instead ask institutions, How are you going to support the family?

I have found that most teachers, doctors, ministers, counselors, and recreation workers sincerely want to support the family, but they don't know how. I suggest that conscientious study of those traits that characterize healthy families might be a very practical, possibly enlightening, first step for institutions to take in order to better support families.

We've come a long way in this book from the woman in the jury box. For those readers who always want an ending to a story, I'm afraid I can't give it. I wasn't selected for jury duty, and I didn't stay around for the trial. How the family as a unit fared on that stand I don't know. But I do know that the questions posed to our colleague by the attorney made us all focus, for a few frenzied moments at least, on our own definition of the healthy family.

Here and now, in a more relaxed atmosphere, let's look at these questions about our own families: How do we rate alongside other families? How healthy are we? How many of the fifteen traits presented in this book do we possess, and in what strength? How can we develop these traits so that our family will be a better place to love and live? Let's begin.

3
Communicating

Trait 1: The healthy family communicates and listens.
Trait 13: The healthy family values table time and conversation.

> I see communication as a huge umbrella that covers and affects
> all that goes on between human beings. Once a human being has
> arrived on this earth, communication is the largest single factor
> determining what kinds of relationships he makes with others
> and what happens to him in the world about him.
> — Virginia Satir

Communicating and listening was chosen as the number one trait
found in healthy families by my 551 survey respondents. This is consistent with the findings of the National Study of Family Strengths and in
the work done on the healthy family by Dr. Jerry M. Lewis of the
Timberlawn Foundation in Dallas.

It's intriguing to ponder the fact that this trait wasn't even considered an important marital trait a generation ago. Why? Why was
communication and listening perceived by today's family professionals to be the single most important characteristic of health in the
family today? One family counselor I surveyed answered the question
for me when he said, "Because without communication you don't
know one another. If you don't know one another, you don't care
about one another, and that's what the family ballgame is all about."

In his column in *Marriage and Family Living,* marriage specialist
David R. Mace noted that before 1970, we really had little understanding of the communication process as it affected family relationships.
He said, "I once made a survey of what I considered to be the twenty-
six best books on marriage published between 1930 and 1970, in order
to find out how they treated the subject. Most of them scarcely mentioned it at all. Of those that did, only a few had any real perception of
its importance."[1]

Today's professionals do understand its importance. "The most
familiar complaint I hear from wives I counsel is 'He won't talk to me,'
and 'He doesn't listen to me,' " said a pastoral marriage counselor.
"And when I share this complaint with their husbands, they don't hear
me, either."

"We have kids in classes whose families are so robotized by television that they literally don't know each other," said a fifth-grade teacher who tried to explain why educators as a group put a much higher value on limited television in the family than the other four professional groups do.

A whole raft of voluntary organizations admit that they exist because of the breakdown of communication in the family. They serve as alternative places where individuals can go to talk, be heard, ventilate feelings, and receive responses. Whether it's a young mother's group, Alcoholics Anonymous, Weight Watchers, or any of the many support-type organizations, the primary need of members is to communicate—with anyone. Better to share oneself with strangers than with nobody.

Even the Boy Scouts are addressing the communication problem in the family. Chief scout executive Jim Tarr explained in a newspaper interview that there is a new emphasis on family communication in the scouting programs: "One of the dilemmas in our world today is that the young get in trouble, and then it's too late to build communication within the family. Therefore, I would hope our programs will reach into homes where parents will understand the scouting program and adapt it to the family," he said.

The phenomenal proliferation and popularity of communication groups such as Parent Effectiveness Training, Systematic Training for Effective Parenting, Parent Awareness, Marriage Encounter, Transactional Analysis, Couple Communication, Parents Anonymous, and literally hundreds of others tell us that the need for effective communication—the sharing of deepest feelings—is not just a need perceived by the professionals. It's also perceived by those many individuals and families who are willing to risk exposure beyond the front door in order to satisfy some of their hunger for intimacy. One of my respondents, a clinical psychologist who works with many families, wrote on her survey, "Perhaps it's because it is an area of specialty for me but I find communication central and key to healthy family relationships. An important aspect of this communication is the ability to name, own, and express feelings, knowing one will not be punished. Dealing openly and gently with anger is important—ability to deal growthfully with conflict is another way of looking at it."

A question we need to deal with here is the one pinpointed for me by an older woman I met who admitted to being mystified by all this talk of communication today. "I think it's exaggerated," she said. "In my day, we didn't worry about it. We just talked."

The question this puzzled woman pinpointed for me is this: Why does family communication top the list of family strengths today when it wasn't even on the list a few years ago?

If an individual in yesterday's family demanded more, he or she was considered strange. Sinclair Lewis's brilliant portrayal of such a woman—Carol Kennicott—in his classic novel *Main Street* bears rereading if we want to fully grasp what it was like to hunger for communication in a society that saw no need for it. Both then and now, this hunger can plant self-doubt. Is there something wrong with me if I need more intimacy in my life? Am I demanding too much if I want more out of marriage than a good provider or good cook?

Today the major function of family is relational. Our needs are emotional, not physical. We want to be valued for more than our ability to bring home a paycheck or to cook and clean. It isn't enough. Our affluence as a people has freed most of us from haunting hunger and the fear of physical survival. We aren't loved today for what we can do, but we still need to be loved and to love. We need to know we're needed and appreciated. We want to share our intimacies, not just physical intimacies but all the intimacies in our lives.

The kind of man our earlier family called for was the masculine one who never feared, doubted, flinched, or—heaven forbid—cried. The kind of woman our earlier family called for was the soft, dependent woman who was ever patient and satisfied with her womanly skills, and who—heaven doubly forbid—never yearned for those things that belonged to the world of men. If either the man or woman experienced feelings traditionally assigned to the other gender, it was best to hide those feelings.

Those traditional sex roles linger on. At a workshop designed for mothers of young children, one young mother disclosed an archetypal problem: the insensitivity of a husband toward his wife and the children when they get sick or are hurting in some way. "My husband gets angry when I get sick," she reported. "And when the kids hurt themselves, he tells them to be tough, not to be pansies and give in to every little hurt. It worries me that when they get older they won't come to him when they're hurting."

They won't, and neither does she now. We probed a little and discovered what I had suspected, that her husband couldn't handle any sign of weakness because it scared him. He was supposed to be in charge at all times. So when his wife got sick, he got angry. He couldn't control her illness. When the kids got hurt, he wouldn't allow himself to be sensitive and caring. He had to become gruff and strong and in charge. Incidentally, guess what kind of father he had? Right—a strong, silent, insensitive man who felt ashamed when he had a stroke and had to be hospitalized because, to him, it was a sign of weakness in a world where men aren't supposed to be weak.

Dr. Avodah K. Offit, psychiatrist, talked about this kind of man in a composite drawn for *McCall's* magazine: "He's rather cold by nature and emotionally ineffectual—the epitome, often, of 'the rational man' who's uncomfortable in the world of feelings. Frequently, he has never *learned* emotional interaction, so he has little insight into it. He always thinks he's right and he never blames himself." Dr. Offit then adds what is a poignant reality. "By the testimony of the women who live with him, he may be a wonderful human being in many other ways. But very little in the domestic power sphere seems to belong to him. Often, he sees his entire role as 'bringing home the bacon.' Everything else simply has to be 'gotten through.' "[2]

Such men are rapidly becoming anachronisms in today's families. They exist, but they aren't good providers in that they don't provide what is needed. In an article in *Marriage and Family Living,* Dr. Bruno Manno reported that in the family " . . . the situation today is not so much one within which marriage, family life, and lifelong intimate relationships between spouses are no longer important, but one within which they have become too important; . . . one within which people's expectations of the physical and psychological rewards of marriage and family life are growing far more rapidly than their capacities to deal with the challenges and problems of human intimacy."[3]

Honest communication calls for courage of a kind different from machismo, and patience of a kind different from motherliness. It means risking ourselves to let another know who we really are underneath all these layers of societal musts, shoulds, oughts, and tsk-tsks.

We're caught between generations. We were taught to be strong, but we know we aren't always strong. And when we aren't, we wish we could share that with the ones we love. We were taught to be satisfied with fulfillment of duty, but we yearn for more than that and know that our yearning won't go away. We realize it's foolish to expect others to know somehow magically how we feel, yet we're hesitant and afraid to say such simple things as "I don't feel appreciated around here," or "I don't think you love me."

Communication is at the top of the family specialists' list because it is basic to loving relationships. It's the energy that fuels the caring, giving, sharing, and affirming. Without genuine listening and sharing of ourselves, we can't know one another. We become a household of roommates who react rather than respond to one another's needs. Let's look carefully at this all-important trait.

Trait 1: The healthy family communicates and listens.

Families ask, "How do we know if we are communicating? What are the signs of good and poor communication in the family?" I perceive these hallmarks in the communicating family.

1. The family exhibits an unusual relationship between the parents.
According to Dr. Jerry M. Lewis—director of the Dallas Timberlawn Psychiatric Center and author of a significant work on healthy families, *No Single Thread*—research data strongly suggests that intimacy, or the capacity of two people to share deep feelings, is strongly correlated with shared power. Rather than dominating one another, healthy spouses complement one another. In an exciting study of families undertaken by his center, he found that in the healthy families, husbands and wives were of equal power. Either could be leader, depending on the circumstances. In the unhealthy families he studied, the dominant spouse had to hide feelings of weakness while the submissive spouse feared being put down if he or she exposed a weakness or fear.

Acknowledging that this finding might be unpopular—touching as it does upon some people's moral conviction that spousal roles must remain in their traditional mold—Dr. Lewis nevertheless insists that equality exists in the healthy marriage. He stresses that children in the healthy family have no question about which parent is boss. Both parents are. If children are asked who is boss, they're likely to respond,

"Sometimes Mom, sometimes Dad." And, in a wonderful statement, Dr. Lewis adds, "If you ask if they're comfortable with this, they look at you as if you're crazy—like there's no other way it ought to be."[4]

My survey respondents echo Dr. Lewis's finding. An administrator in a degreed family program wrote on her survey, "The healthiest families I know are ones in which the mother and father have a strong, loving relationship between themselves. This seems to flow over to the children and even beyond the home. This strong primary relationship seems to breed security in the children, and, in turn, fosters the ability to take risks, to reach out to others, to search for their own answers, become independent, and develop a good self-image."

2. The family has control over television.

Television in the family has been maligned, praised, damned, cherished, and thrown out. It has changed family weekend-living patterns, it has been called the new hearth, and it has more influence on children's values than anything else except their parents. A friend of mine who is a marriage therapist lists football as one of the top five causes of marital discord, competing with money, in-laws, children, and jobs. Television's impact on the family is a book in itself, and a number of books on the subject are on the market for families who feel controlled by the media, who worry about values, consumerism, and passivity brought about by television. For such parents, I recommend a visit to the local library to locate these guides on the use and abuse of television in today's home.

Here, I want specifically to discuss the effect of TV on family communication. Over and over when I'm invited to help families mend their communication ruptures or learn to celebrate together, I hear "But when can we do this?" Probing, I find that these families have literally turned their family-together time over to television. Even those who control the quality of programs watched and set homework-first regulations feel reluctant to intrude upon the individual's right to spend all spare time in front of the set. Or sets. Many families, in the ultimate attempt to offer freedom of choice, avoid clashes over program selection by furnishing a set for each family member. Indeed, one of the women who was most desperate to establish a better sense of communication in her family confided to me that they owned nine sets. Nine sets for seven people.

Whether the breakdown in family communication leads people to excessive viewing or whether excessive television breaks into family lives so pervasively as to literally steal it from them, we don't know. It's the chicken and egg dilemma. But we do know that we can become out of reach to one another when we're in front of a TV set. The term *television widow* is not humorous to thousands whose spouses are absent though present. A woman remarked on a talk show, "I can't get worried about whether there's life after death. I'd be satisfied with life after dinner in our home." A similar situation occurs when a wife is addicted to daytime soaps, making her equally incommunicado to her family.

When someone in the family does want some uninterrupted time to share some problems or feelings, he or she often hears "Shhh, I'm watching TV." That phrase is a strong clue that in that family television is the basic presence, with all other presences considered interruptive. It tells us a lot about the value of persons in that home. In a magazine article, a woman described her television-addicted husband: "He appears to be on a distant planet, and all the earth's equipment cannot penetrate the outer ring of atmosphere. . . ."[5]

One of the techniques I use in family communication workshops is to ask families to make a list of phrases they most commonly hear in their home during a two-week period. One parent was aghast to discover that his family's most familiar comments to one another were "What's on?" and "Move." No need to look further for that family's communication problem! In families like this one, communication isn't hostile—it's just missing. There's little give-and-take between persons when the TV set is constantly intrusive; or when although someone's eyes are on the speaker, his or her attention is on the set. The subtle message passing between family members is "Hurry up and get your message over so I can return to my program."

In a witty vein, Joan Anderson Wilkins told how her family's TV set crashed to the floor accidentally, and her family unexpectedly regained control of family life. "My husband and I talked without the constant drone of the TV behind us. We discussed world affairs, personal affairs, and everybody else's affairs." She went on to explain how her children redeveloped a curiosity about things outside of television in their lives. And then she offered this insightful observation: "After a few days of thinking about TV and family life, I finally

understood why shows like *The Brady Bunch* and *Eight Is Enough* are
so successful. It's because they provide kids with a picture of family life
at its best: where parents participate, people communicate, and living
together seems fun. My children, like millions of others, got pleasure
out of watching those fantasies of simulated family life. All they
needed was a chance to live out this kind of family life."[6] The irony, of
course, is that television was the chief culprit in denying them that experience.

We shouldn't get the impression that television always plays the role
of villain in family communication patterns. Although a 1980 Gallup
Poll undertaken for the White House Conference on Famlies cited the
negative effect of television on families, it also found that the public
sees great potential for television as a help in families. It can be a
tremendous device for initiating discussion between generations on
subjects that aren't likely to come up elsewhere, subjects such as sexuality, sexual mores, corporate ethics, sportsmanship, marital fidelity,
and consumerism.

Even very bad programs can by their badness offer material for
value clarification in the family if members view them together. I
recently observed my sixteen-year-old son and his father viewing a
program in which hazardous driving was part of the hero's
characterization. At one point, my son turned to his dad and asked,
"Is that possible to do with that kind of truck?"

"I don't know," replied my husband, "but it sure is dumb. If that
load shifted. . . ." With that they launched into a discussion on the responsibility of drivers that didn't have to originate from a parental lecture base. I also noted with interest that as the discussion became more
engrossing to them, the TV program became less so, and they eventually turned the sound down in order to continue their conversation.

Parents frequently report this kind of use of television, which, incidentally, is the method that the widely publicized 1972 Surgeon
General's report suggested as the most effective television gate-keeping
by parents. The report suggested that instead of turning off the set,
parents should view programs with their children and make moral
judgments and initiate discussion.

A family counselor pointed out that when a family is able to discuss
the problems and attitudes of a fictional family, individual feelings
and attitudes are not as threatened as when the family looks at itself.

Yet the results are similar. The goal is to be able to risk sharing fears, hopes, and dreams without risking vulnerability. A family that has difficulty sharing fears, hopes, and dreams might seek out specific programs to use as a springboard for deeper levels of family communication and sharing.

In 1981, the A.C. Nielsen Company announced that the average American television set is on for forty-three hours and fifty-two minutes a week. That's more than six hours a day. Whether the family uses television to replace or enhance communication depends on the family. Unfortunately, the level of family communication tends to go down as the level of television goes up, according to the opinion of professionals who work with families.

3. The family listens and responds.

"My parents say they want me to come to them with problems, but when I do they're either busy or they only half listen and keep on doing what they were doing—like shaving or making a grocery list. If a friend of theirs came over to talk, they'd stop, be polite and listen," said one of the children quoted in a *Christian Science Monitor* interview by Ann McCarroll.[7] This child put his finger on the most difficult problem of communicating in families: the inability to listen and respond.

Most of us react rather than respond. When we react, we reflect our own experiences and feelings onto what we've just heard; when we respond, we get into the other person's feelings and are empathetic. Here are a couple of examples to show the difference.

Tom, age 17: "I don't know if I want to go to college. I don't think I'd do very well there."

Father: "Nonsense. Of course you'll do well."

That's reacting. Although this father may think he's fostering confidence, he's actually cutting off communications. He's labeling his son's fear as baseless and telling him he'll do well. He's refusing either to hear his son's fears or to consider his son's feelings, possibly because he can't accept the idea of his son's not attending college. Paradoxically, if the father cared less about college, he probably would be more open and responding, as in this father's handling of the same situation.

Tom: "I don't know if I want to go to college. I don't think I'd do very well there."

Father: "Why not?"

Tom: "Because I'm not that smart."

Father: "Yeah, that's scary. I worried about that, too."

Tom: "Did you ever come close to flunking out?"

Father: "No, but I worried a lot about it before I went because I thought college would be full of brains. Once I got there, I found out that most of the kids were just like me."

This father has responded rather than reacted to his son's fears. Notice what the father did: First, he searched for the reason for Tom's lack of confidence and found it was an academic fear (it could have been fear of leaving home, of a new environment, of peer pressure, of any of a number of things); second, he accepted the fear as legitimate; third, he empathized by admitting to having the same fear when he was Tom's age; and finally, he explained why his, not Tom's, fears turned out to be groundless. He did all of this without denigrating or lecturing Tom.

And that's tough for parents to do. Often we don't want to hear our children's fears because they frighten us or their dreams because they aren't what we have in mind for them. Parents who deny such feelings will allow only surface kinds of conversation. It's fine as long as a child says "School was okay today," but when she says "I'm scared of boys," the parents are uncomfortable, and they react instead of responding. They don't want her to be scared of boys, but since they're afraid they won't handle it well, they react with a pleasant "Oh, you'll outgrow it." She probably will, but what she needs at the moment is someone to hear and understand her pain.

Listening is crucial to communication. Dr. Paul F. Wilczak, director of the Center for Pastoral Ministry in Kansas City, teaches a seven-week course on listening with the heart. His students are parents, counselors, young couples, ministers, and teachers. He says, "Listening with the heart, from the core of our personal reality, is a *major challenge.* . . . A careful empirical study (S. Minuchin and others, *Families of the Slums,* 1967) has documented that multiproblem families are groups of people who do not listen to one another. . . . It has been discovered that in such families no one expects to be heard. They are noisy families where people are used to tuning each other out. Or if on occasion people are heard, they do not expect a response. There is no experience of making contact, of counting as a person, or of making a significant impression. If there is some response, it is not usually relevant. Rather than connect with the other person's message, the response indicates disregard for it and changes the subject."[8]

Listening from the heart is the basis for many of the marriage and family enrichment courses so popular now. It is an integral part of Couple Communication, a program originally put together by three behavioral scientists at the University of Minnesota in the late sixties. They combed the research available on human communication and took from it what could be applied to the average married couple. Removing most of the technical jargon, they developed a twelve-hour course, which is presented to groups of couples by a trained director. Couples who have benefited from the experience are enthusiastic, testifying to its effect on their marriage.

"I always thought we over-communicated," said one participant. "Nobody in our family could get a word in edgewise. When my wife wanted us to take the course, I was against it. Now, I realize we were all talking and nobody was listening. . . ."

Another participant said, "I am learning to listen with my whole being, and it's an intimidating experience. It means I have to give of myself to my wife and children, and it's painful to do that. At first I resented the time it took away from my own interests, but now I realize that the rewards are well worth it."

Robert Benton—director of the movie *Kramer vs. Kramer*, which deals with a father-son relationship—spoke with candor about how directing the movie brought him face-to-face with his own inability to listen to his son. "When I go home and I am sitting with my child and he is very full of something, there is only part of my mind on what he is saying. But a look in his eye tells me he knows I am not there. They know everything, kids. Absolutely everything."[9]

Often children need no more than to know that their parents are listening. They don't really need any active response. They simply want an opportunity to vent some feelings, to expose some opinions, to share some experiences. Pastoral counselor Norman Calloway suggests a counseling procedure for parents: When they listen to a spouse or child, they should ask themselves before responding, "Do I need to do any more than know this?" Often just attentively listening to another's words is all that's required in order to be empathetic. The speaker may not want a solution, just an ear. A five-year plan doesn't have to be designed to meet every problem that's expressed.

In Ann McCarroll's interviews, she ran into fifteen-year-old Bob, who said he had "some mother." And he described what he meant by that. "Each morning she sits with me while I eat breakfast. We talk about anything and everything. She isn't refined or elegant or educated. She's a terrible housekeeper. She uses double negatives. But she's interested in everything I do and she always listens to me — even if she's busy or tired."[10]

That's the kind of listening behavior found in families who experience real communication. Answers to the routine question "How was your day?" are really heard, with the eyes and heart as well as the ears. Nuances are picked up and questions are asked. Every statement isn't met with "That's nice, dear." Members of a family that really listens to one another instinctively know that if people listen to you, they are interested in you. And that's enough for most people.

In probably the most poignant of Ann McCarroll's interviews, a teenager named John summed it up: "The best time I have had with my dad was when burglars broke into our summer cottage at the lake. The police said we should come up to see what was missing. Well, our whole family's made the trip dozens of times, but this time there were just the two of us. It's a six hour drive. I'd never spent six hours alone with him in my whole life. Six hours up, six hours back. No car radio. We really talked. It's like we discovered each other. There's more to him than I thought. It made us friends."

And in an equally poignant postscript, author McCarroll added, "The irony is, the family had a history of fine vacations, outings, and activities."[11]

4. The family recognizes nonverbal messages.

Once one of my sons came home from school and I knew instantly that something was wrong. I ventured a question, "What's wrong, Mike?" and his quick answer, "Nothing," told me that indeed something was amiss. If it wasn't, I knew him well enough to know that he would have looked up questioningly and asked, "Nothing. Why?" His abrupt "Nothing" also told me not to meddle, so I didn't.

But a while later, when he was ready to talk about it, he came and told me he had been the last one chosen that day for football. Remember how painful that was? You stood there praying silently to be chosen and as the list got lower and lower, your stomach cramps got stronger and stronger. And there was an ultimate indignity. If you were really bad, as I was in baseball, even when you were the last one chosen, once in a while the team would ask, "Do we have to take her?"

So when Mike told me he had been the last one chosen, primarily because he was short then and the game was football, I knew how he felt. "That's a terrible feeling," I said, "standing there and watching everyone else get picked."

His head snapped up. It never occurred to him that a parent could have been the last one chosen. He asked a lot of questions, shifting the attention from his pain to my experiences as a child. After a while, he ate a couple of bananas and went out to play.

So often we parents neglect to share with our children our past—and present—feelings of being inadequate, awkward, ugly, not loved, or not treated fairly. Unless we share ourselves with them, they think we've come full-blown to adulthood, never once doubting ourselves. They're much more likely to communicate their feelings to us if they know we experience such feelings, too.

The healthy family responds to feelings as well as to words. "I know how you feel" can be as effective as a dozen admonishments. Dr. Jerry M. Lewis defines empathy as that characteristic in which someone responds to your feelings in such a way that you feel deeply understood. He says, "There is probably no more important dimension in all of human relationship than the capacity for empathy. And healthy families teach empathy."[12]

In the healthy family, members are allowed to be mad, glad, and sad; however, other members aren't always condemned to be around them. There's no crime in being in a bad mood—nor is there betrayal in being happy while someone else is feeling moody. The family recognizes that bad days and good days attack everyone at different times.

Much of our communication—especially our communication of feelings—is nonverbal. When someone tells about an embarrassing incident on the bus, she might be saying "I am such a klutz," and needing reassurance that the rest of us feel the same way at times. In troubled families, the typical reaction to a feeling statement is "Well, you shouldn't feel that way." Not only is communication cut off but the person's feelings are judged. And feelings of all kinds should be acceptable. (Actions are judged, not feelings. Being angry with a sibling may be understandable and acceptable, but hitting him or her isn't.)

Nonverbal expressions of love are the best way to show children that parents love each other. Verbalizing love to children isn't enough. Or even necessary if the nonverbal messages come through clearly. A spouse reaching for the other's hand, a wink, a squeeze on the shoulder, a "How's-your-back-this-morning?", a meaningful glance across the room, a peaceful silence together—all of these tell children that their parents love one another.

Marital specialist David R. Mace stresses that all families are communicating verbally and nonverbally almost continously, and the quality of their communicating processes is vitally important if they want to live together creatively. "The new knowledge we have gained in the past ten years is so precious that I would consider it a tragedy for any responsible family to ignore it," he said.[13]

On the reverse side, the most destructive kind of nonverbal communication in marriage is silence. Silence on the part of a spouse can mean disinterest, hostility, denigration, boredom, or outright war. On the part of a teen or preteen, silence usually indicates pain, sometimes very deep pain. I recall a mother who testified on family needs at a national church hearing. She listened to other parents complain about the quality of religious education offered their teens. Then she said, "I can't get overly worried about what my thirteen-year-old son is or isn't learning in religion class when he hasn't spoken to anyone in the family for three weeks."

This mother recognized prior needs. She knew that simply furnishing a better religion teacher or a more appealing youth group wasn't going to touch the pain that was keeping her son from being a part of their family.

The most common reaction technique of youths in conflict with their families is silence. Often silence is the only reaction acceptable in the family. If youths can't expose what's bothering them for fear of ridicule or censure, or if they aren't allowed to argue, then they will revert to silence. The sad irony discovered by so many family therapists is that parents who seek professional help when their teenager becomes silent have often denied him or her any other route but silence in communicating. And although they won't permit their children to become angry or to reveal doubts or to share depression, they do worry about the silence that results. Rarely do they see any relationships between the two.

Many adolescents feel ugly and unlovable most of the time. They need constant reassurance that they are attractive and loved. I remember particularly the great number of teenage girls I taught in high school who were never made aware of their unique and appealing traits, such as an engaging smile, a special zest, or a keen wit. But they knew about their acne or their extra five pounds, and that was all that counted.

Here, again, let's remember how important it is for parents to admit to times of feeling ugly and unlovable—both in the past and present. Recently, after I'd spoken from a podium in Washington, D.C., with a former Miss America who still looked like one, I went home and despaired to my family, "You know what I had to do today? Stand next to Miss America before 2,000 people." Without pausing for a second, my teenage daughter said sympathetically, "Oh, I'm sorry, Mom." She knew instantly how I felt. We parents should know just as instantly how our children feel much of the time.

Passivity and silence on the part of husbands are most often mentioned by wives as the major problem in their marriage. When in November of 1980 *McCall's* magazine ran an article entitled "When the Man You Love Can't Show His Feelings," it was deluged with letters from women who recognized the marriages described in the article. A follow-up article in its March, 1981, issue indicated the desperation felt by those wives who have husbands who are good in every traditional sense—they're good fathers, good providers, good sons—but who aren't so good in what's most important in today's marriages—developing an intimate relationship.

"I do not feel loved," explained one of the women who wrote. "Now should be the time when we are getting closer together and finding new ways to make life interesting. But there is no communication, only criticism and silence. Is it too late to make a change?"

And then she asked the question posed by most of the women who wrote: Can I turn my back on all we have created just to find happiness? So pervasive was this thread running throughout the women's letters—an expectation of more out of marriage than being provided for and protected, yet feeling guilty for wanting more—that it led the author of this revealing piece, Natalie Gittleson, to label their marriages "on-the-brink." The very fact that these women wrote and with such feeling indicated that they were at a crossroad: Was giving up their otherwise good marriage worth it to find someone with whom they could share themselves?[14]

The impassive father is another tragic example of destructive nonverbal communication in the family. He is often one who was himself fathered by an impassive man. One such father admitted, "I was the son of an impassive father. Dad saw that we never wanted for anything. But my brother Fred and I, well—we somehow never got to really know him. Finally we just quit trying. I suppose you might characterize my impassiveness as hereditary."

We do tend to model ourselves on our parents and their style of parenting, but many couples in healthy families say that they work together so as not to repeat the problems apparent in their own parents' marriage. Impassivity, then, doesn't have to be passed on. Couples can and do overcome it, as difficult as the struggle might be.

Family writer Stuart Covington, in an article in *Marriage and Family Living,* says that without clinical help an impassive father's relationship with his children deteriorates as the years pass. "The gap separating father and children may widen, and what at first were minor problems may escalate into obstacles of frightening proportions," he said.

Covington quotes a family counselor who said, "Every human being has feelings which run the gamut from very pleasant to very painful. If a man has shut himself off from his feelings, he is like the man who would give up the use of his left arm because his right arm works so well. A father can overcome his impassiveness if he himself recognizes it as a problem (not just because someone else sees it as a problem) and is willing to be emotionally honest with himself. It is usually a difficult and painful process and often the support and guidance of a sensitive professional counselor is needed."[15]

The healthy families I know recognize positive nonverbal communication as crucial to family life. They use signs, symbols, body language, smiles, and other physical gestures to express their feelings of caring and love. They deal with silence and withdrawal in a positive, open way. Communication to them doesn't mean talking or listening alone. It includes all the clues to a person's feelings—his bearing, her expression, their resignation. Such families have a highly developed form of communication. Members don't have to say "I'm hurting" or

"I'm in need." A quick glance tells other members that. And they have developed ways of responding without words—ways that indicate empathy and love, whether or not there's an immediate solution to the pain. And that's what counts in the healthy family.

5. The family encourages individual feelings and independent thinking.

It is a paradox that healthy families tend to be alike in their differences, that is, their similarity lies in their ability to encourage and accept the emergence of individual personalities via open sharing of thoughts and feelings. Unhealthy families tend to be less open, less accepting of differences of opinion among members, more interested in thought control. The family must be Republican, or Bronco supporters, or gun-control advocates, and woe to the individual who says "Yes, but . . . ."

In discussing his study on the healthy family, Dr. Jerry M. Lewis called communicating patterns in his healthy families "a joy to witness." He saw very little group-think. He explained that the healthy family encouraged "I" statements, such as "I think..." and "I feel...." According to Dr. Lewis, one way a human being identifies himself or herself as a separate being is by making such individual statements.[16]

Many families break up when an individual member embraces a political or religious affiliation outside of the acceptable family way of thinking and believing. The publicity given youngsters who join cults and other religious groups outside of mainstream religions indicates the depth of this reality. Parents often even hire deprogrammers, who literally kidnap loved ones in order to bring them back home. But these cases are extreme. In other cases, a member might adopt vegetarianism or espouse ecological causes and find himself on the outs with the family.

The healthier the family, the better able it is to accept differing opinions in its midst. Instead of finding these opinions threatening, this family finds them exhilarating. And what Dr. Lewis found is true. It is exciting to witness such a family discussing politics, sports, or the world. Members freely say "I don't agree with you" without risking ridicule or rebuke. They say "I think it's wrong . . ." immediately after Dad says "I think it's right . . ." and Dad listens and responds.

Teachers often are able to identify students who come from such families. These students seem confident that their opinions are respected, even if they aren't shared. Students from families that don't encourage individuality in thought often seem afraid to venture their own thoughts on a subject. Instead, they wait until they discover the tenor of the class's thinking, and then they feel safe to go along. It takes a strong identity to express a belief or a feeling in a group before the group's opinion is known, but people in healthy families establish strong identities early in life.

The give-and-take of good family discussion is valuable for another reason: It gives children practice in articulating their thoughts at home so that eventually they'll feel confident outside the home. What seems to be chaotic, and even contradictory, verbal rambling on the part of preteens during a family conversation is an important prelude to their sorting out their thinking and putting words to their thoughts. Later, they'll be able to do this without verbalizing first, but speaking is the earliest way of discovering one's thoughts on a subject, the "how do I know what I think until I say it" level of articulation.

Rigid families don't understand the dynamics of this give-and-take. Some label it disrespectful and argumentative, others confusing. I like the words of Dr. John Meeks, medical director of the Psychiatric Institute of Montgomery County, Maryland, who claims that argument is a way of life with normally-developing adolescents. "In early adolescence they'll argue with parents loud and long about anything at all; as they grow older the quantity of argument decreases but the quality increases." According to Meeks, arguing is something adolescents need to do. If the argument doesn't become too bitter, they have a good chance to test their own beliefs and feelings. "Incidentally," says Meeks, "parents can expect to 'lose' most of these arguments, because adolescents are not fettered by logic or even reality."[17]

Nor are they likely to exhibit politeness in disagreement. The maturing youth can have wildly bouncing moods, and sometimes family conversation is cursed with the fruit of these moods. Learning how to disagree respectfully is a difficult task, but good families work at it.

Before closing this section, let me stress that encouraging feelings and thoughts in discussion in no way presumes that healthy parents permit unrestricted behaviors on the part of their children. There's a great difference, for example, between permitting a son to express an opinion on marijuana and allowing him to use it. That his opinion conflicts with that of his parents is okay as long as his parents make sure he knows their thinking on the subject. Whether he admits to it or not, he's likely to reflect upon their ideas if he respects them as persons. But beyond that, standards for behavior are still established primarily by parents (although moving toward mutually negotiated standards as children mature), who draw a clear line between individual opinions and subsequent behavior.

Permitting youth to sort out their feelings and thoughts via an open communication system at home gives them some kind of experience in dealing with a bewildering array of behaviors possible when they leave home. If they are free to say "I really don't see anything wrong with premarital sex," and to listen intently when a parent responds, "I understand what you're saying, but how do you feel special if a partner has slept with ten others before you?" then they are likely to recall those parental words when a premarital sexual opportunity comes up later on.

Cutting off discussion of behaviors unacceptable to us, making our young feel guilty for even thinking about values contrary to ours, and insisting upon group-think only makes contrary values more attractive to them. The healthy family risks openness in discussion rather than later regrets in experimental behaviors.

6. The family recognizes turn-off words and put-down phrases.

Some families deliberately use hurtful language in their daily communication. "What did you do all day around here?" can be a red flag to a woman who has spent all day on household tasks that don't show unless they're not done. "If only we had enough money" can be a rebuke to a husband who is working as hard as he can to provide for the family. "Got a new zit, David?" "Flunk any tests today, John?" "Don't pass her the bread. She sure doesn't need it."

Healthy families seem to develop a sensitivity to turn-off words and put-down phrases. They recognize that a comment made in jest to one person may be insulting to another. All of us are sensitive, only on different subjects. A father in one of my parenting groups confided that he could tease his wife about everything but her skiing. "I don't know why she's so sensitive about that, but I back off on it. I can say anything I want to about her cooking, her appearance, her mothering—

whatever. But not her skiing." He shook his head, mystified.

Sometimes we try too hard to discover why a certain sensitivity exists when all we need to know is that it does exist and then respect it. One of my favorite exercises with families is to ask them to reflect upon phrases they most like to hear and those they least like to hear. It's an interesting challenge because we rarely give thought to it.

Recently, for my weekly newspaper column, I invited seventy-five fourth and fifth graders to submit the words they most like to hear from their mothers. Here are five big winners, repeated over and over by almost all the kids:

"I love you."
"Yes."
"Time to eat."
"You can go."
"You can stay up late."

Other favorites included the following:

"I'll help you."
"Your friend can spend the night."
"I'm glad we have such a good daughter."
"You can go out and play."
"Sleep in."
"How was your day?"
"It's Saturday."
"You are my favorite."
"You were good tonight."
"Help me bake a cake."
"We're going to a movie."
"I'm glad I have you."
"You don't have to clean your room."
"I've got a surprise for you."
"You're great."
"Hi, I'm home from work."
"Let's go for a walk."
"You're the best kid in the world."
"Do you want to visit Grandma?"
"I'm sorry."
"I'm glad you're my son."[18]

If I had asked the fourth and fifth graders to list what they don't like to hear, I'm sure they would have given me a list twice as long and it would be apt to include some of these phrases:

"How many times do I have to tell you . . ."

"I don't care who says so."

"Don't argue with me."

"Because I say so."

"Ask your father."

When parents list comments they least like to hear from their children, these often appear:

"Don't ask me."

"Where are my books?"

"I didn't do it."

"It's her turn—I did it last time."

"How come I never get to . . ."

"He started it."

"You never let me do that when I was her age."

And on children's lists of what they least like to hear from one another are the following:

"I'm telling."

"Mom says!"

"I know something you don't know."

"You think you're so big."

"Just see if I ever let you use my bike again."

If there are such things as classic red-flag comments in the family, these would be on the list, along with many more. It's a worthwhile activity for a family to pull itself aside, list the phrases members like most and least to hear, and post them. Often parents aren't even aware of the reaction of their children to certain routine comments. And vice versa. The healthy family pays attention to the impact of its everyday conversation.

Another good exercise to clue a family in on the level of its sensitivity is that of keeping a record for a couple of weeks of the comments heard most often in daily family life. At the end of each day, parents can think of what phrases they've heard more than once that day and tally an approximate number of times they were used. If a family finds that its most-used phrases are of a helpful and caring nature—words such as "How was your day?" and "Can I help?"—then its level of sensitivity is high. If the words most commonly heard are negative—for example, "Shut up" and "Stop it" — then that family needs to pay more attention to its interrelationships, especially the role that communication plays in them.

7. The family interrupts, but equally.

When Dr. Jerry M. Lewis began to study the healthy family, he and his staff videotaped families in the process of problem-solving. The total family was given a question such as "What's the main thing wrong with your family?" Answers would vary from favoritism to lack of money to too much noise, but the answers themselves weren't important to the researchers. What was of significant interest was how the family dealt with problem-solving — who took control, how individuals responded or reacted, what were the put-downs, and whether some members were more entitled to speak than others. Among other results, the researchers found that healthy families were very clear in their communication. These families expected everyone to articulate clearly their words and feelings. Nobody was encouraged to hold back.

But in addition a most interesting discovery emerged. *Members of healthy families interrupted one another more than did members of less healthy families, but no one person got interrupted more than anyone else.* This should make many parents feel better about their family's dinner conversation. One dad reported to me that at their table, they had to take a number to finish a sentence. However, finishing sentences doesn't seem all that important in the communicating family.

So manners, particularly polite conversation techniques, are not high hallmarks of the communicating family. Spontaneity is. The family that communicates well doesn't need to finish its statements — others know what they're going to say. Members aren't sensitive to being interrupted, either. The intensity and spontaneity of the exchange are more important than propriety in conversation.[19]

8. The family develops a pattern of reconciliation.

"We know how to break up, but who the hell ever teaches us to make up?" These words, written in a letter to me from a reader in his thirties, sum up the situation in many families. I had written a column on the need for families to scrutinize their ability to reconcile, and I was astonished at the response to that column. I expect strong reader response on columns on sex education, gun control, and bedwetting, but I never expected it on family reconciliation. Whenever I get such strong response, it's usually a signal from families that I've touched a nerve.

Following up on that reader response, I studied the healthy families pinpointed by professionals and also interviewed several professionals who counsel families. Both groups indicated that there is, indeed, a pattern of reconciliation developed in healthy families that is missing in others. "It usually isn't a kiss-and-make-up situation," explained a family therapist, "but there are certain rituals developed over a long period of time that indicate it's time to get well again. Between husband and wife, it might be a concessionary phrase to which the other is expected to respond in kind. Within a family, it might be that the person who stomps off to his or her room voluntarily reenters the family circle, where something is said to make him or her welcome. The most revealing characteristic lies in how the spouse or the family responds to the first gesture of reconciliation."

When I asked some families how they knew a fight had ended, I got remarkably similar responses from individuals questioned separately. "Everyone comes out of their room," responded every single member of one family. Three members of another family said, "Mom says, 'Anybody want a Pepsi?'" My favorite, though, was the little five-year-old who scratched his head and furrowed his forehead in deep thought after I asked him how he knew the family fight was over. Finally, he said, "Well . . . Daddy gives a great big yawn and says, 'Well. . . .'" This scene is easy to visualize and even somewhat stereotypic of the healthy family in which one parent decides that the unpleasantness needs to end and makes a gesture that comes to be known as the beginning of peace. The great big yawn and the "Well" say a lot more than a stretch to this family. It says it's time to end the fighting and to pull together again as family.

Why have we neglected to teach families the important art of reconciling? I asked the family therapist mentioned earlier. "Because we have pretended that good families don't fight. They do. Everybody does. It's essential to fight for good health in the family. It gets things out into the open. But we need to learn to put ourselves back together—and many families never learn this."

In an attempt to fill this void, I began to include some exercises on reconciliation techniques in family workshops and found them gratefully welcomed by parents. Here's an idea that's ripe for churches, voluntary organizations, and health and parenting groups to offer units and classes on—how to fight and how to reconcile as a family. A 4-H project, a scouting badge, or a session attached to youth league meetings could be devoted to family reconciliation skills.

In my work, I've found that spouses tend to simulate their own parents' method of reconciliation. If, when they were children, a heated argument ended with days of cold silence, they tend to repeat this pattern today. If their parents' arguments always went back to a specific recrimination (as in Erma Bombeck's supreme argument clincher: "Why did your mother wear black to our wedding?"), they're probably going to insert recriminations in their own disagreements. If their parents' fights included physical abuse, they're likely to pass on that horror. (Many abusers had parents who abused one another.)

While the above is depressing, it is helpful to remember that good reconciliation patterns are passed from generation to generation as well. If it's a family policy that nobody goes to bed angry at another—which is the most familiar pattern found in healthy families—it's usually traceable back to an earlier generation. Or if nobody is allowed to hit, that rule is likely to be passed on.

I also found that healthy families know how to time divisive and emotional issues that may cause friction. They don't bring up potentially explosive subjects right before they go out or before bedtime, for instance. Over and over I heard the phrase "the right time." The right time seemed to be one in which there was enough time to discuss the issue heatedly, rationally, and completely—and enough time to reconcile. "You got to solve it right there," said the dad in one of the healthiest families I studied. "Don't let it go on and on. It just causes more problems. Then when it's solved, let it be. No nagging, no remembering."

When I worked with families in Hawaii, they shared with me an old Hawaiian way of setting things right in the family. The whole clan used to gather to get rid of negative feelings about one another. Each person or family was encouraged to bring up those things that needed to be set right among them. Over the centuries rituals for eliminating wrongs were devised. One of the more interesting ones called for the wronged person to draw a picture or symbol of the wrong in the sand. Then the clan invited the person who inflicted the wrong to step forward and ask forgiveness and promise redress. When that was completed, the wronged member wiped the symbol out of the sand. Once that symbol was gone, so was the memory of it, and the family or clan stood together again with no ongoing feuds to destroy their clanship. They were whole again, a family.

As uncomfortable and structured as this might seem to mainland families, it has a kind of counterpart in healthy families, who tend to schedule discussions on divisive issues rather than allow them to explode. In this way, the family has more control over the environment in which to fight and reconcile. Family members aren't victims, totally at the mercy of the emotions of the moment.

Reconciliation is a basic part of communication. It allows the surfacing of occasional discord, unhappy feelings, anger, sadness, disappointment, and frustration. The healthier the family, the more refined its pattern of reconciliation.

These, then, are eight hallmarks of the family that is able to communicate and listen—the trait most often selected by professionals as evident in the healthy families they observe. A family that embodies these hallmarks is likely to be a good communicating family.
1. The family exhibits an unusual relationship between the parents.
2. The family has control over television.
3. The family listens and responds.
4. The family recognizes nonverbal messages.
5. The family encourages individual feelings and independent thinking.
6. The family recognizes turn-off words and put-down phrases.
7. The family interrupts, but equally.
8. The family develops a pattern of reconciliation.

Trait 13: The healthy family values table time and conversation.

My survey respondents valued family table time and conversation so highly that they placed it thirteenth in a list of fifty-six possible traits. Because this trait is so obviously a part of the family communication process, I am discussing it in this chapter.

Traditionally, the family table has been a symbol of socialization.

It's the gathering place for the clan, the one time each day that parents and children are assured of uninterrupted time with one another. It's been said that Tolstoy was so inspired by the love and unity he witnessed when he glimpsed a family at table through a chance opening of the door as he passed on a stairway landing that he wrote *War and Peace,* his saga that centers on the Rostov family.

The family table is more than a literary device or symbol, of course, but it is interesting to study its place in the arts. Cartoonists use drawings of a family at table in order to quickly characterize that family. Breakfast scenes with people hidden behind newspapers show us a certain family style. A round dinner table with lots of people conversing is often used to suggest family closeness. The classic long, narrow table with the matriarch at one end and the patriarch at the other, with perhaps a child or two equidistant, easily indicates distance among family members.

In discussing the problem of family listening and sharing, Dr. Lee Salk, Cornell's popular child psychologist, writes, "Meal time is incredibly important in this regard. People used to talk and listen at meal time, but now they sit in front of their television sets with their dinner. I don't care how busy you are—you can take that time with your children. You can talk about your dreams; you can talk about your day; you can talk about your frustrations. The busier you are, the more valuable meal time is for your child. If we don't spend this time with our youngsters, they are not going to develop healthy attitudes toward family life."[20]

Therapists frequently call upon a patient's memory of the family table during their childhood in order to determine what degree of general communication and interaction there was in the patient's early family life. The patient is asked to draw the shape of the table; to place himself, his parents, and his siblings around it; to describe a typical meal; and, finally, to suggest typical table conversation. Some patients experience a great deal of recall, whereas others can recall nothing. Their childhood tables were either so unpleasant or so unimpressive that they have blocked them out of their memories as adults. Therapists hold that there is a relationship between the love in a home and the richness of the family table. It is to the table that love or discord eventually come.

In many families, the table becomes the place on which to

dump—to dump the day's frustrations, to dump invectives on one another, or to dump silences. In these families, the one daily opportunity to share becomes fraught with tension.

Although my respondents placed family table time high in the traits of the healthy family, the trend is away from families having table time together. Yankelovich, Skelly and White, a research firm specializing in attitudes and life-styles, have found that fast-food dining is becoming a way of life for Americans. According to Florence Skelly, we are eating an average of five times per day and we are eating light and fast. Ironically, while there is a trend toward eating more meals at home, the variety of working patterns in our culture *has led to more unplanned meals that families no longer eat together.*[21] This finding is seconded by George Armelagos, coauthor of *Continuing Passions: The Anthropology of Eating,* who says that fast food is a reflection of a society in which social encounters are short and intense. When asked if the tradition of families eating together is dying, he replied, "Yes. There are so many things we have to do, often with work schedules that don't coincide. Women are working outside the home, and, in general, men and women are becoming more independent."[22]

Independent of what, we might ask? Of our children and spouses? Of our need to share while breaking bread together in the age-old ritual of family life? Or of our need for the closeness and communication that the family table presumes?

Work schedules, organized activities, and other family calendar culprits limit the quantity of family table time, but equally guilty is that old thief of quality family time—television. In an informal study conducted by a Presbyterian ministerial staff, 68 percent of the families interviewed in three churches saw nothing wrong with turning the family table over to television viewing. We have already discussed the difficulty in communicating with the ongoing presence of television in the family circle. If the family table also succumbs to the TV set, hope for a daily period of sharing, caring, and feeling is slim.

Families who do a good job of communicating make the dinner meal an important part of their day. They don't allow personal grudges and unpleasantness to be expressed, even though, as we will see later, they do encourage differences of opinion. These families are very protective of the time allotted to the family dinner hour and often become angry if they're asked to infringe upon it for work or pleasure. A good number of respondents indicated that adults in the healthiest families they know refuse dinner business meetings as a matter of principle. They discourage their children from sports activities that presume upon the dinner hour as a condition for team participation. ("We know which of our swimmers will or won't practice at dinner time," said a coach, with mixed admiration. "Some parents never allow their children to miss dinners. Others don't care at all.") These families pay close attention to the number of times they'll be able to be together in an upcoming week, and they rearrange schedules to be assured of spending this time together. And they never allow television to become part of the menu.

A family counselor commented, "The best way to discover the health of a family is to eat a few meals with them. They can't fake it. Too many ingrained eating patterns. Some are miserable, but others are beautiful to behold."

According to professionals, the family that wants to improve its level of communication should look closely at its attitudes toward the family table. Is family table time and conversation important? Is it optional? Is it open and friendly or warlike and sullen? Is it conducive to sharing more than food — does it encourage the sharing of ideas, feelings, and family intimacies? Is it a battleground between cook and eaters? Does it exist at all?

Expressing sadness over the death of the family table, author George Armelagos said, "Dinner was one of the major times that the parents included children in family and societal affairs. Dinner began with a prayer, which put the food in a symbolic and ritualistic context. Then, in the process of talking, social relationships, attitudes and beliefs were all enforced."[23]

Dinner can still be the daily gathering point for the family, the time when many kinds of sustenance are offered. Although the national trend seems to be away from the family table, the healthy families we studied are making a determined effort to offset that trend.

4
Affirming and Supporting

Trait 2: The healthy family affirms and supports one another.

> Call it a clan, call it a network, call it a tribe, call it a family.
> Whatever you call it, whoever you are, you need one.
> — Jane Howard

The healthy family affirms and supports, according to my survey respondents, who placed this trait second in a list of fifty-six traits. "The good family supports all of its members, not just its father or its parents or a member who's an outstanding athlete," commented one of the responding psychologists. The prominence of this characteristic also shows up in the National Study of Family Strengths, where researchers found that in happy families members show appreciation for one another.

Marriage specialist David R. Mace says that several family studies suggest that this vital characteristic—affirming one another—is the basic cohesive factor in all happy families. He tells of one study done some years ago of really good families in Oklahoma. "The purpose of the study," writes Mace, "was to find out if possible the sources of strength in these 'well' families. Was there something they had in common that had made them function so effectively?

"Yes, there *was* something." Mace continues. "The study found that the members of these families liked each other, and kept on telling each other that they liked each other. They affirmed each other, gave each other a sense of personal worth, and took every reasonable opportunity to speak and act affectionately. The result, very naturally, was that they enjoyed being together and reinforced each other in ways that made their relationships very satisfying."[1]

This is the hunger we all have—to be liked, to be loved, to share our love and our lives—yet many families are unable to satisfy this hunger. For a variety of reasons, they are unable to fulfill this deceptively simple purpose for living together in family.

Most families do have a purpose, however, although it may be hidden from them. In families in which there's a parent with political, executive, or military ambitions, often the family purpose is to further the success goals of that parent. Individual interests and goals are subordinated to the parent's career goals. The family may move eleven times in nine years without complaining, as did a Xerox executive's family whose wife and mother said blatantly, "We are committed to my husband's career. All else is secondary."

In other families the family business, farm, or mere economic survival is the obvious purpose. Each member contributes to the family goal in proportion to his or her ability. Although individual interests and goals aren't necessarily denied, members generally presume that family economics come first. Often a child or spouse has to sacrifice personal ambition, an avocation, or schooling in order to support the family business venture.

Supporting a cause or pursuing a recreational activity are two other purposes frequently found in families. Sometimes families rally around a political movement—working for a candidate, against an issue, or with a specific group. Sometimes families so closely identify with their church life that their own purpose intricately unites with that of the church. And sometimes families are oriented toward leisure, spending most of their nonworking time in recreational activities. They might ski, golf, sail, support a professional football or basketball team, or play in youth or adult league sports.

Families without any sense of purpose tend to become materialistic, even hedonistic. Buying alleviates their hunger for purpose and relationship. If things aren't going well in this family and the parents wonder why they work so hard with so little gratification, well...they can always go shopping. Or move to a larger home. Or redecorate. Or take a trip. Or get a new car.

"We weren't getting along very well so we decided to buy a camper," one mother told me. A camper! If family members aren't getting along very well, why buy a contained area in which to pack them? Because that family, like so many who buy to compensate for missing intimacy, purchased the promise of the camper ads, which show happy families enjoying one another in a beautiful outdoor environment. That's what the family was really seeking, not a shiny new vehicle.

The pattern of buying in order to satisfy deeper longings in a family often becomes cyclic. When the joys of acquisition and the newness of something wear off, old problems and emptiness reemerge. The family begins to pine for another new product, works for it, obtains it—and the cycle continues. Soon the family becomes the economists' definition of a family—a consumer unit.

Several years ago I met a woman with an intriguing career—helping upwardly-mobile families design their future dream homes. She would live with the family for a week or so to get an idea of its life-style; in that way, she was able to relate to the various designers of the home some of the family's needs, whims, and desires. The resulting homes were very expensive, probably costing about $500,000 in today's market. But the astonishing revelation this woman made was that over half of her client couples were divorced within a year of moving into their dream home. "Why?" I asked in disbelief. "Because the home is their last attempt to be happy or to save a crumbling marriage," she replied. "By the time they come to us for their home of a lifetime, often it's a last desperate chance to find out if it will give them happiness."

This unhappy situation of acquisition being a family's purpose is entirely contradictory to what my survey professionals perceive as the central purpose in healthy families. "The best families I see are those in which members care enough about each other to give a sense of support and self-esteem," said a pediatrician. "The kids know they're worthwhile because the family makes them worthwhile."

And a teacher commented, "What a loss to our society that some kids aren't affirmed at home. How can they recognize their goodness and gifts if their own parents don't? If nothing else, I hope your study convinces parents of the need to accept and praise more, scold and tolerate less."

Her words took me back twenty years to the suburban high school in which my husband and I were teaching at the time. We both had as a student a promising young junior from a working class family. When he came to us one day and confided that he was considering quitting school, we were aghast and asked his reasons. He stammered a bit and then admitted the real reason. He had gone home eagerly a week earlier and told his parents that he had made the National Honor Society, the first ever in his family to do so. Their reaction? "Big deal," said his mother. "Why don't you get a job?"

Families today may not be quite so overt, but similar messages—emotional cut-offs, the professionals call them—come through to individuals: What makes you think you're good enough to do it? What makes you think we care? Why aren't you doing what I think is important? Nobody in our family has ever been interested in that. Fat girls can't be cheerleaders. I don't think you have an ear for music. What kind of job could *you* get, Mom? You're not tough enough to go out for that sport. Do you really think you can fix it yourself, dear?

In the healthy family, the individual is affirmed for who he or she is and not for what he or she looks like, has, or does. In such families, emotional cutoffs are nonexistent. Individual members come to the family for affirmation of their being, for support of their projects, and for strength to survive emotionally as well as physically in the many environments outside the home. Dorothy Corkille Briggs explains in *Your Child's Self-Esteem:* "The process of building self-image goes this way: a new reflection, a new experience, or a bit of new growth leads to a new success or failure, which in turn leads to a new or revised statement about the *self*. In this fashion, each person's self-concept usually evolves throughout his lifetime."[2] The value of a supportive family during this evolutionary process is inestimable.

A young Olympian athlete said in a TV interview, "I always had my parents' support—even when I knew they disagreed with me." This kind of support emerges constantly in good families. Members support one another, for better or for worse, in similarity and in differences. Dr. Urie Bronfenbrenner defines a family as *a group which possesses and implements an irrational commitment to the well-being of its members.*[3] *Irrational* is an important word here. It means that although we may not understand or agree with a particular stand taken by one of our children or siblings, we'll defend that person's right to take that stand and may even do the dishes for that person when he or she is pushed for time. Irrational means that although we may not want Mom to go back to school or work, we celebrate her A's and we fold the laundry without being asked. And it means that even though we may be disappointed when Dad's work takes him out of town and away from us, we pretend it's okay so he won't feel guilty.

The word *irrational* means more. It means that the squeaky concert presented by third graders playing recorders is as important as the near-professional jazz concert of the high-school senior, that the girl who is fat feels lovable in spite of it, and that when an election is lost or a prized spot on the team isn't won, the family doesn't value the loser less.

This need for affirmation extends far beyond small children and their need for support. A recent British study found that the survival rate of heart patients in an intensive-care unit was no higher than that of similar patients treated at home, surrounded by family and friends. According to work done by Dr. Leonard Duhl of Berkeley and the work of other medical specialists, people who are connected to others in personal relationship and through communities are the ones most capable of dealing with illness.[4]

Educators are paying close attention to a study conducted by Dr. Jack Pascoe, a pediatrician in the School of Medicine at the University of North Carolina, who found that children who are talked to, held, and praised tend to develop intellectually more rapidly than children who do not receive as much warmth and affection. Dr. Pascoe studied the families of eighty children born premature or sick and who had been in intensive-care units for a length of time before joining their families.

Visiting the families of these children over a two-year period, the researcher examined the children and interviewed their mothers, noting particularly the amount of family and social support the mother received, the child's intellectual level, and the home environment. His conclusion? That mothers who received a high level of emotional support themselves gave their children more tender care and encouragement than mothers in families that didn't give them emotional support. The most important source of their support were husbands and other family members.

Despite such obstacles as living in rural areas, lacking for money, and having to care for a sick child, these families — devoid of material wealth and rich in emotional support — enjoyed their children and did a good job of rearing them. The children in families like these scored significantly higher on intelligence tests than those who came from less stimulating and caring families.[5]

Many quiet, unassuming families are models of support and affirmation. Teachers and church personnel are particularly aware of the children who come from affirming homes. The children may be very different in looks, ability, and personality, but they all are alike in feeling good about themselves. What is it about these families that makes them affirming and supportive? Here are some obvious hallmarks.

1. The parents have good self-esteem.
Insecure and doubting parents are not likely to instill attitudes of

self-worth in their children. Unfortunately, many such parents believe they can. They focus upon their children when they need to focus first on themselves. In an article on choosing a spouse wisely, psychologist Michael Cavanagh asks persons about to be married: "Are you confident of your own worth? People with confidence in their own worth approach others assuming that they will be liked and accepted until they learn otherwise. Such individuals have a serene appreciation for their own goodness and recognize that their faults and weaknesses are outweighed by their likeability or loveableness."

Dr. Cavanagh goes on to explain that people who fear rejection assume that, sooner or later, other persons will discover something negative in them and not want to be with them anymore. "When a relationship does not work out, they explain, 'I knew that after you got to know me, you wouldn't like me,' which reinforces their own feeling of rejectability. An individual with a good self-concept states, 'It's all right that it didn't work out, because the other person wanted me to be somebody I'm not,' or 'It's too bad the relationship didn't work out but I feel the other person is losing more than I am.' "[6]

If we aren't esteemed at home, we'll seek it elsewhere—at work, in peer groups, or in voluntary organizations. It's common for women to enter the work force to increase their sense of self-worth. "I know my job isn't that exciting," a young mother said, "typing all day, you know, but I'm good at it and I'm valued at work. I know I'm worth something *there*." She didn't have to tell us that she wasn't valued much at home.

Unfortunately, in our society we judge people's value by their income. The more society rewards people financially, the more worth we accord them. Thus, we find some men and women in a frenzy-like drive to get to the top of their field, even if it means losing their families along the way. When they arrive, theirs is a Pyrrhic victory because their worth is still pegged on what they do rather than on what they are. They discover that too late. Sportsmen, politicians, stars—how many have publicly regretted sacrificing their families, who would have loved them for who they *are*, in exchange for public adulation, which is fleeting and based on what a person *does*?

In good families parents feel good about themselves. If they don't, they recognize their problems and do something about them. I know a man who felt undervalued in his work. Before long, this situation began to affect his family life. His eroding self-worth rubbed off on his wife and children, particularly his formerly confident teenage son, who began to show signs of insecurity at school and in friendships. After a time, the couple decided that the job, for all its money and financial security, wasn't worth either the feelings of doubt it was instilling in the husband or the subsequent fallout on family life. The man quit his job to take a less well-paying but more satisfying one. That was four years ago, and when I recently asked him if he regretted it, he replied with a strong no. "I wish I had done it sooner," he said. "I think if I would have stayed there, our family life would have gone down the drain. After worrying day after day about whether I could do the job well enough to please the boss, I started to believe I couldn't do it. It wasn't until I got out that I realized it was my boss's problem, not mine."

It takes a lot of courage to begin again at age forty-five, but people who need to experience more self-worth frequently find that courage. Probably the example we're most familiar with is the wife-mother who never finished college and decides to go back to school in her thirties or forties. After twenty or so years away, she isn't sure she can do the work. She knows she may be the odd one in a classroom of young coeds. She realizes that the family is going to have to move over and make space for her during the homework hour and that she'll be less available to them. But she also recognizes her deep need to prove that she can do it—for her sense of self-worth.

Sometimes her loving family—who has valued her—doesn't understand her motive. Family members are hurt because she needs more than them alone. They need to listen to the words that have issued from the lips of thousands of women in similar circumstances: "I know I am valuable as a wife and mother. Now I want to find out if I'm worth something out there. I have to do this."

I have to do this—a rallying cry for those adults who reach a point in life when their doubts and insecurities from childhood, resulting in a lack of self-esteem in adulthood, drive them to test the validity of their self-worth. Healthy families recognize and support a parent's search for self-esteem. Unhealthy ones block it, often selfishly. And it's true that it may indeed mean less money, less availability, a move, a risk that the parent will find other people more interesting than they are.

There's a wonderful anecdote about a forty-four-year-old mother who decided that at long last she would begin college. Her children were stunned. "You'll be forty-eight when you're finished," they cried. "I'll be forty-eight anyway," she replied.

I speak with the authority of personal experience about the fact that families can be heroic when it comes to supporting a father who changes careers or a mother who broadens hers. As a wife and mother of three children and a person whose career includes firm writing deadlines and a travel schedule, I realize the boost that my family's support and affirmation gives me in my work. It frees me so that I can do the best possible job "out there." About once a month I go out of state to lecture. Not only does the family naturally assume household duties while I'm gone but they also assume nurturing and supporting roles as well. My sixteen-year-old son shows a parental concern for his twelve-year-old brother, asking about his day and helping with his homework. When I return home, they ask the right questions. They seem happy to see me and to hear of any small successes or failures I may have experienced. And I am always glad to return to them because I need their support and affirmation. I don't have to leave to get it.

2. Everyone is expected to affirm and support.

I meet families in which the mother is the sole source of emotional support, which is sad because this is an area in which it's as vital to give as to receive. In these families, the children don't show much interest or support in each other's activities. The father may focus on his work and come home to relax, not to be bothered with the children's activities, interests, and triumphs. He leaves that to Mom.

In family workshops or retreats, when we call upon the family to rate members in order of their supportive nature, many a family is surprised to discover, upon reflection, that in its family life the mother serves as the total emotional support system while the father serves as the total financial support system. It's important for families to evaluate how they function in order to avoid an imbalance of support.

Dr. Gary Stollak, a psychologist who specializes in child and family, stresses the importance of two parents in the nurturing and affirming process. "When two adults are actively involved in child care, youngsters simply have a better crack at finding a talent or interest that meshes with one held by a parent, so winning them the warm glow of parental approval and encouragement." He extends this to sibling rivalry as well. "Brothers and sisters quarrel precisely because they feel elbowed off the path of the parents' warm rays of attention. The more paths that open up, the less likely a kid is to feel he must push his brother or sister out of the way to get emotional goodies. And Dad, with a different set of interests and enthusiasms than Mom, opens up a whole new avenue for them."[7]

An equally interesting observation by Urie Bronfenbrenner is that children are the most important source of parental support. Although our culture tends to promote the reverse, both parents and children should serve as support systems and recipients. It isn't a case of the parents doing the supporting and the children doing the receiving but a case of both doing both in strong family systems.

It's a pleasure to be with a supportive family in its natural setting. There's a genuine interest exhibited in what each member has done during the day. A dinner I sat in on recently went like this:

"Was your history test as tough as you thought it would be, Rich?"

"Yeah, worse. But I think I did okay on it. I sure didn't ace it."

"Did he ask about the stuff you were studying last night? The League of Nations and all that?"

"No, at least not for the members and nonmembers—the stuff I memorized. But he asked why the United States voted the way it did."

"Bet you got that one."

"Yeah. But I'm glad we talked about it at supper or I wouldn't have. Say, did you find out about this weekend yet, Dad?"

"Yes. I can't go to the mountains. I've got a meeting."

"About what?"

"I have to meet with the sales reps of a home computer company on Saturday and tell them about our product."

"Why? What do they want to know about industrial rivets?"

"They're looking for a small company to use in their sales campaign—to show other small companies how a bunch of their computers would help them make more money. If they pick ours, we get free computers from them, so it's worth it."

"Sounds like a good deal."

"Could be. Cross your fingers. Sorry about the mountains."

"That's okay. Maybe we can go fishing instead. When will the meeting be over?"

"Should be over by noon. Anybody else have anything on Saturday?"

Heads shake all the way around.

"Mom, if we go fishing, do you want to go?"

"Do I have to cook or do I get to read while you fish?" Laughter.

"We'll all cook . . . but you can clean up." More laughter.

The conversation went on like this throughout the meal. Eventually each member was questioned specifically about his or her day—and not the general "How-was-your-day?-Oh,-fine" routine which passes for interest in many families. Topics from the previous day, such as the history test, were remembered and discussed—a sure sign to a child that his or her day's work is interesting enough to be recalled. Dad's meeting, which could have drawn recriminating frowns, was treated as a topic of interest, and together the family chose an alternate recreation, clearly telling Dad that he was supported in his decision to hold the meeting. Others' schedules were taken into consideration before a fishing trip was settled upon, and Mom's feelings about the choice were invited. Aside from the general humor in the conversation, the most refreshing aspect of this family at table was its genuine interest in what all members were doing, from a mundane account of a third-grade-recess football game to an explanation of a parent's work.

In too many families, this just doesn't happen. Members focus only on themselves and their own needs, precisely because others don't. They aren't aware of what's going on in one another's lives, so they can't show interest in the daily living out of those lives. Interest generates support. Lack of interest generates lack of support. Those who work with many families remark on the great difference between the supportive and nonsupportive family. "It's the difference between a family and a group of roommates," explained a family counselor. "The person from a really supportive family doesn't have to go it alone. That person is part of something bigger—a family that cares enough to let him or her know he or she is okay."

In a newspaper interview, some healthy families in America's mobile executive class said that a support system was crucial to them in their constant need to adjust to new living circumstances. A woman who had moved almost yearly said, "It takes a strong, intact family to survive. In front of others I put up a guard. I'm rarely vulnerable to others. Most girls who are transient are used to hiding their feelings. It's for your own survival. As long as you have support at home, you don't need anything else."

3. The family realizes support doesn't mean pressure.

Dr. Henry Fischer, prominent Denver-area child psychologist and family counselor, once told me two basic problems of parents with whom he meets in practice are that they are not in their children's lives enough or that they are in their children's lives too much. That's the fine line that families tread. How much support and affirmation are good? When does support turn into pressure on the child or the spouse to become something someone else wants them to be? A day at the youth league ballpark can demonstrate just about every level of parental support imaginable, from anger at having to be there to bullying the child for failing to perform up to parental expectations.

Healthy families seem to find that right level of support for each member. They realize that some children need to be encouraged and prodded while others need to learn to develop realistic goals and to control their expectations of themselves. Truly knowing each child and his or her capabilities, confidence, and pressure level is foundational to determining the best level of support.

"My parents don't put me down when I lose," said nine-year-old ski racer Preston Mendenhall of Aspen. "All of us on the team have a good time. Winning is great but having fun is more important."[8] Many of us live with more pressure than we should, but too much pressure can be especially devastating for children. Growing suicide rates and increasing chemical dependency among young people point to our youths' inability to survive the many pressures that family and culture place upon them. The pressures may be subtle ones, but they're real nevertheless. Maybe it's an expectation of talent that just isn't there or of academic achievement beyond the student's ability or desire. Perhaps it's a hope that the child will become the individual the parent wanted to be.

Children pick up parental disappointment quickly, as much as we may try to mask it. "You didn't make the team?" in the wrong tone of voice won't be offset by a "That's too bad, Bob." A comment about a friend's achievement or beauty can be taken by children—sometimes justifiably—to be a criticism of them. Elaborate rationalizations of others' achievements by parents don't help either. For example, "Well, her parents paid for the best tennis coach around. No wonder she won."

It's important to note here the existence of the superachiever in many families. This is a child (or a parent) who doesn't have unusual gifts but is so motivated by some inner determination to succeed that parents are confused about their role. Should they automatically support such a child in all his or her endeavors, even when they know it will lead to disappointment for that child and perhaps a damaged self-image?

Again, good families seem to keep goals in perspective and motivation under scrutiny. "Why is it so important to this child to win, to be tops in everything?" they ask themselves. Parents in healthy families frequently sense that such a child needs more personal attention and reassurance than their less achieving, less motivated children, even though a natural parental reaction is to furnish less for the child who is already superachieving.

A mother confided in me that one of their children caused her and her husband a good deal of distress. The child set impossible standards and goals for himself, and then when he didn't reach them, he proclaimed he was justified in his low self-esteem. "See, I can't do anything!" he would react bitterly. For a while they only reassured him of his worth, but eventually they began to take a hand in his life by permitting him some of the pressured activities he seemed to search out or denying others to him. It worked. He hadn't been ready for the responsibility of selecting his own activities. Once he was freed of making those choices and realized he didn't have to do everything, he relaxed and became much more enjoyable, both to himself and others.

High self-esteem includes accepting one's limitations. Denying them only leads to greater problems because self-images that can't be lived up to lead inevitably to failure, which in turn fosters poor self-esteem. Joan B. Lindroth, writing in *Marriage and Family Living,* explained, "A child must be taught to think well of himself or herself in a healthy and realistic way. By recognizing and emphasizing a child's talents and attributes, yet being aware of his or her imperfections, a parent can help a child develop a healthy balance between a complete lack of self-confidence and an overinflated ego. A show of ability or a job well-done by the child should always be praised."

According to Lindroth, shortcomings should be viewed in the proper perspective, neither glossed over nor pointed out in a way so negative as to destroy self-confidence. "When Jimmy is downcast after striking out with the bases loaded, remind him how well he played outfield and impress upon him that each team member contributes different talents. Above all, avoid comparing him with other children, especially siblings. . . . A youngster must learn to accept his or her limitations, but the emphasis should always be on recognizing and improving existing strengths."[9]

4. The family's basic mood is positive.

Family specialists speak of a family personality, or mood, which is as unique to each family as a mood is to an individual. Dr. Jerry M. Lewis explains that this mood is the one on which the family operates when all is going well. How it survives its stresses depends upon its basic mood. In some families, according to Lewis, even when all is going as well as can be expected, the basic mood is one of depression.[10]

Not so in good families. One of its hallmarks is hope, a looking-forward quality. Stresses are considered temporary, although they may last years, and the healthy family seems to dredge up the resources to deal with them. One of the more positive families I have met in my work has been beset by problems: loss of job, poverty-level existence, discrimination, emergency health problems, drug addiction, and an unwed pregnancy. Yet, the family is basically hopeful, living out a sort of gratitude that things aren't worse than they are and that as long as family members have one another, they can go on.

Members of families such as this one use many forms of support. They listen and they discuss, but they also make overt gestures of support. For example, when a daughter's homework isn't going well, the rest of the family tries to help. Or when a son gets up late, the rest pitch in and see that he gets out the door in time, one handing him a hastily prepared lunch, another rounding up his books or briefcase, and yet another picking up his trail of discarded clothing and possessions. Or when a parent has had a trying day, this family supports by relieving him or her from routine questions and duties. They sense that on this particular day this parent needs more support than usual.

This family presents an achievable ideal of family life, unlike some television families in which members spend their entire day concerned for one another. Members of the healthy families I surveyed, in fact, tended to be individualistic in nature—that is, each member had his or her own interests and life—but together members supplied extra amounts of visible support to one another when it was needed.

(As a later chapter on responsibility submits, active family support should *not* be used to shore up a slacker. On the contrary, the way that the healthy family supports a member who refuses to be responsible is to force that person to face the consequences of his or her irresponsibility. In this family, if a child is consistently late to school, family members do less rather than more to get him or her to school on time. Their emotional support lies in withdrawing physical support.)

Probably the most obvious way family members can show support is by praising one another and by letting each member know how much he or she is cared for. In this area, the American family isn't as bad off as many believe. According to a 1979 Gallup Youth Survey, parental words of love are much more common than parental words of wisdom. Teens surveyed were asked, "Did either of your parents happen to do any of the following with you during the past twenty-four hours? Help with your homework? Praise you for something you did? Hug or kiss you? Tell you they love you? Talk with you about your activities during the day?"

Three out of four teens said they had discussed their day's activities with at least one parent; 58 percent had received parental words of praise; half had gotten a hug or kiss; and a slightly smaller number had heard "I love you" from at least one parent.

Interestingly, only 20 percent had been helped with their homework by parents. (This may say less about parental support than parental ability, however.) Teens from white-collar backgrounds were more likely to hear words of praise or get hugs than their classmates from blue-collar homes. Not surprisingly, the better students, regardless of background, answered yes to the five questions in greater numbers than did those of average or below-average academic standing.

The most marked difference, though, was in the praise category. Simply put, the more that students received praise from their parents, the better able they were to achieve.[11] This shouldn't surprise us when we consider how essential praise is to our own well-being. We need it from friends, from people at work, and in our families. We remember praise long after the deliverer has given it. I recently met a woman in the supermart whom I had taught as an adult student in a professional writing class eight years earlier. She had to reintroduce herself to me because I had completely forgotten her. After we spoke for a minute or two, she said, "I have always remembered you because you said I had a nice sense of wit in my writing." (At that moment, I needed one myself, because I couldn't even remember her, much less her wit.)

According to Linda Tschirhart Sanford, author of family-related materials, a frequent mistake parents make is to remain silent when they could praise a child for something. Parents are better at pointing out failures than successes to their children. "But if mistakes and successes do not receive equal attention, chances are good any youngster will lose interest in his finer qualities and become discouraged over the disproportionate focus on his human frailties," says this parent educator. "And if parents' praise is genuine and accurate, children will learn self-love, not conceit," she adds. [12]

Parents' reluctance to praise their children may well be based on just such a fear of encouraging conceit. Many of today's parents grew up when praise was not considered a positive parenting virtue. Praise spoiled children, made them vain. It ran contrary to the religious principle of humility and the cultural virtue of modesty. Many modern parents were taught to offset compliments with such denigrating remarks as "Oh, this old dress?" "Anybody could do it," "I was just lucky," and "You ought to see my friend do this."

Praise works wonders in the family. I use a technique in family retreats in which families pull apart and each member tells what he or she prizes about every other member. This activity is remembered long after the retreat ends. I witnessed one particular family as they went around their circle mentioning gifts that were appreciated. "Dad is always able to understand. He doesn't shout first and ask questions later," said one, and the others nodded. "Mom keeps the family together. She has ideas for things like this retreat and sees that we do things together." Another nod. On to the children: "Paul is always in a good mood." "Gary tells super good jokes and is always so funny." "Martha teases us in a way to make us laugh."

These recognitions of even very little talents are significant to us because they came from the family who lives with us daily. If a family has never done any exercise like this one, I suggest establishing a time yearly to do it—perhaps while in the car on vacation, on New Year's Day, or during any other annual event. If the families I work with are any yardstick, this activity might turn out to be one of your family's most cherished check-up traditions.

Families who have a practice of praising, of helping one another without being asked, of being able to say "You're neat" and other forms of "I love you" have a basically positive mood. Life is seen as a pleasant experience to be enjoyed, not a daily chore to be endured.

In his book *Encounters with the Self,* Don Hamachek writes, "Whether parents are aware of it or not, through their daily life-styles and the *consistency* of their behavior they teach their children how to blend, for better or worse, the basic ingredients for living—how to deal with anxiety, failure, how to handle money, make friends, *be* a friend, how to resolve conflicts and make decisions, how to love and be loved.[13]

5. The family supports its institutions, but not automatically.

An old, approved attitude in our culture said that if a child experienced difficulty at school, he or she could expect to experience more difficulty at home. In a conflict between teacher and child, the teacher was automatically right, and the child was not even allowed to explain his or her side of the problem. Parents with this attitude even bragged, "If my kid gets in trouble at school, he's in for more trouble at home."

Children were not allowed to complain about boring Sunday school lessons, insensitive pastors, or religious rituals they didn't understand. Encounters with unsympathetic doctors, frightening hospital experiences, painful dental visits—all these were expected and were considered a part of the toughening required in the growing-up experience. The prime motivation for parental behavior in this regard, though, was less that of personal insensitivity and more that of providing unquestioning institutional support.

Our country has always promoted the idea that good families and effective parents support their institutions without question. Much of the anguish of the sixties occurred when parents felt compelled to choose sides with their young over respect and obedience to the institutions in their lives—government, schools, law, and church. Even today we find a strong thread of patriotism involved in parental support for the various institutions. This attitude implies that a family who questions its government, school, or church is asking for problems. Its children will likely grow up without morals and proper respect for tradition.

In contrast, we find families who completely write off the institutions as self-serving, inhumane, uncaring, and corrupt. They promote the attitude to their children that schools are no damn good, all church personnel are hypocritical, doctors are out to gouge them, government is corrupt, and, in fact, no institution can be trusted. These are the parents Dr. Bruno Bettelheim referred to when he said, "We send our children to school to make their way into the system, and then we tell them the system is lousy."

Healthy families look with a much more balanced eye at the institutions that affect their lives. They support the school and the teachers, but they also support their children. When the two conflict, they check out the situation and may well end up supporting the child over the institution. Sometimes they're labeled troublesome by the schools when they do this, but they recognize the importance of being fair. They know that if they automatically choose the school and teacher, they merely drive children away from education and foster in them a distrust of the adults in their lives, who seem to be in a conspiracy against them.

Educator and teacher-trainer Martin Weiss explains that because the school system is so sophisticated today, parents need guidance on how to steer their children through school. "In days gone by," he said, "parents did not question the schools, but today the education of a child is far too important to be left to the school alone." His wife and associate Helen Weiss concurred. "This is not an adversary position, but a supportive position. Parents should always be involved as much as they can. The school doesn't know their kid. They do."[14]

It's a rare parent who hasn't experienced the trauma of a child who hates school, at least temporarily. The healthy family patiently seeks out underlying causes. Is it a social problem? Perhaps a child is being ridiculed or doesn't have any friends. Perhaps it's an out-and-out dislike of a teacher who seems to be picking on the child. Perhaps it's a reason totally unrelated to the classroom but brought to school by the child from elsewhere.

Author Ralph Keyes has written a book called *Is There Life After High School?* in which he presents some convincing arguments to the effect that the remainder of our lives are spent reacting to what we were or weren't in our high school years.[15] If we didn't make cheerleader in high school, we spend later years trying to prove to ourselves and others that we're attractive and popular. If we didn't make the team, the student council, or the clique of snobbish students, we might try desperately to compensate for this in college or the work world. That's why class reunions are so fraught with anxiety. Some people want to go back and show their classmates they made it while others refuse to attend because they didn't.

It isn't very helpful to tell our children that school isn't that important. To them, at that moment, it is. It is their milieu, the most important environment in their lives, except maybe their families. (For some children school compensates somewhat for an unhealthy family life.) It is in school that children are accepted or rejected, that they are part of their peer culture or left out, and here is where they begin a lifetime journey of enjoying learning or hating it. An insensitive teacher or an unpleasant learning environment can destroy a child's faith in his or her school and ultimately in his or her person, so caring parents cannot ignore problems. Automatically writing off schools as being valueless and insensitive isn't a constructive attitude for parents, either. This attitude merely tells children that their parents are sending them to an institution that can't be trusted but that they are expected to make the best of it.

Finding that fine line between support of a teacher and school and support of a child can be difficult. Parents are rarely sure they have taken the right stance. Should they insist that the child remain with the teacher and learn to get along, or will the teacher cause real emotional damage in their child? Should they switch schools? Go over the teacher's head to the principal, knowing that the child might suffer for it? What should they do about social problems—butt in or stay out?

I know a family with a gifted child who began to complain about school. At first, his parents brushed off his complaints about school precisely because he was such a good student, and they felt it might be just normal childhood griping. When he developed physical problems—gnawing his knuckles and developing an ulcer at age ten—they decided to check into the classroom. There they discovered that the teacher was immensely threatened by this bright child and openly referred to him in class as "Mr. Know-it-all." The parents immediately transferred their son to a different school. His life then became livable and his physical problems disappeared, but the parents deeply regretted that they hadn't taken the action earlier.

On the other side of the playground, there is a set of parents who are so into their children's school life that the kids are actually embarrassed. They dare not breathe a complaint, a fear, or a difficulty, or their mother is pounding on the principal's door. Such parents automatically assume that bad education is going on in all of their children's classes every year. This assumption puts terrible pressure upon their children, and they begin to hate school, which in turn justifies the parents' behavior.

Support of church can be as traumatic, especially for families who put a high value on religion but find themselves facing an unhealthy situation in their local church. Probably most questions about support for church arise over whether or not teens have to regularly attend church services or youth group meetings. Again, the healthier the family, the less automatic the support. Good parents don't insist that children attend bad classes or appreciate mediocre sermons just because the classes or sermons are associated with church.

Whenever there's a conflict situation with the personnel in an institution—whether it's with an unjust police officer, an unfair teacher, or an insensitive minister—good parents check into the situation and attempt to remedy it if they can. They don't remove themselves from the responsibility of keeping institutions and the people in them accountable. Our institutions exist to serve us. When they stop serving us or don't serve us as well as we deserve, then we need to look into what's going on and work for improvement.

Family affirmation and support are not luxuries but necessities in our lives. If we don't experience them as children, we may spend the rest of our lives seeking them from strangers. Someone has said that every child would be a success in *some* family. That's probably true, but children need to be successes in their *own* families, whoever they are. In healthy families, children invariably are.

In summary, the five hallmarks of an affirming and supportive family are the following:
1. The parents have good self-esteem.
2. Everyone is expected to affirm and support.
3. The family realizes support doesn't mean pressure.
4. The family's basic mood is positive.
5. The family supports its institutions, but not automatically.

5
Respecting Others

Trait 3: The healthy family teaches respect for others.

> There was no respect for youth when I was young, and now I am
> old, there is no respect for age—I missed it coming and going.
> —J. B. Priestley

"In our home, we were expected to be respectful and hospitable to
everyone who came," said an immensely successful businessman. "One
day when my parents were away, some traveling missionaries knocked
on the door and asked if they could come in. Torn between two parental injunctions—don't talk to strangers; always respect others—we
finally decided to let them in. We were only nine and eleven at the time,
but we sat and listened to them proselytize for over two hours. I'll
never forget how my parents handled it when they came home. They
politely thanked the missionaries and ushered them out. Then they
thanked us for being respectful and listening to them for so long. It
wasn't until the next day that they brought up the question of letting
strangers into your home and what to do when respect bumps into personal safety."

Although that conflict between respect for others and concern for
safety is an increasing dilemma in modern society, respect for others is
certainly an integral part of the healthy family according to my survey
respondents, who placed it third in the list of fifty-six traits. Some of
their comments deserve sharing.

"Thanks for the opportunity to contribute in this very small way,"
wrote a pastoral counselor. "The trait that stands out for me and really
encompasses most of the ones I've checked is the respect for persons
that healthy families have—especially parents for their children and,
consequently, children for Mom and Dad and parents for each other.
All are *not* equal in terms of responsibilities and duties, but all are *persons,* which does, I feel, result in whole new ways of relating within the
family, ways more personal and less formal. This kind of respect is not
superficial or pretended. It is real and deliberate."

A family therapist penned, "Respect for others begins within the

home where individuals are respected for their uniqueness and then is
spread out from there."

A YMCA director remarked, "Respect wears many faces. We see it
in self-respect, respect for team members, respect for coaches and
referees, and respect for those on the other team. It's most obvious
when it's missing."

"Families either teach respect or they don't teach it," wrote a family
counselor. "In our practice, we rarely find a family where one member
respects people and the others don't. Respect doesn't seem to be either
innate or automatic but rather something that is modeled and
learned."

In talking about respect in general, so many respondents specifically
mentioned respect for individual differences within the family that I
consider that kind of respect to be the foundational hallmark of
families where respect for others is taught.

1. The family respects individual differences within the family.

Individuality is prized in the healthy family. There are no "different"
children in the sense of "Tim is our different one," or "We don't know
where we got Karen." Remarks such as these, even though they're
usually made by parents in a jesting tone, are often veiled put-downs
of differences. The healthy family makes room for a wide variety of
personalities, interests, and differences. This family may include a
scholar, an athlete, and an artist, and instead of emphasizing differences, it emphasizes the richness that this diversity brings to the
family. "We're so lucky," said a mother in front of her family at a reunion, "because we get to be part of a lot of different things like soccer,
drama, and jazz band. If all of us were alike, think what we'd be
missing."

Yet, we often foster conformity as a value in our culture. In writing
on this, Reverend Thomas E. Legere says, "A sure way to strike terror
in the heart of a parent is to tell him or her that their child is not 'well
adjusted.' In this country, in particular, we seem to regard 'adjustment' as one of our national values. . . . It seems to me that making a
fetish out of 'adjustment' is a sure way to encourage mediocrity.
Greatness in any way, shape or form is usually accomplished by people
who are a little bit different than the rest of the world." He said that
Albert Einstein was always considered weird. "When he went up to

receive his Nobel Prize he wore a nice tuxedo. But he forgot to wear sox or tie his shoes. Was he 'well adjusted'?"[1]

Many families attempt to create a clan with like interests, like attitudes, and like behaviors. If a child in a family that is heavily involved in a youth league doesn't want to play or even to attend the many games scheduled, often he or she is made to feel left out. Since nobody likes to feel that way, the child, in order to alleviate the pressure, may pretend to like the activity. "We have a lot of half-hearted players because their parents think they should play," said a sandlot baseball coach. "Then when they don't play eagerly or well, their parents blame them for not putting their all into it. Their 'all' was never in it in the first place."

Music-minded parents can be just as rigid. If they enjoyed band or orchestra in their past, they can be insistent about their child participating in music, even if the child doesn't like it. Parents who place a high value on academics often put impossible pressures on children who either can't or aren't motivated to make high grades. If a boy from such a family is inclined toward auto mechanics—as happened in a family I once met—he can be made to experience unnecessary trauma and alienation. This boy's parents, by their attitudes, told him his avocation was unacceptable as a future for him. In other words, they couldn't accept him as he was. A high school counselor has said of such situations, "They're more common than you think. A lot of grown-ups are unhappy in their work today because their parents didn't let them choose to be what they wanted to be. They may be successful, but they're not happy."

This might explain in part the increasingly familiar phenomenon of second careers. Former school principals are becoming bailiffs, doctors are turning into writers, and accountants are opening restaurants. After career changes, many admit that they greatly disliked their previous career even though they were considered successful by society. The good news is that there's a trend in our culture away from job success and toward work satisfaction. Our society is showing signs of placing a higher value on the latter, even if it means less money and less social prestige. My respondents mirrored this societal trend when they placed "the healthy family values work satisfaction" high on the final list, twentieth in a field of fifty-six characteristics.

But there's more to individual uniqueness than interests. A

healthy family also accepts widely different personality styles among its members. Everyone doesn't have to be quiet and reserved or loquacious and outgoing. Shyness is accepted, not ridiculed. An introvert feels comfortable in the midst of an otherwise extroverted family.

Ellen Galinsky, author of *Between Generations: The Six Stages of Parenthood,* says that during pregnancy parents-to-be dream up scenarios with a mystery star, their baby. They deeply identify with this child and often think of giving him or her everything that was missing in their own childhood. At birth, though, "the baby tells us he is very different from us, and as he grows up, we see he is a very separate individual," she says. This process can be smooth or rocky depending upon how well parents can accept reality. One mother in Galinsky's study found that her daughter loved a toy she had hated as a child. She said, "I looked at my husband and he looked at me. I said, 'Well, we'd better get used to this. She's going to like a lot of things that we don't!' "[2]

Disappointment in children who have traits inherited from us can cause parents to withhold respect for those children. Linda Tschirhart Sanford writes, "From the time we conceive our children, we may secretly hope that certain qualities of ours or our mate's will be passed along to a child. On the other hand, we sometimes don't bargain for the continuation of less-than-desired traits. When we see in our children what we don't like in ourselves, we can react in one of two ways. If we have a poor self-concept, we likely feel threatened by the 'mirror' our child's behavior holds up to us. We may try to punish our child, in the name of love, with the goal of eradicating the flaw that makes us so uncomfortable. When we do this, we lessen the value the child places on himself and on his parents. . . . On the other hand, if we evaluate ourselves positively, we might help our children recognize a problem and teach them how to work toward its resolution without impairing their sense of worth."[3]

This tendency to wipe out personality traits is particularly strong in divorced families, where one parent may constantly harp on a trait inherited from the other, absent parent. The message comes through to the child clearly: "You're acting like your father and you know what happened to him." Hardly designed to make a child proud of himself or his father.

Behavior is another area of difference among family members. I'm not talking here about rules but style. Some of us like to sleep late in the morning, some like to watch the sun rise. Some of us always arrive at an event early, some are always late. Some love dressing up to go out, some hate it. Some spend their money, some save it. Yet, we find ourselves married to each other or born into a family with a variety of personal styles.

Accommodating different personal styles can be one of the most trying areas of family life, but healthy families try to respect differing behavioral styles as much as possible. They don't mock the family member who wants to sleep in Saturday even though the rest of them may be up and active; they simply tiptoe past the sleeper's door. They make an attempt to be punctual in order to preserve the sanity of the member who feels uncomfortable if late. Gregarious breakfast eaters don't force a slow waker to talk. Those who enjoy taking it easy don't chide the person who likes to be always busy.

Family members in a healthy family learn to live with one another. And once a pattern of respect for individual styles is established in a family, it becomes rather automatic. No one feels odd if he or she isn't in the majority.

Probably the ultimate refinement in respect for individuality in the family surfaces in the area of attitudes. Unfortunately, some families do not allow disagreement in attitudes about such things as work, politics, health, faith, and friends. Other families insist on attitude agreement even about mundane subjects. For example, a family in which most members freely exchange gossip may hoot out of the family circle any member who thinks that gossip should be substantiated before being passed along. A family with a liberal orientation can feel strained when an emerging adolescent begins to think along conservative lines.

The healthy family accepts differences of opinion and—as we discussed earlier when talking about communication—even encourages them. Parents in this family recognize that their young people will be influenced by teachers, television, and the outside world and may adopt ideas and beliefs different from their parents.

When a child does adopt new opinions, parents can be heartbroken. They seem especially vulnerable to heartbreak if a child rejects their religious beliefs, perhaps adopting new ones. The more religion means to the parents, the more devastating a change of religious interest can be.

But healthy families can handle the situation. I know a Jewish family who lived in a largely gentile community. Although the parents were deeply hurt when their children, one by one, drifted into Christian youth groups, they allowed this searching and experimentation, never permitting it to become a battlefield in their home. Eventually, all of their grown children returned to their original faith, but for some of them, it took years to do so. Those years between weren't easy for the parents, but it's likely that had they insisted that their children remain true to their faith during their searching years, their children wouldn't have returned.

This is a familiar part of my work with families. Rarely does a lecture of mine end without parents approaching me to confide that one or more of their children has left the church and to ask how they can bring them back into the fold. One of the most widely reprinted chapters I've ever written is one dealing with adolescent/parent faith relationships called "He's Losing My Faith" (*Who, Me, Teach My Child Religion?* Winston Press).[4] Catholic parents who were reared in an age when parents were made responsible for the lifelong faith commitments of their children often consider themselves failures if their grown children do not believe exactly as they do. They do not understand that no one can take upon himself or herself the lifelong faith commitment of another person.

I remember reading an insightful piece about family differences by Janet Lowe of The Copley News Service. Her article really was a unique love letter between a grown daughter and her father. In it the daughter wrote about how her environmentalist activities conflicted with her free-enterprise-minded father. She pointed out that he himself had taught her during her childhood not to go along with the crowd. She reminded him that when she was in high school and reluctantly ironing yards and yards of petticoats in order to be part of the peer fashion of the fifties, he had discouraged her from wearing them if she disliked them so. He emphasized to her that individuality is a human right. Yet, here he was, years later, saddened by her involvement in Sierra Club, an environmentalist organization, because it didn't mesh with his conservatism. Her letter was a loving thank you to this man, who taught her to respect herself by daring to be different, whether it was in a matter of petticoats or pollution.

As children become young adults, they may—are even likely to—think differently from their parents on subjects such as consumerism, work, education, vegetarianism, premarital sex, health, diet, exercise, government, draft, patriotism, taxes, race relations, and childrearing.

Good families work at allowing and respecting differences of opinion and belief in their midst. Because they do so, their children are more likely to respect others when they grow up and away from the family. Families who are rigid and don't permit contrary attitudes and beliefs to enter the family circle tend to send out into society rigid children, who do not respect differences in others' beliefs.

A letter to the nationally syndicated column "Dear Abby" made an interesting point a few years ago.

> Dear Abby: KEEPING THE PEACE wrote to say that she and her husband's family had vast disagreements when it came to politics and related social issues, so in order to keep every family gathering from erupting into a noisy battle she kept her mouth shut. She said, "Afterward I felt guilty because my children are old enough to understand the talk, and I don't want some of the erroneous and bigoted statements made by my husband's family to go unchallenged."
>
> You replied, "A noisy battle involving politics is much healthier for children than the choked-off silence you're maintaining in the interest of peace and quiet. Silence implies agreement."
>
> Abby, I grew up in a politically active family and I consider the experience valuable. I highly recommend that KEEPING THE PEACE should challenge any views she considers bigoted or wrong. She owes it not only to herself, but to her children. Coincidentally, the day I read that provocative item in your column, I saw the following quote displayed. . . . "It is better to debate a question without settling it than to settle a question without debating it." (Joseph Jourbert)[5]

Columnist Erma Bombeck was referring to rigid parenting when she wrote a column about letting go of children as they mature. In it, she asks parents how they view their children. "Are they like a finely gilded mirror that reflects the image of their owner in every way? On the day the owner looks in and sees a flaw, a crack, a distortion, one tiny idea or attitude that is different from his own, he casts it aside and declares himself a failure."[6]

We have a lot of parents walking around who have declared themselves failures for that very reason—their children don't mirror them exactly. These parents cannot accept differences. They don't respect the right of each child to become an individual.

As siblings grow up and have their own families, the ways in which they differ become more obvious. If as children they were taught to respect one another's differences, they are likely as adults to respect them. If they were taught that differences are unhealthy, they are not apt to remain friends as adults, especially if one of them deviates in any way from childhood norms.

Dr. Helgola G. Ross, University of Cincinnati psychologist, warns that whatever labels we and our siblings may have worn as children, chances are we're still wearing them today. And those labels may account for whatever difficulties we and our siblings continue to have. "We collected data on adults into their nineties and found that the name tags remain," reports Dr. Ross, who has studied sibling relationships intensively. "This can be good or bad, depending on the particular label."

Other family specialists second her words. They find that in some families children are not allowed to become individuals either while in the nest or out of it. If they make a move later in life to change into the persons they want to be, they're apt to be castigated by the rest of the family; and the result is guilt and confusion.

2. The family knows that self-respect means just that—respect for self.

My mother used to have a refrain that began "No self-respecting person would . . ." and then she would end with "What will other people say?" She never saw her contradiction, but it was more a cultural hangover than anything else. Self-respect in an earlier age was based on community standards. It wasn't self-respect at all. True self-respect implies that one knows oneself well enough to act on principle. It further implies that one likes oneself well enough to have confidence in acting on principle.

Lack of self respect is the basis for enslavement to a peer group—teen or adult. When we lack confidence in our own judgments and are insecure if we aren't exactly like everyone else, then we drift toward a group consensus. Juvenile authorities tell us about kids of ten or eleven years who become involved in drugs, alcoholism, and vandalism because they don't have enough self-respect to say initially "I don't want to be part of that." They're desperately afraid that if they do, they'll be drummed out of the group, and they can't stand that possibility. Yet, many admit that they didn't find their early experimentation with alcohol or chemicals pleasant. They went along with it simply because it promised acceptance.

I once took a course in Jungian dream analysis and after a number of lectures, each participant was invited to tell about a dream. One woman related her dream about skiing, which is big in our state of Colorado. The skilled analyst asked penetrating questions, choosing certain elements of her dream that symbolized deeper meanings. The sequence went something like this:

He: What does a ski pole mean to you?

She: Something to help me ski, to keep my balance, to push me along.

He: And the bright blue ski outfit in your dream? What does that mean to you?

She: Something pretty, flashy, stylish—that would be worn by a model or someone.

He: And the top of the mountain?

She (pausing for a moment): It means fear; it means something to get down, to conquer.

In this way the analyst gently led her to the meaning of her dream. To her astonishment, the woman found that she really hated to ski, although it was the basis for her family's social life. She protested that all of their friends skied; that their activities, clothing, and life-style were intricately bound up with skiing; and that she herself was a very vocal supporter of the sport.

But her last reflection was very telling. She said, "Until just now, I didn't realize how much I disliked skiing itself. I know I'm supposed to like it because my husband and our friends love it, but I hate getting off that lift and coming down those slopes. I'm in terror all the way down. I've been calling it a thrill, but it's really a terror. I'm relieved when I reach bottom, and I stall getting back on the lift as long as possible." She paused again, this time longer, and then asked, "How can all this be when I really thought I liked it?"

It was apparent that this woman had submerged her feelings and desires in an effort to please her husband and the group. She had played the game of liking skiing long enough to convince herself that she really did. She hadn't respected herself enough to be honest. Now she feared losing her social life and her husband's company.

In contrast to her, I can think of a family who spends a lot of time camping in the mountains. Each family member enjoys his or her own activity there. Dad loves fishing, Mom likes an opportunity to wander off alone and pick wildflowers while communing with nature, one child brings a whole library and curls up on a lawn chair near the potato chips, another suntans, and two others spend hours throwing rocks into the stream. When this family vacations in winter months, two members downhill ski, two cross-country ski, yet another shops, and the reader mentioned earlier brings her library and curls up with her potato chips near the fireplace. This family's individual recreational preferences are respected within the perimeters of a larger social grouping.

3. The family accords respect to all groups, not just specifically-approved ones.

Probably one of the most difficult responsibilities parents have is to teach their children to respect people with whom the parents disagree or whom they basically fear. Racism rears its ugly head here. Otherwise good and loving parents frequently bump into their own bigotry in this area. What happens when parents teach children to love all of humankind while they themselves can't stand Blacks or Latinos or Mormons or Native Americans or Republicans or liberals or people with freckles? Then the respect they've taught is really selected, limited respect. They're saying to their families, "Respect other people . . . except . . . ."

Healthy families exhibit a willingness to respect individuals while not necessarily implying approval of their behavior. Homosexuality is a good case in point. In the past several years, we have seen the emotional distress this and other like issues have produced in society. Why? Because we are on the brink of maturing enough to face the consequences of the contradiction between our words and our actions in regard to homosexuality. If we hold that politically all are equal and that religiously all are worthy of love, and then proceed to deny equality and love to large groups because their standards and life-styles differ from ours, we create tensions within ourselves that spread to tensions in the larger society.

A lot of parents who got swept up in the issue of homosexuality during the Anita Bryant crusade against it became very uncomfortable with themselves. They began by believing they were fighting evil, acting on God's behalf to rid the world of some unacceptable human beings. They ended up bewildered and depressed because they found evil in themselves in the form of attitudes which were contrary to the religious and democratic ideas they'd always professed to believe. This self-discovery wasn't pleasant.

Healthy families teach respect for all individuals regardless of how they differ one from the other. They teach that each human being has inviolable rights, the most basic of which is the right to be respected as a human being. But the healthy family goes beyond this. It helps its members to distinguish between respect and approval. For example, children from good families are taught to respect homosexual persons, though they may not be taught to approve of homosexuality itself. These children wholeheartedly disapprove of homosexual life-styles and sexual preferences, but they will not be among those who throw rocks at homosexuals or refuse to allow them to work.

Historically, society chooses the groups upon which it places its seal of approval. It's difficult for young people living in today's high-divorce-rate culture to understand the intolerance for divorce prevalent in society just a generation ago. Family members who were divorced were not welcome in many families. Divorce was a stigma which reflected upon the divorced person's parents and family. In just a few short years, we've gone from rejecting completely the mere idea of a divorced president to Gerald Ford's actual presidency, in which three of the four partners in the presidential/vice-presidential team were married more than once. The institution of divorce didn't change, but society's tolerance of it certainly did.

Teaching respect for all humans regardless of their ideology is much harder than it appears to be. The American Civil Liberties Union (ACLU) is a much-maligned organization that exists to insure the rights of all people in our nation. Because of its dedication to that cause, it frequently disappoints its own members. For years it was accused of supporting primarily radical liberals, but many of them screamed foul when the organization defended the right of the Ku Klux Klan to hold a march.

The ACLU simply mirrors the dilemma found on a smaller scale in families who are trying to teach children to respect individuals with whom they disagree. A father reported that he saw the most noticeable sign of maturity in his college freshman son when his son confided that his best friend at college was a conservative, and then went on to say, "But he's a really nice guy, Dad. I think you'd like him." This son had been a highly opinionated young man who had gone off to college accepting or rejecting persons on the basis of what their affiliations were rather than on their beings.

The really healthy family likes to bring its members into contact with a variety of people, whether through organizations, travel, work, or church. In contrast, dogmatic and righteous families, many of whom consider themselves healthy, protect their beliefs and attitudes by surrounding themselves with others like themselves. And sometimes, unfortunately, these kinds of families gather under the umbrella of church and country.

4. The family respects individual decisions.

In the healthy family, as in the healthy organization, individuals are encouraged to make decisions appropriate to their age and station and to live with the consequences. Child psychologist Rudolph Dreikurs offers one of the most effective approaches to childrearing I know of. His philosophy is rooted in what he calls *logical consequences*. He says that just as adults are responsible for the consequences of their decisions, so should children be held accountable for theirs.[7]

Who makes decisions in a family is crucial to many areas of family life. Should children be allowed to make decisions which impact the family? For example, if a child decides to choose a particular extra-curricular activity that requires him or her to be in town on Saturdays, what happens if the family wants to go out of town? What about an older offspring who wants to choose what high-school courses to take? Should he or she be allowed to take only goof-off courses if the parents and teachers know that the child is capable of handling the more difficult ones? This was a classic stand-off in some families in my teaching days. I remember one junior who quit school just to prove to his parents that he was his own person—and all his parents had wanted was what was best for him.

Healthy families tend to allow decision-making on the part of children in those areas for which the children must accept the entire consequences. They can spend their allowance in any way they wish, for instance, but if they run out, they will have no money until next week. What they choose to do during free time, whether they want to take a certain kind of lessons, which shoes they want to buy (within reason)—decisions like these are gradually turned over to the children as they are able to make and live with the results.

However, good parents tend to remain a part of the decision-making that impacts their children's social life, education, and health. They are often firm in denying their children contact with certain friends. They insist upon certain academic classes and standards of achievement. They require specific health measures, such as adequate sleep, a balanced diet, dental and other preventative care.

"These parents don't cop out," said a high-school principal. "They know their kids, what they're doing, and what they're capable of. They keep a tight rein on them, but not too tight." He then went on to tell story after story about students who had been in difficulty and trouble for weeks and even months before parents detected anything. "A lot of parents pretend that they're being open and democratic when they're really abdicating responsibility," he said.

"Well, what about choices and decisions in areas like course selection?" I asked him.

"I'd say the healthy families choose together. If a kid selects only goof-off classes, these parents insist upon balance. And sometimes the reverse is true. A kid sets impossible expectations and the parent has to say, 'No, you can't do all that. It isn't right for you.' "

This approach to family decision-making is emphasized by Dr. Jerry M. Lewis. In his work, he found that although the healthiest parents listen respectfully to the input of their children on decisions to be made, ultimately the parents make the final decisions that impact the family.

Troubled families either don't allow any decision-making, allow too much, or make individuals feel guilty for making decisions. A family therapist commented that parents will often tell a child it's his or her choice and then criticize the choice. "If it's the child's choice, then he or she should not be made to feel guilty about it," he said. He told of a mother/daughter pair who were having tremendous emotional conflicts. The mother intended to send her daughter to see him professionally, but he insisted upon seeing them both. The basic problem was rooted in the mother's inability to allow her daughter to make decisions. Yet, she considered herself to be democratic. She gave her daughter the money to buy clothing but took all the joy out of the purchase by criticizing her daughter's choices. She gave her daughter the freedom to choose activities and then harped on what poor activities she had chosen.

In some marriages spouses aren't allowed to make decisions without criticism or belittlement. "Did you spend our money on that?" and "When I decide what we think, I'll tell you" are typical put-down comments heard in such marriages. Both men and women are becoming more protective of their rights, inside and outside the home, and are refusing to accept automatic decisions made by their spouses, which causes great tension in some marriages. For example, no longer can a husband come home and announce "We're moving," disregarding the rest of the family's feelings and needs, and expect to have a harmonious and loving family.

Several highly mobile American family wives indicated to me that the reason their many family moves went smoothly is that they were part of the decision-making process which precipitated the move. Once they had agreed to the move, they then became active supporters of it, thus freeing their spouses to face and focus on new job challenges. Many also mentioned that some moves had been turned down, moves that they felt wouldn't have been good for the family.

5. The family shows respect to those outside the family.

Healthy families tend to *show* respect by their actions, not just teach about it. They reach out to others in need. If a frail person with a cane is trying to negotiate his or her way through a large crowd, they take the initiative and help. If a mother is overwhelmed trying to handle several small children, they come to her aid. If the breeze seems to bother others on the bus, they close their window, regardless of how pleasant it might be to feel the wind blowing through their hair. Their teens don't play loud, blaring radios in contained public places. When they go to a meeting and a lone person is putting up folding chairs, they automatically help out. There is a distinct difference in attitude between the healthy and not-so-healthy family in this matter of respect, yet both may think themselves respectful. One is *actively* respectful, the other committed to respect primarily in terms of teaching it.

Teachers, recreation directors, and juvenile authorities point out that a great number of children today have parents who don't model respect for others. "Look at some parents at organized sports," said a little-league sponsor. "They shout obscenities at their kid, the coach, the referee, and each other. Then they wonder why their children don't show them more respect."

"I worry about the absence of respect among children today," commented an elementary school principal. "They don't seem to care if they humiliate peers or offend adults. We have many, many children who refuse to respect teachers other than their own. They show their disrespect in many ways—offensive signals, obscenities, refusal to obey simple orders unless the orders are accompanied with a threat, willingness to hog the ball or the court . . . . We're forced to wonder what kind of respect is modeled at home."

I asked her if there were children who are respectful, and if so, what traits set them apart. "Yes, of course there are. Children from some families tend to respect others. They don't have to be teacher's pet and that sort of thing, but they behave respectfully toward others. They wait their turn while others push ahead in line; they don't bully other children; and they respect teachers, secretary, and custodian, people like that." She paused, thoughtfully. "It's not particular traits they hold— it's just basic respect for others. Either it's instilled or not. And it's difficult for us to instill it if it isn't evident in the family."

Let's turn to the subject of respect within the family. Why is it that in some families there is a basic respect between children and parents and among siblings, while in other families the lack of respect is so obvious that it makes visitors uncomfortable? In the latter, children talk back to their parents in unbelievable language, spouses speak in derogatory tones to each other, and parents are more likely to swear at their children than hug them.

Dr. Wayne W. Dyer speaks effectively on this issue. He received a letter from a mother which said, in part, "My children are very disrespectful toward me—unmanageable in the home, running roughshod over me. What can I do?"

Dr. Dyer responded, "A mother who receives disrespectful treatment from a child, regardless of the age of the offspring, must deal directly and firmly with the behavior. First look at your own behavior and ask yourself, 'Why am I allowing myself to be treated this way?' Yes, that's correct, you do get treated the way you teach others to treat you."

He went on to explain that for a long time the mother may have been teaching her children that she was willing to tolerate their disrespect, showing them that she would continue to be a good and pleasant mother even if they treated her badly. "If you are going to end the insolence," said Dr. Dyer, "then don't come up with excuses for the child—such as blaming your husband or yourself for wrongdoing when the youngster was an infant. Retracing your earlier steps will not change the child's behavior today."

Dr. Dyer then suggested a sequence of attitudes and ways to react on her part that she would need to master in order to begin to receive respect from her children. These attitudes included self-respect. "When you receive a crude reaction from a child, tell the child, 'I have a great deal of respect for myself, and I will not tolerate anyone treating me the way you do. I can't really force you to change, but I won't stay here and listen to this kind of talk from you.' "

He then advised a course of action that seems normal to healthy parents and outrageous to insecure ones. He suggested that to really teach children that you won't tolerate disrespect, especially if they are chronically rude, the most effective strategy is to stop performing services for them. "He will soon get the message: If I treat Mom with disrespect, then she won't wash my clothes. Why should she?" He warns that parents may feel pangs of guilt at first but he continues, "Remember that it is important for you to serve as a model, for your children, of a person who possesses self-respect. And you can't respect yourself if you continue to wait on a child hand and foot though he abuses you."[8]

Dr. Dyer's sound words are lived out in subtle ways in the strong family. A mother shared with her parenting group the idea that respect doesn't just happen but has to be forced sometimes. "I drove up with a load of groceries one day and my teenage son was mowing the lawn. I called to him and asked him to carry in my groceries and he said he didn't have time because he had to finish the lawn, eat dinner, and get to practice. So I hauled in the groceries myself.

"But when he came in forty-five minutes later and asked about dinner, I said I didn't have time to prepare it because I had to haul in the groceries. He had to make his own dinner and he was late for practice, but he got the point."

Parents model respect. If they don't insist upon it for themselves, they aren't likely to get it. And if they don't get it, other authorities, such as teachers, counselors, ministers, and police aren't likely to get it either.

Not only do parents have to demand that respect be shown to them but they also have to show respect for their children as well. As I mentioned earlier, this means respect for differing opinions, individuality, and decision-making. It also means physical respect toward their children—speaking to children as politely as they speak to others; asking, not ordering, them to do a chore; eliminating abusive language and actions; never humiliating children in front of others—behaviors that are common in some families and never found in others. Parents who respect their children don't talk about them as humorous objects, don't belittle them, don't make them the victims of their own mistakes, and don't search out their faults and weaknesses as a subject of conversation.

Parents in healthy families say that teaching children to *show* respect takes attention and time. They deal with disrespect immediately when it comes up. Sometimes disrespect is intentional; often a child or spouse is unaware of it. The caring family usually gives the benefit of the doubt and approaches the area of disrespect openly: "There wasn't any hot water left for John this morning. Please, each of you take a shorter shower tomorrow so he doesn't have to shampoo with cold water again." If John faces cold water the following day, this family might limit members to every-other-day showering to prove its intent. The unhealthy family might allow the situation to continue, at the same time allowing abusive charges and countercharges over it to destroy family peace and respect for one another.

Husband and wife often show disrespect for each other by interrupting, belittling, or, as one husband put it, "by paying no attention whatsoever to what I say." He esplained that in public, as well as at home, his wife never responded when he said something. "It's as if I never even said anything. What can I do?" He was feeling justifiably put down because she did pay attention to other people. Obviously, this lack of respect revealed deep marital discord, and this couple needed professional help. But in many marriages, spouses adopt a disrespectful style of responding or not responding to another's needs and attempts to communicate that might not be so much intentional as it is habitual.

If a man has grown up in a home in which the father never accorded the mother any respect regarding her political opinions or any other opinions, he may well treat his wife in the same way, even though he may love her deeply. If a woman embraces a certain mode of thinking that regards all men as little boys, she may mother her spouse to distraction and not even be aware of his discomfort in this role. Disrespectful attitudes and behaviors that are perceived by one or the other spouse need to be surfaced, not submerged. Marriages have been known to break up over disrespectful eating habits.

The healthy family begins, then, by insisting upon respect for one another in the home, and after that they extend respect beyond the home. "Would you do that at home?" is still an appropriate question to ask, because what goes on in the home in the name of respect or disrespect spreads outward to our larger society in general.

6. The family respects the property of others.

In talking with parents about respect for property, I was interested to discover that most families have to deal with petty shoplifting, destruction of property, and thieving from one another with most of their children at some stage in their lives. Parent after parent shared with me the one or two incidents of disrespect for property in their children's formative years and told how they handled the incidents. How parents handle such an incident seems to be pivotal in whether or not it's repeated.

Classic is the case of the child who takes candy or a toy from the shelves of the store while Mom is shopping. Not so classic is how the parents handle it. If they take the child back to the spot, insist that he or she return the stolen item or reimburse store personnel for it, and also require that the child live with the consequences of his or her actions—usually intense embarrassment—they don't generally have the situation repeated.

If, as so many parents do in these circumstances, they remove the child from the scene of the action and scold him or her all the way home, perhaps after reimbursing the shop themselves, they are not forcing the child to face the real consequences of his or her actions, which may well be repeated. The parents accept what should be the child's consequences, humiliation, and responsibility for future behavior while the child merely endures a chastisement from them.

Parents I talk to also commonly tell me about incidents of spontaneous vandalism. A street light is broken by a group of active kids on the way home from practice; a car antenna is broken off the neighbor's Ford, either willfully or accidentally; a neighbor's flowers are picked; a library book is filled with drawings—what's to be done about these somewhat archetypal transgressions? They are not merely childish pranks. They can be early signs of what can become habitual behavior—*if permitted*.

Healthy families tend not to permit it. They take the child by the hand to the neighbor to explain about the flower and apologize. They probe where the antenna came from, then insist that the child visit the car owner, make an apology, and offer restitution from his or her own resources. Or they take the child to the library to pay for the book that was ruined. The difference between the family that teaches respect for other's property and the one that ignores property destruction is that the former takes the time and effort to get it stopped at inception.

What is petty theft in childhood can become accomplished acquisition in adolescence and serious crime in later years if parents don't take action. Occasionally, a teen will come home with an expensive item like a watch or radio and remark that a friend "gave it to me." The alert parent asks a lot of questions and does a bit of checking, even if it infringes upon the respect I talked about earlier. Ignoring intuition is a commonly regretted parental fault.

In summary, the hallmarks of a family that teaches respect include the following:

1. The family respects individual differences within the family.
2. The family knows that self-respect means just that—respect for self.
3. The family accords respect to all groups, not just specifically approved ones.
4. The family respects individual decisions.
5. The family shows respect to those outside the family.
6. The family respects the property of others.

6
Trusting

Trait 4: The healthy family develops a sense of trust.

If you can't trust your mother, who can you trust?
— Classic Americana

If there's a second classic trust statement in families, it's "You don't trust me." That familiar complaint is heard at some time or another by most parents. It often causes us to be defensive because we don't want to face the unpleasant possibility that it might be true. How to deal with that complaint is discussed later in this chapter. The fact that my professional respondents placed a sense of trust as fourth in a list of fifty-six characteristics of the healthy family should indicate to us how important it is for us to examine closely this valuable family commodity.

In some families, members aren't sure about one another. Are they really loved, or are they merely tolerated because they happen to belong to the family? Can they trust their parents (or children) to do what they do because they *love* them? Can they be sure of anyone? Will they still be seeking security and love at age eighty?

In the healthy family, trust is recognized as a precious possession, carefully developed and nurtured as both children and parents progress through the various stages of family life together. It begins at birth when infants have to turn themselves entirely over to an adult. If this adult acts in a loving and fondling manner, the infant gradually begins to trust her or him. This process is called bonding and is presently a very popular topic among psychologists and sociologists, who do not always agree on the preferred gender of the bonding adult or the length of time necessary to create a bond strong enough in infants that they feel free to trust other adults who may assume part of their care.

Erik Erikson names trust as the first and foundational of his eight ages of man. According to this honored psychologist, "the infant's first social achievement is his willingness to let the mother out of sight without undue anxiety or rage, because she has become an inner certainty as well as an outer predictability."[1]

Inner certainty and outer predictability—a pair of phrases tightly linked and so basic to our lifelong health that if we lack either, we become essentially different persons than if we are fortunate enough to receive both, not only in infancy but throughout our lifetime. We need an inner certainty that tells us we are loved enough to be able to establish an outer predictability, or trust in others, during our lives.

If this loving and nurturing is absent the first several months or maybe years of a child's life, it may be impossible to establish in later years. We see legions of adults walking around with insecurities dating back to their early family life, perhaps to an era of childcaring where nurture was considered spoiling and loving was considered pampering. When something negative occurs in these adults' lives, such as a love spurned or a job lost, they can feel an enormous sense of rejection, which then re-engages those basic feelings of unlovedness and insecurity. Many of these people are pathetic in that they *expect* to be spurned. When it happens, it simply reinforces old, negative feelings about themselves. "Who could love me anyway?" they say.

Erikson wrote, "In psychopathology the absence of basic trust can best be studied in infantile schizophrenia, while lifelong underlying weakness of such trust is apparent in adult personalities in whom withdrawal into schizoid and depressive states is habitual. The re-establishment of a state of trust has been found to be the basic requirement for therapy in these cases."[2]

As troubled families discover, this reestablishment of trust can be long, painful, and disappointing. When one spouse breaks marital trust, for example, it can plunge the remaining partner into the depths of self-loathing, even if the erring partner's infidelity has more to do with circumstances than rejection of spouse. This is one of the highest costs of infidelity—not what it does to the marriage as much as what it does to the sense of self-worth of the person erred against.

Ashley Montagu writes, "The ability to love, and also to respond to love, has its origin in the experience of maternal love during infancy and early childhood—and the inability to love, except as an act of aggression, results from the absence of that primal bond and the frustration of that human need. In matters of the heart, not only is it better to give than to receive; it is essential to give in order to receive—for it is only the lovable, only the caring who will be cared about."[3]

Early bonding and trust, then, are essential to establishing a deep sense of trust within the infant. But Erikson warns that large amounts of food and fondling aren't enough. "Let it be said here that the amount of trust derived from earliest infantile experience does not seem to depend on absolute quantities of food or demonstrations of love, but rather on the quality of the maternal relationship. Mothers create a sense of trust in their children by that kind of administration which in its quality combines sensitive care of the baby's individual needs and a firm sense of personal trustworthiness within the trusted framework of their culture's life-style. This later combines with a sense of being 'all right', of being oneself, and of becoming what other people trust one will become."[4]

Today Erikson's automatic presumption that the infant requires specifically a mother instead of either parent serving as the bonding adult is highly controversial. Although some respected professionals hold that it is crucial for the mother to be home with the infant the first two years of life, others maintain only that a constant caring adult—mother or otherwise—be with the infant during the first three months of life. The longitudinal data isn't in yet. We simply don't know how great numbers of children will fare as adults if they didn't have a full-time parent at home during those early months.

While there's little agreement among those who study children and families on this issue of bonding, we are becoming aware of a variety of ways that cultures and families are trying to deal with it. In some Scandinavian countries, for example, laws require that employers grant *either* the mother or father a leave of up to two years after the birth of a child without losing jobs or jeopardizing promotions. When children are older, these same laws permit either parent to work a shorter work day, more congruent with the school day, so that a parent can be home when the children are home. Employers are required to grant a certain number of sick days for working parents—for themselves, yes, but also for sick children. (Sick children present a real dilemma for working parents in America.)

Many couples work out shifts in their jobs so that one parent can be home at all times, a better solution for the baby than the marriage perhaps, but one that points out the commitment of these couples to parenting in the early, particularly crucial stages of child development. Surrogate parents are also commonly used, the most popular being grandma. In the Black family particularly, grandma establishes a close, lifelong relationship with her grandchildren, a relationship missing in many white, middle-class families. Often in Black families grandma is the early caregiver to these children whose parents, out of either necessity or desire, have to go to work. The grandchildren develop a basic trust in grandma in their infancy years, that "inner certainty" of her "outer predictability" that Erikson talked about. Families other than Black use grandma in this role, too, of course, but not as often.

I was fortunate in having a long conversation about this subject with a Black woman in South Carolina, who worked part-time in a retreat center. She and her husband both had worked when their children were young, so her mother had cared for her children. Now this woman has assumed the same role with her own children, rearing some of her grandchildren. The fact that all of these children had mothers who were not home full-time when they were young didn't seem to matter—as long as grandma was there, furnishing love, trust, and security. As the children grew up and away, they came back for support and affirmation both from their own parents and from grandma, their surrogate parent.

But grandmas are hard to come by for everyone. Many grandmas work themselves. Some live thousands of miles away. Others, understandably, don't want to return to caregiving twenty-five years after they have nurtured their own children through these stages.

Another, more common surrogate parent is that person our society calls the *Babysitter*. I'm deliberately capitalizing this word in order to distinguish this sitter from the occasional sitter who comes in to relieve the parents to go to a movie. The Babysitter is that person Alvin Toffler refers to as the professional parent in our midst—one who loves children and would rather spend time with them than doing anything else. These women—and most of them are women—work, only their work is for other parents, filling (for better or for worse) a surrogate-parent role with the infant. When parents find a loving Babysitter, she becomes more precious to them than the proverbial gold. I know of two cases in which such Babysitters were approached and asked about their availability and agreement to serve in this role before the couples undertook pregnancies.

Not many parents are lucky enough or affluent enough to be able to find and hire such a Babysitter. Most parents have to settle for someone who cares for a number of children and can't allocate a great deal of time to any one infant. These are the working parents who have to make a decision between financial and career security and the baby. In the healthy family, the decision is usually in favor of the baby.

"I didn't want to give up my job, but there was no question of who was going to raise my baby," a young career woman said to me. "I can always go back to work, but I can't make up later for what my baby needs now."

I didn't ask on the survey instrument about the importance of having a full-time parent at home during infancy, so I had to interview to get insights on this. Almost to a person, professionals who work closely with families indicated that the healthier the family, the more likelihood there was of having one of the child's parents at home full-time during early infancy.

Parents have a moral responsibility to be there, according to Stanley Hauerwas of Notre Dame. "Children, if they are to be both morally and socially responsible and potentially self-reflective adults, must be reared in a highly charged emotional setting in which they are loved in a manner that establishes basic trust. This requires the continuing presence of specific beloved others, for it is only through powerful, eroticized relations with such specific others, parents or their permanent, not temporary, surrogates that the child will be nurtured and protected in a way that allows his or her creation of self and others to be structured and mediated by parental care and concern. It is only through the child's internalization of specific others that he or she can later identify with non-familial human beings. These ties cannot emerge in abstract, diffuse, non-familialized settings. This is the moral imperative which animates the family reconstruction mode."[5]

However parents work out satisfactory bonding periods, once basic trust has been established, it must be nurtured throughout the entire period of family life. Because trust is so intangible, many families are unsure of the quality or depth of the trust level among their members. Here are some of the hallmarks displayed by families who have achieved deep levels of trust.

1. The husband and wife trust each other deeply.
In his work on the healthy family, Dr. Jerry M. Lewis found many differences among the families he studied, but he didn't find a single case of infidelity. It just didn't occur in healthy families. In confidential

interviews with spouses, he found that this fidelity was due not to lack of opportunity but to a felt need to preserve trust between husband and wife.[6]

Some time ago when I was doing extensive interviews and research for an article on whether marriage can survive infidelity, I found that there is a strong relationship between true intimacy and fidelity and that there are many levels of intimacy in marriage. Couples whose only intimacy is sexual are shattered by sexual infidelity because it destroys the basis of their relationship. However, most couples seek a richer meaning of marital intimacy; for them, intimacy must include sharing of deep human feelings of love, fear, hope, joy, disappointment. They learn to risk their vulnerability, and that, according to counselors, is the basis for intimacy—the willingness to risk exposing our true selves to one another. This risk is in direct proportion to the level of trust operating between spouses.

To a couple who is able to achieve this kind of union, infidelity has a much broader meaning than sexual infidelity only. To such a couple infidelity means that an unfaithful spouse is sharing his or her intimate self, confiding thoughts, hopes, and dreams, to a third person. This kind of infidelity can be as disastrous in some marriages as sexual infidelity is to others.

Trust, then, is foundational in the healthy marriage—and not just trust in a sexual sense. The traditional gossip that says "She can't trust her husband" or "He can't trust his wife around other men" has always implied unfaithful sexual behavior. Today's husbands and wives can feel betrayed if their spouses seek fulfillment in work, television, football, fishing, friends, the soaps, causes, or organizations. An obvious enthusiasm for these activities—an enthusiasm which is absent in regard to the partner—can cause great pain. Confidence, or trust, is broken. In speaking of marital infidelity, a trained pastoral counselor said, "I wouldn't want to be misunderstood on this, but sexual infidelity *can* lead a couple to a better marriage *if* they take it as a warning signal and allow themselves to look at what has happened to their trust in one another."

That's a pretty extreme way to rebuild trust. A number of little exercises I have used with couples in parenting seminars have helped them to evaluate their level of trust in one another. These couples are astonished at how quickly the trust that is taken for granted in marriage can deteriorate. "It's little things," said a husband. "She asks probing questions that tell me she isn't sure I'm telling the truth. I ask probing questions on where the money went. And our mistrust just escalates."

Healthy couples don't allow this disintegration of trust to develop. They know that family trust emanates from spousal trust. If a man doesn't trust his wife, his children aren't likely to trust their mother. If a woman confides her lack of trust in her husband to her own mother or children, this will also shake their trust in him—and possibly in her, as well.

Any married person knows that it isn't easy to trust one another in all things. At times I've hated to admit to a dented fender and have been sorely tempted to attribute it to some unknown coward passing through a parking lot. I suspect there are areas where my husband has felt equally hesitant to tell me things.

I know a woman who counts on her husband's chronic forgetfulness in order to acquire an expensive wardrobe for herself. If he asks her about a new dress, she replies, "Yes, I showed you this when I got it. Don't you remember?" and he hastily apologizes. Or she replies, "I've had this a long time. You just don't pay any attention to what I wear." This effectively prevents him from questioning her further and turns him from the offensive to the defensive. What's most offensive to me is the lack of trust this woman affords her husband by sharing her strategy humorously with groups of women.

Trust or lack of it shows up in myriad little ways between partners. If he says he'll be home at a certain time, can she trust him to be there? Can she be trusted to keep their personal life confidential, or does she share it with her friends? Trust, once the cornerstone of a couple's courtship, can either erode or mature in marriage. In healthy families, it develops and matures.

2. The children are gradually given more opportunity to earn trust.
When children are toddlers, it's difficult to trust them with anything. We can *tell* them not to turn on the gas jets or to be careful with the baby, but we can't really trust them to behave in that way. We have to stick around to be sure. Many parents are still doing that when the toddler turns teen. They don't trust their emerging adolescents because they haven't presented them with gradual opportunities for

earning trust. So the parents stick around, monitoring the young person's life, asking probing questions, and sending out signals that say "We can't trust you."

In the healthy family, parents design situations for the children, as they mature, to gradually earn more trust. Once the toddler can be trusted with the baby, they stop the close parental hovering, and the toddler then is given a specific responsibility like holding the bottle, which requires even more trust. When that's established, the toddler-turned-four might be trusted to keep his or her eye on the baby outside, and so on.

One of the most difficult questions for me to answer when I am out-of-state conducting a workshop is "Who is watching your children while you're gone?" Implicit in this question is the idea that children must always be watched—not just guarded from dangers but watched for misbehaviors and improper actions. Mistrust.

Because I do leave home, I have had to trust my children early on with responsibilities such as getting themselves up and making their own breakfast occasionally, and this trust has paid off. Today, they eat healthy breakfasts whether their mother is in town or not because they have become accustomed to eating them. They're proud of their culinary achievement, and so am I. (My sixteen-year-old son can make a better omelette than I can.) They don't fall apart when I leave because they can make reasonable decisions regarding their daily lives. If they need help in making those decisions, I trust them to go to their dad, a caring neighbor, or a friend.

But my trust in their competence didn't just happen. My husband and I go through a lot of hassles at times, forcing the children to assume those responsibilities that create trust. In spite of what they say, many kids really prefer that their parents take on the responsibility for their behavior, rather than learn to be trustworthy themselves. "I have trust in you" tells children that they are responsible persons, and they can't place the blame for their actions or inactions on others.

We have a joke in our family: "Watch out when Mom says 'I have faith in you. . . .'" Once after I said it, one of my sons responded, "You keep that faith, Mom. I don't want it." He verbalized how many people, including adults, feel about trust—they'd rather not make the effort to behave in a way that earns trust from others.

"I have to go back to the office tonight because they're counting on me," says the tired father. But his children are observing his example of trustworthy behavior. As adults, we don't always want that trust in us, either. At times it would be a lot easier to say "Give it to somebody else. I don't want to be that trustworthy." Easier, but not better.

I am saddened by the many parents who admit they can't trust their nine- or ten-year-old child to come home after school and complete a necessary little household chore such as turning on the crock pot, or follow simple directions intended to show courtesy to others in the family.

At a workshop for young mothers, our sharing about trust often turns into a recital of distrust. "My son's never where he says he'll be when I come to pick him up after practice," complained one mother. Gently we led her into recognizing that her behavior told him he didn't have to be there. She acted as if she just presumed he wouldn't be there. We encouraged her to next time trust her son to be at the place agreed upon at the time promised, and if he wasn't, she should immediately return home and await his call.

It happened exactly that way. When her son called, the mother said, "I was there at the time and place we set." (Implication: I trusted you.) "I waited a few minutes and then realized that you must have decided instead to walk home." (Implication: You broke trust.) "I'm getting dinner now, so you better not linger along the way. If you hustle, you can get home before dark."

When this mom returned to the workshop the following week, she was jubilant. She had had the courage to force her child to endure the consequences of his actions. After that incident, her son was there when and where he said he would be. He now could be trusted in this small matter.

Small matters expand into large matters in families. For example, when this same child reaches his driving years, he must be trusted with the safety of others, with getting himself home on time, and with assuming responsibility for the car. His parents can't operate on distrust for sixteen years and then suddenly turn a responsibility this heavy over to him. It isn't fair to him. Yet, it's when they can't trust their teenagers, that many parents for the first time turn their thoughts to trust.

When younger children do untrustworthy things, the consequences are annoying but not dangerous. So sometimes parents let it pass. For example, don't make an issue out of a "little lie," as parents so often term it. But getting by with little lies simply teaches children that lying is harmless if no one gets hurt. It gives children practice for big lies later on. It devalues trust as a personal trait worthy of their developing between themselves and others, particularly their parents.

When I taught sophomores, I once questioned a student about her behavior. She wavered before answering because she knew she'd have to face the consequences of her action (which I've long since forgotten). Later, she told me, "I wanted to lie, but I figured that truth is the best thing I've got going for me." I think she capsulized the issue of trustworthiness in that sentence. Truth is the best thing we've got going. When parents permit a child to get by with a lie and don't use the opportunity to build personal trustworthiness, they are really taking something from that child. They are removing some self-respect, some confidence, some trust. The child trusts parents to do what is best for him or her, and as parents, we have to assume that responsibility whether it's pleasant or otherwise.

I recall reading a minister's words about his mother's trust in him when he was a child. It seems that one day when he walked into his home, he heard his mother say on the phone, "I know Ralph didn't do it because I know he wouldn't do it." As it turned out, it was some cranky neighbor complaining about something insignificant, but the minister said overhearing his mother express such complete trust in him that she didn't even question him on the issue was at once reassuring and distressing. Reassuring because he knew he was trusted, but distressing because he knew that he had to be trustworthy in the future as well.

Parents have to be sure, though, that they don't use this technique as a parental copout. Some parents refuse to believe authorities who have witnessed their child in a misdemeanor. "I know my child wouldn't do that," they say. There's a fine line between justifiable trust and defensive parenting.

Too much trust too soon is equally hazardous. Television and our frenetic pace of life often push children into premature life experiences that we trust they can handle. A respected child psychoanalyst warns about this danger. "Children who are pushed into adult experience do not become precociously mature," he says. "On the contrary, they cling to childhood longer, perhaps all their lives."

3. Family members don't play the trust-trap game.

Parents can get trapped easily in this issue of trust. When they set a rule or disallow permission, they're often accused of not trusting their young. "You don't trust me" can be one of the most unsettling charges issued by adolescents and preadolescents (right up there with "You didn't tell me to bring the car *back*").

This charge puts parents on the defensive because there is some truth in it. Sometimes we don't trust our children in certain circumstances. If we can't always trust ourselves to behave in a certain way, how can we always trust others? We parents tend to react to the charge in one of two ways. We become defensive: "I do too trust you; I just don't trust your friends." Or we become apologetic: "I don't want you to think that . . ." and "I didn't mean to imply that . . . ." Neither reaction is effective, and we don't feel very good about falling into either of them. So, after being put on the defensive for a while, we get angry, and then the youngster is triumphant because he or she suspected all along that we didn't have a good reason for saying no, and our anger proves this suspicion to be correct.

Healthy families don't buy into the trust trap, especially when the decisions being made have really very little to do with trust, decisions such as Friday night curfew or who gets the car. Parents in these families refuse to argue trust at times like this and firmly put the trap away with a response such as "Trust isn't at issue here. Who got the car *last* weekend?" Or, "This isn't a matter of trust. You have to work tomorrow; that's the reason we expect you to be in by twelve."

Some parents use a wonderful technique with their children when discussing the issues that really are a matter of trust. (I borrow the technique frequently.) When their children first charge "You don't trust me," they turn it around and respond, "And you don't trust me if you think I'm doing this because I don't care about you. I love you, you see. It isn't always easy, but I love you." The words don't have to be exact, but the technique works because it puts youngsters on the defensive. They are forced to confront the same charge that they've just hurled at their parents, that of lack of love. (When kids say "You don't trust me" they're implying "You don't love me, or you would let me do this.")

When the parents turn it around and tell a daughter, for instance, that she is loved for herself, not because of their authority over her, she is disarmed. What can she say? How can any of us react with anger to "I love you"? One parent whose child threw a "If you really loved me, you'd let me go" comment to her came right back with "You're right—and I'm also letting you *not* go because I really love you."

The trust trap begins in a family long before it's clearly articulated. Its early vestiges show up in comments like "Everybody else is going" or "Nobody else's mother makes them (wear boots or go to the dentist or clean their room)." These comments involving trust are easily dealt with by confident parents, but I am astonished at how many parents allow young children to push them around with statements like these. The kids are implying "You don't love me enough to let me be like everyone else," or "You're only making me do this because you're big, mean, and power hungry, not because you love me." I try to get young parents to consider exactly what the child is saying to them before they respond to him or her. I've found that once they realize the intent of the child's words, they respond much more confidently and firmly. In short, they trust in their own judgment.

In earlier chapters we talked about self-worth and self-respect. Here we need to realize there's a corollary virtue: self-trust. When parents trust in their own love for their children and have confidence in their right to parent out of that love, then the trust trap can't get set.

4. The family doesn't break trust for the amusement of others.

Members of healthy families tend to guard information that might hurt or humiliate one of their members if it were known outside the home. A big brother doesn't tell the sandlot bunch that his little brother wets the bed now and then, even though he's tempted in the heat of a disagreement with that brother. An older sister doesn't share with friends on the school bus the contents of her younger sister's phone call the night before. Parents don't tell amusing stories about their kids, stories likely to be retold in a number of homes where the children are known. Husbands and wives don't talk about each other's idiosyncrasies.

Unfortunately, this extremely destructive form of family mistrust is found in too many families. Members simply can't trust one another with confidences. They have to guard their conversations. They must constantly warn, "Now don't tell anybody about this." It's pretty obvious that you cannot develop intimacies in such a family.

A mother shared with me a story about how she had suddenly become aware that she'd broken trust with her daughter. One day she'd phoned her teenage daughter to ask her to make some potato salad before she went out with friends. The salad was intended for a family gathering the following day. When the mother came home, the salad was made—but in such a hurry that there was literally a whole potato in it. The girl hadn't taken time to chop the ingredients well, to say the least. She'd given the salad a couple of hasty stirs, tossed in some mayonnaise, and put it in the refrigerator.

"I thought the salad was so ridiculously funny, I left it that way and showed it to relatives the next day," the mother continued. "But after I had showed it to about the fourth group that came in, my daughter asked, 'If it's so awful, why are you showing it to everyone?' I didn't know how to answer. She was right. I was ridiculing her because I was angry about her sloppy job. I should have chosen some other way to admonish her. I apologized to her later. I really felt bad about that."

This mother pinpointed a very common reason for the sharing of family failures with others, even if done in jest. Often it's used as a way to get even, to make up for disappointing behaviors, to express anger indirectly. It would have been far better for that mother to insist that the girl make another salad rather than to react the way she did.

Teens can be as guilty of this disloyalty as parents are. Some teens constantly betray parental confidences and mimic behaviors for the amusement of their friends. High-school teachers often can pick out a few students each year whose chief source of entertaining conversation with peers is the ridicule of their parents, including even their parents' most intimate conversations.

5. The family realizes that broken trust can be mended.

I suspect all of us have done things that break trust with others. We've told a half truth, revealed a family confidence, or omitted an important fact. Yet, in spite of our occasional lapses into untrustworthiness, we still want to be trustworthy persons. We want another chance.

Healthy families give their family members second, third, and thirtieth chances because the development of trust is so important to them. They continue to show basic trust in the children's character and judgment, even though the children break trust sometimes. The parents behave toward their children like the couple I know whose son got into every imaginable kind of scrape during his adolescent years. This couple dredged up renewed trust in their son after each incident he was involved in, although at times their doing so seemed heroic. They didn't imply that they trusted their erring son's actions at all times, but they did imply that they believed he would be trustworthy someday because he loved them and they him. It paid off. Their son, now thirty, is loving, whole, and productive. He said to them recently, "I don't know why I behaved the way I did. But if you had given up on me, I would have given up on myself, and God knows where I would be today."

For healthy parents, the idea of giving up on their children is foreign to their idea of family. To them, rebuilding trust is an integral part of family life. They know that members will slip and betray others' trust at times, but they also know that members need to be given another chance to prove their trustworthiness, and another, and often another.

Not-so-healthy families tend for years to harp back on incidents of betrayed trust. A child or parent is never allowed to forget an early transgression. "We never could believe you," "Remember the time," and "You just can't be trusted" are ways to write off a family member's later attempts at proving himself or herself trustworthy. The member just gives up. No matter what the member does, he or she can't really be trusted because of a mistake made five years earlier.

6. Parents as well as children are trustworthy.

In some families, trust is for children only. The parents expect to be trusted simply because they are parents, even though they can't always be trusted to carry out their promise.

Both lack of trust and great trust in parents showed up in interviews I conducted with people who grew up in mobile families. "I never could believe my dad when he said this was our last move," one interviewee said. "Because he said it every move. I ended up going to four different high schools and finally I got to a point where I'd nod and say 'Sure, Dad' when he'd apologize for the upcoming move, tell me what a good deal it was for the family, and promise this would be our last move." This twenty-eight-year-old remembers his teenage years as misery.

However, a daughter of a military man, speaking of the same era in her life, had been much impressed by her father's rejection of a promising promotion because he didn't feel the move would be good for the family at that time. "It told me clearly that he had our best interests at heart," said this young mother. "We all trusted him to do what was best for us, not best for his career. He probably didn't go as far in the Air Force as he could have, but he did in his family."

Stanley Hauerwas tells us about the need of parents themselves to experience trust and security. He says, ". . . in order to provide such trust and security for their children, parents, in turn, must experience trust and security themselves in their relations with one another and the 'outside world.' As Erik Erikson argued years ago, parents who are frustrated and demeaned, rendered helpless in worklife and citizenship, will have great difficulty instilling such bedrock beliefs, ways of being, inside the family."[7] When parents can't trust the world, they find it hard to trust themselves, and, in turn, are less trustworthy to their children.

Parents can betray their children's love and trust in little ways, such as failing to show up for a school program or a visitation, or in tragic ways, such as various forms of child abuse.

One of the most common disappointments in the life of single-parent children occurs when the father fails to show up on visitation day after he has promised the children he would. "At first this happened only occasionally," said a single mother. "Then it became somewhat routine, and it was terrible on the kids because they couldn't count on him and they would vacillate between great anger and great relief every Saturday. I got so I hated Friday because they'd begin gnawing their knuckles and wondering, 'Will he come like he said he would?'" This kind of wavering trustworthiness is very hard on children. They feel betrayed, but they also feel guilty if they get angry with their absent parent.

Parents need to have confidence in their own authority as parents, and children need to be able to trust their parents to act in their best interests, not to think first of their (the parents') social reputation. Popular columnist Erma Bombeck, in a column I mentioned earlier, asked parents how they regarded their children. "Are they like a used car? You maintain it for years and when you are ready to sell it to someone else, you feel a great responsibility to keep it running or it reflects on you? (That is why some parents never let their children marry good friends.)"[8]

The tragic outcomes of many children of public figures, particularly movie stars and politicians, show the results of this kind of parenting, in which the needs and problems of children take a back seat to the public image and needs of the parents. The children are unable in their formative years to build that faith so essential in healthy parent-child relationships.

Some of the grown children of politicians complain that their family's image was polished up beyond reality during reelection time when their politician-parent would arrange to pose for pictures with loving spouse, children, and dog in front of a picket fence surrounding the humble family home. Even though the children hadn't seen their dad or mom for months because of business or legislative sessions, they were pulled out for family togetherness scenes or a TV spot. The children got the picture, in more ways than one. As grownups, they realized they had been used — and *trustworthy* parents don't use their children.

Dr. Charles William Wahl, psychiatrist, psychoanalyst, and UCLA professor, wrote, "A basic need of any child is working identification with loving and cherishing parents. It is common for successful people to have unsuccessful children. The problem is that highly successful individuals have less time to devote to their children. That's true not only of actors, but politicians, academicians, ministers as well. Half the kids in communes who have dropped out of the competitive world have come from well-to-do families. I suspect that a good many of them are the victims of parental neglect."[9]

Another common way parents can fail in the area of trust is by perpetrating myths about themselves, especially what I term the "I never—I always" myths that hook some parents. "I never got into trouble when I was young" or "I always had a good report card" tell the child that the parent is either lying or the world's first perfect human being. Stories that have a Walter Mittyesque hue are also suspect; it's not easy to believe that Dad singlehandedly won World War II, or that Mom captured the heart of every male in her high school. Kids recognize that these stories are myths, even though they often pretend to believe them. But a little of their trust in their parents is eroded. Adults in the healthier families I studied were honest with their children about their own childhoods and backgrounds. "I figure it's tough enough for children today just to compete with one another," said a father. "Why make them compete with their parents at that age?"

In the healthy family, parents first work at being trustworthy themselves. Husbands and wives want to be trusted by their spouse to be constant in love, and then together as parents they carry this trust over to their children. They don't expect their children to be the only ones concerned about trustworthiness in the family. They want to be counted on to be there as loving, caring parents whenever their children need them. And their trustworthiness can be counted on for a lifetime.

In summary, the hallmarks of a family that trusts are as follows:
1. The husband and wife trust each other deeply.
2. The children are gradually given more opportunity to earn trust.
3. Family members don't play the trust-trap game.
4. The family doesn't break trust for the amusement of others.
5. The family realizes that broken trust can be mended.
6. Parents as well as children are trustworthy.

7
Sharing Time

Trait 5: The healthy family has a sense of play and humor.

Trait 9: The healthy family has a balance of interaction among members.

Trait 14: The healthy family shares leisure time.

Family jokes, though rightly cursed by strangers, are the bond that keeps most families alive.   — Stella Benson

In this chapter, I am combining three of the traits that my survey respondents placed in their list of the traits that characterize healthy families. The three traits presented are a sense of play and humor (number 5 on the list), a balance of interaction among members (number 9), and the sharing of leisure time (number 14). Each of these traits shares a common thread — *the use of family time.* Interestingly, two of the six traits isolated in the National Study of Family Strengths also had to do with family time and activities: Happy families are committed to the family group; happy families spend time together.[1]

How a family uses — or misuses — its collective time is so crucial that it in some way impacts each of the traits that characterize the healthy family. Let's look at some of the ways in which it impacts them.

Communication and listening, the top trait, is often missing in families who have lost control of their time together. In an incisive article called "Fast Folk," which appeared in the October 1979 issue of *Harpers,* Louis T. Grant dissects an article published earlier in *Woman's Day* in which the life-style of one working mother is praised and presented as a model of sorts. Listen to this woman's life. She rushes from home to work in the morning, eating yogurt in the car for breakfast; has lunch at the spa where she works out; leaves child care to her husband, who also has a managerial position forty miles the other side of home; pilots a small plane in her leisure time for pleasure; teaches on the side a class at a local women's college; leaves the kids with Grandma; leaves the kids with sitters; leaves the kids. . . . Grant likens this life-style, which he calls "fast folk," to keeping up with the gerbils. In his immensely perceptive piece, he illustrates the shallowness of relationships in a fast-folk family. There's no time in such a family for one another, for intimacy, for communication, for listening. That's for slowpokes. And, the author points out, "children are slowpokes."[2]

The second-most-named trait, *affirmation and support,* also suffers in the family that is so overscheduled that it has little time to affirm and support one another. Grant and others refer to the phenomenon of "sunset fatigue," that tiredness at the end of the day, when we're just too drained to support those we love most and whom we may be seeing for the first time that day. Our own needs are too great. It's the time of the day when we need loved ones to support us, and they need us to support them—but we've both run out of energy.

In interviews with career men about their marriages and families, Lynn Balster Liontos and Demetri Liontos asked, "What about the end of a workday—is coming home a problem for any of you?" The men answered with a resounding yes. One replied, "For us it's a problem. It's almost a daily thing. And I haven't figured out just what it is. Like frequently I'll stop and get Barbara at work. But both of us seem to have trouble letting go of our workday, focusing on one another. And we both seem to resent the other person not focusing on us or not being able to listen very well."[3]

Frankly, this man is too bright not to figure what it is that's causing the friction. Remember that the primary function of the modern family—the reason people marry and have children today—is relational. We want a relationship of loving, caring, and sharing with one another—and that's a two-way relationship. We need to be loved back, supported, and affirmed. If there's no time for that support, there's no time for that relationship to thrive.

A second man interviewed admitted, "Coming home is a real clash for us, too." A clash! Reading that comment gives one a sense of the pathos present in families in which work and other activities consume the time available and do away with the dream of coming home together to mutual support, love, and family harmony.

Respect for one another and *trust,* third and fourth in the list of healthy-family traits, also depend upon the time available to us in the modern family. If it's a fast-folk family, individual needs and personal confidences are not even heard, much less encouraged and responded to. Life in these supposedly successful families swirls around competing and being on top, not needing and responding. Children go off to their organized sports and compete. Parents must win at work. There's an ongoing need to triumph over impossible schedules. Attention to basic respect for one another's needs and to developing a trust level becomes secondary, and in the very troubled family completely sacrificed.

The traits that are discussed in later chapters are also affected and underscored by time. *A strong sense of family* takes time to develop and nurture. Traditions, storytelling, ancestor gathering, visits to the elderly, trips to the cemetery—all take time and as a result conflict with that insatiable time-gulper, work. In a study of corporate life in America, Diane Rothbard Margolis quotes a manager who said, "What happens is this. You fit your family around the corporation. You say, 'You always have to be available and if I'm called on then everything revolves around it.' I do it and then the family life adjusts."[4]

Shared responsibility can't exist in the family if one or more members have little time to be responsible, either for doing physical chores or responding to emotional needs. A *sense of right and wrong* and a *shared religious core* demand time for spiritual nurturing, praying, worshiping, and supporting church activities.

Respect for privacy includes allowing each family member some time that's private. In speaking about the single-parent family, Dr. Robert S. Weiss says the need for private time—an hour of personal time at the end of the day—is the greatest need a single parent has. This parent feels enormous resentment against the children if they call upon him or her during that precious time. If the kids are ill or need homework help then, the single parent can dissolve in stress.[5] (I submit that a parent in a two-parent family—where private time is sometimes even harder to find—can also dissolve when private time is denied her.)

Service to others, our twelfth trait, is self-evident in its reliance on available time. So is number thirteen, *table time and conversation,* which I've already discussed in conjunction with communication. The final trait, *admits to and seeks help with problems,* presumes time is available. Identification of what the problems are within the family can be a long, painstaking process, and working together to overcome them can take even longer. If the family is unwilling to allocate time from other activities to do so, the problems are not identified and never solved. "We didn't have time for marriage counseling," a man explained with irony. "We only had time for a divorce." Other families can't find the time to sit down with a child in need and hear his or her problems—or even to do something such as meet with juvenile authorities for family counseling after a bout of vandalism or shoplifting in their family.

Lack of time, then, might be the most pervasive enemy the healthy family has. Help is sorely needed on time control and stress management in families because the pressures of stress escalate yearly. *Family stress* is a new word in town, a sibling to and perhaps an offshoot from *executive stress,* that debilitating disease that ruins not only individuals but families as well since work stresses bounce back on the family.

Familiar symptoms of a constantly stressful family life include the following:
—a continual sense of urgency and hurry; no time to release and relax
—an underlying tension that causes lots of sharp words, sibling quarrels, marital misunderstandings
—a preoccupation to escape to one's room, car, garage, out to lunch
—a constant feeling of frustration about not getting things done
—a sense that time is passing too quickly; that children are growing up too fast
—a nagging desire to find a simpler life.

Some stress is healthy, of course. It's an important element of mental health. The depressed person tries to block out stress—either by sleeping all the time or by deadening stress with drugs, alcohol, or maybe work. A successful religious educator who found herself in this last category reflected after counseling and retirement, "All the time I thought I was being dynamic and instead I was just plain old stressful."

How did we reach this stress state in our culture? We like to drift back into selective nostalgia and ponder the classic pastoral existences of families living earlier in our century. Families sat on front porches. We don't have front porches anymore. They walked down to the town square for a band concert. We don't have town squares anymore; we have malls. We don't have band concerts outside on a summer evening; we have Muzak to soothe us every moment of the day, whether we're in an elevator or on hold on the telephone.

Our nation's shift from an agrarian to a computer society is the main reason why we moved from a slow-paced, family-based culture to one of fast folk and family stress. But this foundational shift occurred over three decades of time, and the drastically different events of each decade greatly contributed to our present situation of great family stress. Let's look at each decade's event.

First, there was the Great Depression of the thirties, which forced families to concentrate on survival. If a family had no bread, fun and relationships were low priority. Our parents and grandparents had to forego many of the pleasures of family fun just to keep the family fed. Leisure time meant the possibility of a second job. The healthy family during the Depression was one that was fed, sheltered, and cared for by parents who loved each other and their children but didn't have left-over energy to demonstrate it in tangible ways beyond providing mere sustenance.

Then there was the decade of the forties, in which our nation focused on World War II. The family fabric was abruptly stretched out of traditional shape by sons going off to war, women going off for the first time to war plants, and the whole nation coming together in kinship against common enemies. The family of the forties gave up its members to its nation because the nation's need was greater.

But the fifties is the decade most pertinent to us in our scrutiny of the history of family stress. When the American family began its great move to the suburbs in the fifties, it began losing its battle with time. Along with the patio and the two-car garage came lessons, youth leagues, and commuting. The dining room, symbol of family unity, eventually gave way to the family room with its symbol of separation, the TV set. Loneliness, the separation of family from relatives, and an abundance of available time conspired to produce a model of wife and mother who eventually turned into today's woman, with her rush to volunteer or return to college or enter the work world.

Today we live with the results of that rush. Today's women are not necessarily giving up what their mothers had—they're simply attempting to add what their dads had. And today's dads? After a pause in the sixties during which a generation of college students "copped out" and took a look at values, priorities, and time, the men are now back in the grey flannel rush, most of them.

I am one of those considered lucky by our culture, in that I can have my job and be in my home, too. Looking at it from a different perspective, though, I am one for whom both are always very present. My life isn't divided into neat compartments of work and home. Because I work at home, my deadlines are interruptible by family and my family by deadlines. Routine responsibilities have led me precariously close to a high stress level at times.

I recall a day during which I spent some time in looking from the clock to the calendar and back again, frustration rising. I stared hard at both, as if the dilemma of having to be in first one place and then another—without having a car to reach either place—would resolve itself if I really concentrated on it, willing it to resolution. I had had it all worked out earlier; that was the maddening part. I would pick up my son in time to get him to the soccer field, but on the way I would stop at the travel agency to pick up my next day's ticket. Then, while he was at soccer, I would fetch my daughter from school and drop her off at the clinic for her allergy shot. At the clinic, I would study my notes for the weekend. Just a routine day in the family—until the car broke down. I decided to dial my husband's office to see if there was a slim chance he could get home early—like in ten minutes. Busy signal. I sat down close to tears. . . .

If that sounds familiar, it's because thousands of American parents find themselves situated between two points on the compass of family life today: the clock and the calendar. As long as everything works well, like the aptly proverbial clockwork, we can keep running the mechanism of an overly busy family life. But let just one hitch present itself—a sick child, an unexpected caller, a coughing appliance—and our carefully constructed schedules collapse and give release to countless pressures and tensions held in check by organization.

In retrospect, I ask myself, "Why did I fall apart that day the car decided it needed a sabbatical?" If my son missed a soccer practice, it was only 1 in 25 scheduled for that season and 125 in his school career. If my daughter wasn't there for her allergy shot, the clinic wouldn't close down. (It *would* charge. Nonfunctioning cars rate little sympathy from the medical profession.) When I called the travel agent to explain my ticket dilemma, she responded cheerfully, "No problem. I'll drop it off on my way home."

Why, then, my reaction? Because I had failed. As a middle-class parent, I am expected to be where my culture dictates. On that particular day, the culture said that my son needed to be at soccer practice in order to be a healthy and fulfilled American male. It also said clearly that he should be driven because the time allowance between the end of school and the beginning of practice was too short to walk or ride his bike. (Perhaps if he did, he wouldn't need soccer to keep him fit in suburbia.) It said that the good parent furnishes adequate medical care, and in my daughter's case, this means bi-monthly allergy shots. Nothing dramatic, but each shot requires a trip to the clinic fifteen minutes away and an indefinite wait, sometimes for twenty minutes, sometimes forty, during a time the rest of the family is loaded with activities and appointments to keep. The culture says that I can work, even hints that I must work outside the home to be fulfilled. It also just plain dictates that a high percentage of our mothers *must* work during these inflationary years in order to meet such family expenses as soccer shorts, allergy shots, and car repairs. So I needed a car to pick up my ticket to give a lecture to fulfill myself and defray expenses.

Kenneth Keniston, in his book *All Our Children: The American Family Under Pressure,* addresses the frustration parents feel as they try to fulfill cultural dictates: ". . . the parent today is usually a coordinator without voice or authority, a maestro trying to conduct an orchestra of players who have never met and who play from a multitude of different scores, each in a notation the conductor cannot read. If parents are frustrated, it is no wonder: for although they have the responsibility for their children's lives, they hardly ever have the voice, the authority, or the power to make others listen to them."[6]

How did we get into this box? Where is it written that our family is better off attending meetings, signing up for lessons, joining a discussion club, working out at the spa, and generally being a slave to the family calendar rather than spending quiet and relaxed time together occasionally?

As a result of my work with parents—initially in the area of moral and religious development of children and later gradually expanded to the many peripheral issues of family life in the public arena—I am convinced that the family's loss of control of its time is one of its most volatile and frustrating problems today. It underlies many foundational problems in the hurting family and exacerbates the more common problems in other families.

Many families, competent in other professional and family areas, feel helpless when it comes to controlling their family's pace of life. Listening to society's contradictory messages—"You should be at this meeting; you should spend more time with your family!"—parents live in a continual state of guilt. One thirty-two-year-old editor told me, "I feel guilty when I'm not working, and I feel guilty when I'm not spending time with the family." She turned palms upward and shook her head in resignation. Another parent confessed, "On Saturday mornings, I'm glad when my wife asks me to drive the kids somewhere because I can sneak by the office and look through the mail."

The institutions in our lives—instead of helping parents learn to control family life by prioritizing, by evaluating, by carefully selecting any family activities, and by learning to say no—often encourage the reverse. Schools foster all sorts of activities to keep family members busily away from one another, and the child who isn't involved in those activities feels left out. Churches have such a complete calendar of religious education classes, organizations, and activities that the family loyal to its church must of necessity be a fragmented family, its members rarely seeing one another because one member always seems to be at church. The Mormons recently made news by limiting their family church time to a three-hour block on Sunday! This in addition to extensive weekday meetings and lessons—all coming from a church known particularly for its emphasis on family. Contradictions like these are common in our culture.

Recreation districts produce catalogs of self-fulfillment courses—yoga, swimming, embroidery, woodworking, and parenting—to lure the family to the calendar. Organized youth and adult sports with their myriad of practice schedules insure that thousands of families will not dine together in the evening, and national organizations such as scouts and 4-H have professed goals of bringing the family closer together by, paradoxically, taking it away from home to attend meetings, go on trips, and do projects.

Why do we succumb to this barrage of calendar-cluttering activity when we sense underneath that it isn't what's best for our family? When we know that our best times occur when we get away together, relax, and enjoy ourselves and one another? Worse, why are we ourselves often part of the problem, developing workshops, planning meetings, and lengthening kids' sports seasons, all the while complaining about our family's pace of life?

Why? Because we bought into that mentality fostered by the fifties that the healthier the family, the more *involved* it was. In fact, involvement was the pivotal word in family life. The healthy family was involved in home, neighborhood, community, church, self-fulfillment, youth leagues, local schools, Jaycees, League of Women Voters—and that's just touching the first layer of possibilities.

We are beginning to sense the error in our fifties thinking and realize that the stress rampant in families today is the ultimate danger in involvement. The 551 family professionals I surveyed tell us, loud and clear, that the healthy family spends more time *together*, and not more time involved in activities that steal members from one another. They give a much higher priority to such traits as the development of play and humor, family interaction, and shared leisure time than they do to those traditionally accepted traits of the good family: strong work ethic, college, financial security, home ownership, much activity in community affairs, and volunteerism.

It's important to note the very low value today's professionals placed on these traditional traits of the good family. Only 30 of the 551 respondents marked that the healthy family owns its own home while over ten times that number chose "has a sense of play and humor." In a society where volunteerism is equated with patriotism, only 74 of the 551 respondents marked it as a trait found in the healthy families with whom they work. (And the majority of those who marked it worked in voluntary organizations.)

This is an incredible shift. It is telling the family to look to itself for meaning, sustenance, and healing, rather than look to society and its many invitations for self-fulfillment outside of the home. In an effort to do that, let's look at each of this chapter's traits, all of them closely linked to the family's use of time.

Trait 5: The healthy family has a sense of play and humor.

This trait, prioritized high on the respondents' list, implies that families need to possess two separate but related characteristics. They need an ability to divorce themselves from work and other responsibilities, to get away; they also need to develop their capacity for enjoyment. Some families are stunted in this development. Either they embrace a modern-day work ethic—work is sacred and pleasure is frivolous—or they equate play with expense. "We don't have the money to have fun," complained one family studied. Apparently, this family is dependent, as so many are, upon expensive culturally induced pastimes, such as movies, skiing, and dining out, rather than upon developing the play that is within them as a family unit.

There's a third category as well, the family that turns play into work. There's a cynicism that holds that the English play at work and Americans work at play. A glance at the inordinate amount of time spent in our society in planning and executing our play bears out that comment.

Good families seem able to keep their work and play in perspective. Like the people in the early agricultural communities, when they work, they work hard and when they play, they play hard. They feel no guilt when they reward themselves by relaxing.

A sense of humor in the family also keeps things in perspective and works as an antidote to drudgery, depression, and conflict within families. Members of families that have a sense of humor can say to themselves, "I am not the center of the universe or even of this family. This situation I'm in is not going to change my life. I can laugh about it." Members who have this distance on themselves help defuse potentially explosive family situations.

A sense of humor seems to be an either/or thing in families. Some families develop a fine sense of humor. They are a joy to be around. Others have very little humor. They aren't as much in demand.

Here are some hallmarks of families who have a sense of play and humor.

1. The family pays heed to its need to play.

The primary hallmark of this family seems to be its absence of guilt at times of play. Individuals and the family collectively give themselves permission to sit back, relax, dream, and enjoy. Further, they schedule play times onto the calendar; they don't wait for free time, a mistake made by the family that doesn't find time to play. "Someday we will . . ." or "When we get a free day . . ." are familiar themes in the work-oriented family. Children and parents alike know it's never going to happen, but just expressing the hope seems to be enough.

The family that pays attention to its need for play usually schedules something every couple of weeks or so. It plans a reunion of sorts, a picnic, a volleyball game, or a museum trip. Or this family might save a Sunday for fishing, the beach, or auto races. Or it becomes part of such ongoing groups as those dedicated to mountain climbing, building model airplanes, or bowling.

Members of this kind of family come to expect their play times and to enjoy them. In Colorado, for instance, there's a group of families who reenact early mountain life. They love history, and they dress up in apparel authentic to the early days of exploration, mining, and trapping. Even their babies are dressed and carried as babies were then. These families come to historical functions in communities around Colorado and to parades and picnics—and they have a wonderful time. Each summer they rendezvous in the mountains and invite others to join them. It's fun to watch these families with microwaves back home put up their tepees and light flint fires, and enjoy their pleasure together. The guilt found among so many individuals and families whenever they aren't working is absent from this group.

Incidentally, families who have a healthy sense of play tend to pass that sense along to their children while, conversely, those families who are work-obsessed tend to pass along to their children their own discomfort and/or guilt at play.

"Why is it that I have to give my leftover time to my family?" complained one of the career men interviewed by the Liontoses. "My prime time goes to people I'm not intimate with, people who could do without my tie—except for the money relationship. My family I presume upon. But how long can I do that before Lisa turns fourteen and doesn't tell me what's happening at school or with her boyfriend and I say, 'Why don't you ever talk to me?' and she says, 'Because I've been getting leftover time for fourteen years.'"

There's one family style for handling play that I haven't yet mentioned. It's the family that cannot or does not play during the work year, but instead gathers together all its deferred family play time and uses it for an annual two- or three-week vacation. Or, in a variation, this family may work and study hard during three weekends a month but get away and enjoy the one remaining weekend in total abandonment of work. This family's basic style, which often is adopted because of work demands, is that of saving up its play time.

Some families seem to make this style of play work for them. They can let go and abandon themselves entirely to the relaxation and recreation of a single period of time. And they are able to put off play longer than others *as long as they know it's coming*. The drawback of this style for other families is that it introduces an element of work in their play. They feel required to relax at a given time whether they

want to or not. Their play almost is regarded as another work commitment, that is, it's on the calendar so it must be observed. I know a
family who shares a mountain condo with three other families. This
family has to use the condo the second weekend of every month if they
want to use it at all. At times, the family forces itself to go, even when
its members would rather stay in town for an event.

2. *The family recognizes its stress level.*

Our pace of life is partially determined by demands of society,
school, and work, but a good deal of it is determined by family
members themselves. When I work with parents on family stress
management, I tend to see those who feel stress and want to learn
more about controlling it. If there's one feeling these parents have in
common, it's their feeling of helplessness. They don't feel entitled to
control many of the controllables in their family life. "I just get so
weary of trying to coordinate—that's all I seem to do," said a mother
of four school-age children, near tears. Others nodded in agreement,
as if this is the way life must be.

I once went around a circle of twenty or so mothers and asked their
concerns about family stress, making a list on the blackboard as each
offered comments such as "I never seem to get my work done," or "I
know we're supposed to see one another, but how?" or "I don't have
any time for myself." By the time the circle was completed, the board
was full, but it visually proved the point that I wanted these parents to
recognize: We want to do everything, but we can't, so we feel
guilty—in other words, we set ourselves up for failure.

I shared with the mothers a clipping from the newspaper about a
woman whose husband sued for child custody on the basis that she
was an unfit mother. The main point he cited to prove this lack of
fitness was that "she fell apart just because our son left his coat on the
school bus." I went around the circle and asked my twenty women to
answer the following questions about this woman they had never met
or even heard about prior to that day:
—How many children did she have?
—What time of day was it when she fell apart?
—What day?
—Give me five things she had done that day.
—Tell me two activities that conflicted.

—How much time had she spent on herself that day?
—How many children were sick?
—How many repairpersons didn't show up?
—What did her mother say to her on the phone?
—How many coats had her children lost that year?
—Why was it imperative that her son have his coat that weekend?

By the time we had group answers, we were all laughing. We all knew that woman very well, and we didn't wonder at all that she "fell apart" over a little matter such as her son leaving his coat on the bus. We also awarded her custody of the child but gave her husband visiting privileges—on the days the six children were sick.

Today's parent is encouraged to spend a great deal of time and interest on each child, on his or her spouse, and on himself or herself. Yet, the amount of time available remains finite and constant. Instead of looking at our aspirations realistically and scaling them down, we set impossible standards for ourselves. When we can't meet them, we feel as if we have failed. Stress accompanies each feeling of failure. We're like the two men in a pond of quicksand. One turns to the other and says, "You can stop worrying about the quicksand. Here comes a crocodile." The only thing that takes our mind off one stress is another.

The only way we are going to control stress is by learning to select and control our activities. We have to accept deep within ourselves that we can't be superwomen and supermen, that we can't accomplish all that we would like, and that we aren't failures if everything isn't "done," whether it's at work or at home. This is hard to do. It's easy to accept these ideas intellectually, but emotionally it's a constant battle.

All across America the same dilemma repeats itself in other phases of family life. Intellectually parents want to play more with each other and their children, but emotionally they know they should be doing something more "worthwhile." I suspect our guilt goes back to our puritanism, which H. L. Mencken defined as "the haunting fear that someone, somewhere, may be happy."

What constitutes too much stress varies from individual to individual and, in our case, from family to family. What is zest to one family is stress to another. The family that has its stress level under control is the one who can recognize symptoms of stress, such as constant harriedness, short tempers, distractability, and ongoing tension, and pull back and say, "Let's look at what's happening here. How can we get ourselves under control?" They may cancel some activities, drop some memberships, or get out of town together, but they do *something* to alleviate the situation. Families who don't take charge feel victimized. They're afraid to say no to others who infringe upon their time. They don't have the courage to drop activities, and they don't give themselves the right to prioritize. Therefore, they don't just *feel* helpless, they *are* helpless.

3. The family doesn't equate play with spending money.

One of the most positive aspects of recreation and relaxation for the family is that it's as possible to experience in low-income families as it is in more affluent families. In fact, true family recreation is often more evident in low-income families. Poorer families have much wisdom to share with the not-so-poor in this area of family life. Those who live a simpler life-style know they don't have to have a lot of money in order to have a good time. Casual front-porch gatherings at dusk supply the same kind of pleasurable communication that a dinner party supplies, but it doesn't take all-day stress and a hefty entertainment budget to achieve. Picnics, ball games, potlucks, hikes, a day in the mountains or at the beach—all of these are inexpensive, often requiring only transportation.

Some families are able to make group work fun, whether the job is an annual cleanup or a painting or gardening spree. Members work as a unit, laughing and playing as they work—the same method used in the barn raisings or quilting bees of old. Other families have a strict division between work and fun. Their attitude is that work should not be fun—fun comes later.

Some families are beginning to cluster together for such simple pleasures as sing-alongs, caroling, square dancing, play readings, volleyball, crafts and cooking projects, and the like. I know of five families who share a garden and have a harvest festival among themselves. They also can and preserve their produce together, but most of all they have fun and companionship doing something that they might otherwise find lonely and burdensome.

In my state of Colorado, skiing is the popular winter sport, but with lift tickets running about fifteen dollars a day, the minimum for which our family can ski is seventy-five dollars. Add to that amount any equipment rental or purchase, transportation, and meals, and it adds up to a once- or twice-a-year entertainment. Yet, many families feel deprived if they aren't skiing. Instead of finding alternative and cheap sources of winter entertainment, such as ice skating, cross-country skiing, or sledding, they feel cheated and sorry for themselves. They can't envision family fun without spending lots of money. Healthy families can. They find alternatives, and they enjoy them together.

4. The family uses humor positively.

There's increasing evidence that humor and laughter are therapeutic for all of us. Norman Cousins, in his widely discussed book, *Anatomy of an Illness,* tells his story of being diagnosed as having a debilitating, incurable illness. With the help of one of his physicians, he set up a program for himself that was based on humor, enjoyment, and laughter. He rented humorous films to view, read funny books, went to comedies at the theater, and spent time with friends who liked to laugh. And he got well.[7]

The wellness movement, which is gaining so much respectable attention today, claims that humor is basic to good health. People who like to laugh experience less stress, probably because they use laughter as a tool to deflect stress. University of Nebraska researcher Nick Stinnett points out that when trouble comes, it has to be shared with the family, and if the problems shared are not balanced by shared pleasures, "in time people come to associate family life with problems rather than with enjoyable things." We see that in a great number of families today.

In good families humor is used to defuse potentially stressful situations. These families tend to hang on to a quip that recalls an earlier humorous family episode. Spoken at the right time, it can relieve tensions that build up. Often these little remarks mean nothing to outsiders—they don't even make sense to them—but to the family, they are invaluable in maintaining family health and equilibrium. For example, one family I interviewed reported that several years earlier one of their sons had punched his brother "because he was thinking bad things about me." For years, this family has benefited from that line. Whenever one member is acting badly for no good reason, someone else in the family will say, "Who's thinking bad things about you?" That little remark tells the offender to shape up and become responsible for his or her own bad mood. No lectures are necessary, and tension is safely released.

Sometimes a family who comes for counseling will tell a therapist that they have a great sense of humor, but it becomes quickly apparent that their humor is based on ridicule. Healthy families tend to laugh *with* one another while unhealthy families laugh *at* one another. Parents in healthy families simply don't allow the latter. Personal shortcomings aren't material for family jests.

Some families are able to produce a free enough atmosphere that individuals can share humor at their own expense, that is, they can laugh at themselves. Usually such an atmosphere comes about because the parents are able to poke fun at themselves. "Do you know what happened to me today?" says a parent and tells about some ridiculous goof he or she made. A few days later, a child is likely to say "I felt so foolish today in English class when . . . ."

Laughter has been around forever, according to psychiatrist William Fry of Stanford, who studies its impact on our lives, but we're just beginning to understand what a dramatic impact it can have on human beings and why. Laughter is serious business to Fry, who explains that tests on humans prove that humor is a tremendous boon to physical health. Laughing steps up the pulse rate, activates muscles, enervates circulation of blood, and increases oxygen intake—all effects that match the beneficial aspects of physical exercise. But more important, laughter causes remarkable physical relaxation, the reverse of stress, which can kill through hypertension and coronaries. Fry points out that humor and fury cannot coexist. "Mirth defuses rages," he says. "Anger demands a serious attitude, but humor banishes the tightness and severity necessary for anger. If mirth is experienced, rage is impossible."[8]

Some families can laugh at themselves, others can't. Some use humor positively, others destructively. Healthy families tend to fit in the first category. Once again, the hallmarks of a family with a sense of play and humor are the following:

1. The family pays heed to its need to play.
2. The family recognizes its stress level.
3. The family doesn't equate play with spending money.
4. The family uses humor positively.

Trait 9: The healthy family has a balance of interaction among members.

Nobel prize winner, Mother Teresa, said of today's modern family, "I think the world today is upside-down, and is suffering so much, because there is so very little love in the homes and in family life. We have no time for our children, we have no time for each other; there is no time to enjoy each other." One of the characteristics of the healthy family is that there is a balance of time spent with individuals so that they can learn to know, appreciate, and love one another. It's awfully hard to love someone you don't know, yet many families expect to be able to do so.

Nick Stinnett, researcher in the National Study of Family Strengths, says, "Like everyone else, people in happy families sometimes are hassled and have problems in their work or social lives. But when these people found their life-styles becoming fragmented, when they weren't spending enough time together — or weren't enjoying it when they were together — they made their families the top priority for a while. They crossed other things off the list to make more time for the family. And they tried to relieve themselves of unnecessary stress from outside."[9]

In speaking to the reality of the present-but-absent father in our society, Jim Guy Tucker, director of the 1980 White House Conference on Families, quoted a statistic: "Men spend twice as much time with children as they did twenty years ago but that merely means that they have increased from six to twelve minutes daily." As mothers move out into the work world and/or the single world, they are faced with the same dilemma — time allocation. If these mothers are upwardly mobile (an euphemism for successful), they must be willing to spend more time at work, to be on call at odd hours, and to be above asking for time off for family needs and occasions.

A few years ago, *The Wall Street Journal* carried an article about the emerging corporate stance in regard to divorced executives. It seems that on the management and corporate level, all other things equal, many corporations will now choose a divorced person over a happily married one because the divorced person has fewer family demands on his or her time. This is an astounding shift from just a generation ago when large corporations routinely interviewed the wives of potential executives before offering their husbands positions in order to judge the health of the marriage and the likelihood of the wife to be supportive of their goals for her husband. Those corporate executives quoted in the *Journal* article indicated that the divorced man is more desirable because he's able to work without distractions and competition from his family for his time.

The *Wall Street Journal* article quoted a company chairman who wanted to fill a hectic executive post in his company. He instructed his recruiters, "Find me someone who is as unhappily married as I am, so he'll really devote himself to the task at hand." The man eventually hired for the $100,000-a-year East Coast job had a stable, but hopelessly dreary, marriage. He liked nothing more than to escape from his family by spending Sundays in the office. Another executive told a Midwestern company chairman that his wife would file for divorce if he took the job offered but that he wanted it anyway. The chairman replied, "Go ahead. I don't care what you do on your own time—just raise our sales 30 percent." The executive got the job—and the divorce.[10]

Work, more than anything else, gets in the way of strong family relationships, whether it's the father's, mother's, or children's work. Once a teenager gets a part-time job, a family's life-style and its members' availability to one another changes, sometimes slightly but often drastically. A mother in a workshop I gave in San Antonio strongly discouraged the American practice of sending teens off to part-time work as soon as they are able to earn. Speaking from her own family experience, she shared with other parents the effect work had had on her children and her family. "We had three teens and they all had jobs. The result was that for four years we were never together. Yet, we were all home, supposedly a family. The job just isn't worth it if you lose your family in the process." She added the wry observation that their youngsters were working toward college but became so dependent upon their earnings that they were unwilling to give them up for college, "so it was all for little purpose, anyway."

Still, some families, even those with complicated work and activity schedules, seem to be able to work out a satisfying balance of time with one another. Two hallmarks identify these families.

1. The family does not allow work and other activities to infringe routinely upon family time.

The key word here is *routinely*. Many jobs call for periodic times when unusual effort is expected. For the salesperson, it's the holiday shopping rush. For the auto worker, it's the annual changeover in design. For the CPA, it's April 15, the income tax deadline. For the doctor, plumber, or military person, it's an emergency in their respective fields. For the writer, it's the big deadline. For the farmer, it's the harvest; for the student, exam time; and for the politician, the weeks just prior to an election.

At times like these, healthy families rally around their working person and support him or her in tangible physical ways and in supportive emotional ways. Family problems aren't brought up when the worker is so exhausted from long hours at work that he or she can't focus on them but are postponed, if possible, until the overtime period has passed. Chores and responsibilities are quietly assumed by others in the family. A parent from Chicago reported, "The day our family came of age was the day our thirteen-year-old said to his sister, 'Go ahead and write your English paper. I'll do the dishes.'"

But even though the healthy family supports its members temporarily caught up in the emergency or overtime nature of work, it does not permit routine work to interfere with family interaction. The healthy family doesn't automatically accept the idea that work always comes first. It expects the parents to be present for graduations and tonsillectomies, and those parents wouldn't consider being elsewhere. It presumes that dinner belongs to the family. It refuses Sunday or holiday work. It even refuses *to fight for* the worker's presence. It presumes that the worker belongs to the family during nonwork hours and refuses to allow itself to get caught up in the guilt-struggle laid on by management—that devastating guilt experienced by so many workers, who feel guilty when they're working and equally guilty when they're not.

A pastoral counselor shared with me the story of a man who had promised his son they would go fishing after dinner one night. During dinner, he was called away from the table by an associate who asked him to come in and look at something in the office. He declined pleasantly but firmly. "Somebody else can give you input on this, but nobody else can be a father to my son tonight," he said. This so impressed his son that he shared the story with the pastor.

This is a reaction typical of the worker in a healthy family. Yes, work is important, but not first. When work becomes the most important thing in a family member's life, often it's because that person is having problems in the family that he or she is trying to avoid. In the

Liontoses' interviews, one interviewee referred to this avoidance: "You know, it's been said that there are three life tasks—work, love, and friendship. And there's a tendency for a person to compensate in one if another isn't going well. So if you're having a hard time with your wife, you go to a bar for friendship or you stay at work. If your job isn't going well, you want more nurturing from your wife or family or your friends. Whatever isn't going well, you dump into the other two."

In our society work is often attributed a religious value in that it is considered the prime activity after which all else follows. Not so in the good family. In fact, I discovered a surprising number of men in healthy families who had changed jobs or careers because of the conflict they experienced between work expectations and family time. One couple in particular stays in my memory. The husband was a successful manager in some phase of camera production, the father of four, the husband of a woman who had gone back to college and then had begun to teach. Several times he passed up promotions that would have been personally satisfying and better paid but which would have required him to work weekends, travel, and generally be available whenever the company wanted him. Finally, he was given the word: either he must move on up, or move out in order to make room for someone else more interested in the corporate climb. He made a choice to leave this secure and satisfying job and found another. "It only pays three-quarters of what my old job did, but the pressures are so much less that it's like being given another chance—living another lifetime," he said. His family agreed. Even though he had successfully resisted workaholism in his company, it was an ongoing struggle accompanied by guilt.

We're beginning to find many examples of men like this one who was willing to earn less so that he could enjoy more life with his family and personal interests.

There seems to be a point in the lives of men such as these when they stop working long enough to evaluate their lives. They observe that their children are growing up and realize that they will soon be gone. "At times I want to shake myself and say, 'Listen, this is the *only* time he will be twelve years old,'" said Bob Benton of his son. "I wish I could put a brick on my boy's head and that he would stay the same size, just the way he is now. . . ."

Has there ever been a parent who hasn't felt like that at some time?

Yet, children won't stop growing and these men know it. They also know that their wives need them throughout the entire marital relationship, not just at retirement time. One of the men interviewed by Lynn and Demetri Liontos summed it up by saying, "It's strange, but all those years when intimacy is an issue—when we should get our relationships rooted down—we lay aside and work like hell. Then we end up forty and hollow. So what if we make $40,000 a year?"[11]

Researchers, alerted to the relationship between work and the quality of family life, have found that control of the work schedule is the bottom-line factor in balanced family interactions. Dr. Graham Staines of the University of Michigan found that family events and activities are built around work time and work rhythms. Long working hours per day and excessive days per week are predictably hard on the family, but being able to work variable hours from day to day is better for children than working the standard hours because it enables parents to find time to attend to personal and family matters. "The key issue," said Dr. Staines, "is the degree of control the employee has over his work schedule."[12]

The institutions in our lives have an overdue responsibility to help alleviate this struggle between reverence for work and concern about family health. In my second chapter I stressed my hope that the findings of the research upon which this book is based would force institutions to reflect upon their various responsibilities to foster in families those characteristics of healthy families. Businesses, churches, voluntary organizations, military life-styles—all are potential thieves of a family's rightful time together. "There's a real institutional impediment to the two-career family," stresses Jodi Wetzel, who holds workshops on the topic. "They still behave as if everyone has a traditional family—father-breadwinner, mother-homemaker, even though that's not the case." She cited Bureau of Labor statistics indicating that 53 percent of our families have two wage earners and only 15 percent make up the traditional family structure. More than half the mothers with children under six are in the work force.[13]

Some institutions, recognizing their responsibilities to two-wage-earner families, do a variety of things to enhance the amount of time a family can spend together. Some businesses have implemented flextime, a system of late arrival or early dismissal from work so that a parent can spend more before- or after-school time with children. I

know of a company that dropped its experimentation with a four-day
work week of ten hours a day when its workers found such a work
week not compatible with their family schedules. (Parents on this
work schedule rarely saw their children during the work week.) More
and more companies are offering day care on company premises so
that parents can have lunch with their children and are spared driving
miles out of the way to the babysitters.

Churches, schools, and voluntary organizations can bring families
in on calendar planning. Too often, plans are made from a managerial
or administrative perspective, not a family perspective. Schools that
don't open their doors until nine o'clock or close down half days for
teachers' meetings are ignoring the very real pressures these policies
place on the eight-to-five parents. What do they do when their six-
year-old is turned loose one afternoon a month? Take off work? How
do they juggle and struggle to find child care from 7:30 to 9:00 A.M.?

Why not some attention to child care at school, the logical environment? "Because we aren't in the business of babysitting," say the
educators. Perhaps with over half of our children living in two-career
families, we need to get into that business. Schools, after all, are prod-
ucts of families, not determinants. If the taxpayers call for and financially support early-morning or after-school child care, why not use
the facilities in which the children already are?

Some churches do try to help out families by planning their activities to take place at the same time, thus only one evening a week for
youth, adult education, and the religious education of children. Or
they plan education and other activities in conjunction with Sunday
worship. It's tougher on their staffs but easier on families.

Voluntary organizations have yet to overcome their tendency to
schedule activities at times that are inopportune for the family, or
even, I'm afraid, to recognize that they have a responsibility to the
family in this matter. So dependent are they upon volunteer coaches
that they allow the coaches to determine practice schedules that affect
anywhere from ten to twenty families in a given sport. That's ten or
twenty families who don't see one another in any tangible way a couple
of days a week. Some families attempt to handle the situation by involving the whole family in practices and games, an idea that most of
the league officials welcome and promote as healthy.

But all of this is contrary to what my respondents said about families needing time together. What's the answer for families unwilling or unable to become a support system for one child's seasonal activity? There's a long overdue need to study seriously what effects these leagues and practices have on family life, and if there's no alternative to infringing upon the one time sacrosanct to the family as a unit—the dinner hour—then we need at least to teach families about their potential cost to family health. It may come as a sobering revelation to thousands of parents that contrary to the positive family image fostered by these organized youth activities, the family, in fact, suffers from them.

What is more valuable for a child—participation in organized activities or the opportunity to live in a family that spends time together? Family time, according to most people who work with families. "I see too many kids who had Little League coaches for parents," said a pediatrician. "Why don't their parents realize that if they take the time they spend driving kids to practices and watching games and spend it with their children they all would be better off? How important is playing twleve baseball games or twenty hockey games to them twenty-five years later when they don't remember having had a family?"

Author John M. Drescher in his book, *If I Were Starting My Family Again,* stated boldly that he would spend more time with his children. "A group of three hundred seventh- and eighth-grade boys kept accurate records on how much time their fathers actually spent with them over a two-week period," Drescher wrote. "Most saw their father only at the dinner table. A number never saw their father for days at a time. The average time father and son were alone together for an entire week was seven and one-half minutes."[14]

Seven and one-half minutes! Yet, we pretend that in that amount of time a young adolescent and his father are able to establish a close relationship, one that will be helpful for the boy in his growing up. How?

Church, organized activities, and school, then, all vie for family time. But the most constant and most influential institution to be reckoned with is work. The family that keeps its work commitments under control is apt to be healthier than the family that subordinates its time to the parents' work patterns.

2. The family actively discourages the formation of coalitions and cliques within the family.

Dr. Jerry M. Lewis in his family studies found that healthy families don't have any little coalitions formed between certain members. Lewis says that in some not-so-healthy families there are obvious coalitions in which two or more members of the family pull apart and form a clique. (Common coalitions are mother/son or daddy/daughter.) He reiterates that in his healthy families the number one relationship is that of the parents and that the kids accept this as normal.

But even parents can form a coalition. In some families, I have found that it's an us-against-them proposition, the parents against the children. The parents and the children each try to one-up the other. The parents talk of their parenting tools as weapons, and the children gloat when they put something over on their parents, instead of working things out together.

Since the *couple relationship* is foundational to all other relationships in the family, let's look at that relationship first. As I pointed out earlier, husbands and wives in a healthy couple relationship have equal power. Neither husband nor wife wishes to dominate the other; rather, they seek to complement each other. The ability of two grown people, who have freely chosen each other, to share equal power is a significantly healthy characteristic. These couples, in Dr. Lewis's words, are "charged up," that is, they seem to support each other and other family members with an enthusiasm not found in couples with an unequal relationship.[15]

When the couple relationship is hurting, parents often turn to a particular child for friendship, and then the family begins choosing up social sides. "What are you and Tom doing Sunday?" a wife may ask her partner, implying that she and her teenage daughter, her special friend, will be doing something separately. Little confidences are shared. Eventually, a close, even intimate, relationship can develop between one parent and one child, often to the exclusion of the others. Mom begins to talk to her son about her disappointments in his father. Daddy finds a friend in his daughter, whom he visibly cherishes more than he does her mother. These parent-child coalitions are distinctly unhealthy for both the persons involved in them and the persons excluded from them.

In a letter to a woman's magazine, a woman wrote, "I am having a hard time fighting depression. I also weigh 25 pounds more than I should because I eat out of boredom and loneliness. One problem is that my husband spends more time with our children than with me. I feel so unloved. . . ."

Another common coalition is the one formed between one spouse and his or her parents. Often a wife will spend inordinate amounts of time and share deep confidences with her own mother, who lives nearby. Or a son will never really leave his birth family after he has a family of his own. What his parents think about his job or about world affairs is more important to him than what his wife and children think.

Coalitions between siblings are the most common and less hazardous of family coalitions because they tend to be more fleeting. It's normal for coalitions to exist between siblings of similar ages and sexes, but these are mainly built around play and interest patterns at a given age. Therefore, parents need not be concerned if their six- and eight-year-old sons are spending the majority of their time hunting frogs and snakes together to the exclusion of older or younger siblings. Or if two teens share music, school, and activity interests as well as personal confidences. That's natural.

However, there is danger to the family unit whenever two or three siblings establish a basic trust unit to the complete exclusion of the rest of the family. Coalition members may use private language and tell private jokes, both of which can disrupt the trust level of the entire family. Other family members are gradually forced into a coalition of their own, and soon no one receives affirmation and support except within his or her own group. The situation begins to resemble a group of roommates or opposing team members who form subgroups for support and friendship.

We don't find this exclusivity in the healthy family. Coalitions aren't permitted to exist, primarily because of the recognized hazard to the sense of family and to the need members have for shared support and love. Parents in healthy families tend to keep a sharp eye out for potential cliques and get them stopped at the first sign. One couple told me about the problem they had when their college freshman son returned home for the summer. Their other three sons, who had experienced a year of no older brother bossing them around, immediately formed a coalition to thwart any attempt their older brother might make to reassert power once he came home. The parents were baffled when they realized that instead of welcoming him back into their previously pleasant family, these three had formed a tight little unit designed to let him know he wasn't welcome. Five days after the son's return, the parents called a family conference and invited feelings to surface. The younger boys exposed their feelings and strategy. The older brother let them know that while he was away he had really rather enjoyed not having to be an older brother, and things began to be put right again. But the parents were the ones who sensed the coalition and put a stop to it before it became threatening to the family.

The essential reason for developing good sibling relationships is often misunderstood. Brothers and sisters don't exist primarily for lifelong relationships but for support for one another when they are young. They exist to learn from one another within the family unit as children. Then, as they mature, they need each other less. When they leave home to found families of their own, they should focus on their family of construction, not their family of origin. When brothers and sisters become adults, then they can choose whether or not to be friends.

I asked parents in good families how they viewed their own sibling relationships. Many of them indicated peripheral relationships with their grown siblings due to geography and differences in interest, but the majority of them mentioned that there were strong bonds when they were younger. Their relationships with their brothers and sisters had helped them to learn how later on to foster strong relationships among their own children.

Margaret Mead once observed that she noticed a cycle operative with sisters in our society. Sisters who are close as children and teens tend to pull apart and become competitors, she said, during marriage and early years of parenting. However, she observed that once the sisters' children began growing up and away from the home, then the grown sisters tended to become friends again, much closer even than they were as teens. I have noticed the same pattern. It's almost as if the sisters are able to say to one another, "We don't need to compete any longer. We can be friends."

According to Dr. Helgola Ross, who has studied sibling relationships, we need to put a bit more time into developing lifelong support relationships with our siblings. "Since we started work, we've learned how many people are aware of what closeness in sibling relationships can do," says Dr. Ross. "There's upheaval in our society. We move around more than before, marriages don't last as long as they used to, families break up. There's a greater need for more intimate relationships today. We've found that friends are considered important but are left behind when a person moves away. Even mates are sometimes left fairly easily. But sibling relationships are usually maintained even if you live far apart and don't see each other for years."[16]

Imbalanced parent/child relationships frequently occur when Dad is always at work. Mom and the children may form a tight little unit which excludes him. This happens frequently to men who travel a lot. They have to reestablish themselves in their families each time they return. A family counselor calls this "a family way of getting even." It is probably most noticeable in the military, where families are constantly being left. The military member, on the other hand, feels constantly pulled. He is being fought over by his superiors on one side and by his family on the other.

But men aren't the only ones who can have an imbalanced relationship with their families. Women who live in the world of work outside the home as well as the world of family often have to choose between the two worlds at crucial times. I am familiar with the tightrope act such women have to perform. Come with me through this scene which took place recently in my life. Because I have to schedule lectures so far in advance, I never know when I accept an invitation just what will be going on in my children's lives when the invitation comes due. So it was that I had agreed six months in advance to teach a session on family resources at a local college on a certain Tuesday night in May. Then I discovered that our oldest son, Pat, had a jazz band concert that very evening. Not wanting to miss the concert or to disappoint him, I said that perhaps I could go to dress rehearsal, scheduled for the evening before the jazz concert. Immediately our youngest son, Dan, said, "But that's the night of *my* band concert." So I ended up going to Dan's dress rehearsal on Monday morning at his elementary school, sitting with kindergartners and teachers, and then attending Pat's dress rehearsal Monday evening—all so that I could teach Tuesday evening as planned. Such a scene as this is not uncommon to either working men or women—this constant juggling so that children know they are important enough for us to want to establish individual relationships as well as family units.

Regrettably, more and more women are beginning to mimic success-oriented men in their climbs up the career ladder. Remember the woman I earlier referred to in "Fast Folk"? Author Louis T. Grant said, "Out of sympathy for Charlotte I'd like to hold a mirror up to her so she could see the blur she represents in her daughters' lives. . . ." He quotes her as saying, "When something happens at home, Chris (her husband) copes, I don't. Not even last winter when the kids seemed to have one strep throat after another. Nothing ever rattles Chris."[17] She is apparently proud of the fact that children's needs and crises don't interfere with her successful career and incredibly busy life. The point here is not whether Charlotte should work. The point is that there has already developed a coalition in that family, a triad of daughters and daddy, which will lead, if unchanged, to an imbalance in relationship and probably to the kind of maternal relationship that a colleague of mine calls the "Aunt Mommy Syndrome."

Often parents will confess that they have paid little attention to the amount of interaction time operating between and among individuals within their family, so I use a little device to help them evaluate the amount of time, or at least I call their attention to it. I suggest that they keep a simple record, jotting down at the close of each day how much time each family member has spent with each other member of the family. It isn't as difficult as it seems. At the end of a week or two, patterns begin to emerge. In the healthy family, the time spent seems about equal among members. In others, an imbalance appears. Usually where there's an imbalance, there's one member, usually but not always a child, who spends an inordinate amount of time alone. Usually this is the one least pleasant to be around and also the person who most needs interaction and socialization.

Again, the hallmarks of the family that has a balance of interaction among members are as follows:
1. The family does not allow work and other activities to infringe routinely upon family time.
2. The family actively discourages the formation of coalitions and cliques within the family.

Trait 14: The healthy family shares leisure time.

Surely one of the ironies of our fast-paced culture is that it calls for more leisure time in order to offset ever-increasing pressures, while at the same time it reduces the amount of time available to us. Louis T.

Grant explains this paradox: "As the national treadmill speeds up, everyone adjusts his pace and so no one's the wiser, just a little more exhausted, irritable, and depressed."

The value of leisure time was collectively ranked number fourteen in the list of healthy-family traits by four out of five of the professional groups. As I mentioned in an earlier chapter, one professional group—the health and medical professionals—rated this trait significantly lower than the other groups did.

Whatever the reason for the health professionals' variance, the trait was prized enough by the four other groups to give it a position in the top fifteen characteristics. That there's a need in our families for leisure-time activities, for a chance to refresh ourselves, is so obvious that I won't go into it here. But *how* the family views and manages its leisure time is another matter.

We found great diversity among families in this area of leisure. Individuals in some families regard their nonworking time as their private possession, not to be infringed upon by other members of the family. Other families—the we-always-do-everything-together families—presumed just the opposite extreme. We found some families who did do just that on weekends. The entire family, from five-year-old and teens to mother and father, grocery shopped together, discussing each purchase, holding conversations at the cereal section, making the week's menu together, and so on. They went to garage sales and sandlot games *en masse*. Most families, however, exhibited a combination: some individual leisure-time activities and some shared family activities.

Where does the healthy family fit into this picture? I found six hallmarks that characterize the family who shares its leisure time in a healthy way.

1. The family keeps its collective leisure time in balance.

In interviews with people who work closely with families, I didn't find a single professional—not even those in voluntary organizations—who felt it healthy for the family to spend all or even most of its leisure time in shared activity. "Then it becomes forced activity," said a family counselor. "I see families like this. They say, 'I don't know what's wrong. We do everything together.' That's what's wrong."

On the other hand, many otherwise healthy families give up trying to have any shared family leisure. They abdicate to the crowded calendar and forget about trying to find a time when they can all go to the beach or even share a TV special. It's just too difficult to manage in the family who has succumbed to the plethora of activities with which the American family is bombarded. Researcher Graham Staines, in his study on the impact of work schedules on family life, concludes, "The quality of time spent with the family is important, but so is quantity—at least to parents and most probably to children. I'm not saying that parents should spend 100 hours with their kids, but simply that you can't ignore the issue of the quantity of time spent with children."[18]

Balance is the key. How much time is the right amount? It differs from family to family, but I found that most contented families tend to share at least one leisure activity weekly. It may be just a backyard volleyball game or front-porch sitting in the evening. It may be a planned activity like family fishing or shopping (a surprising number of American families list shopping as their shared leisure time activity).

These families also tend to get away together, whether it's to visit grandparents overnight or to take an annual vacation. They seem to feel the need for unity that travel can bring to families. "I think the best investment in our family's health is going to the cabin in the Northwoods every summer," said a working class father, who indicated that the family voluntarily forgoes other entertainment during the year so as to be able to afford two weeks in the lake area of northern Wisconsin.

His wife concurred, adding, "When we get away from home and our own friends and interests and TV shows, we seem to enjoy each other more." What she said about the importance of time away together was echoed by many of the parents quizzed. Single-parent families particularly stressed the need to share some leisure time together, a luxury in the family where so much time is spent at just completing day-to-day responsibilities. "If I'm at home, I can't relax," said a single mother of four. "There's always something crying to be done. So we go to my parents for a weekend about once a month. It's probably silly—it's only across town—but we all love it because there we can relax and talk and play cards and things like that."

Healthy families seem to be able to work out the teen dilemma by varying the activities shared by the family. Parents of teens know well the difficulty of enjoying a family activity when their teens don't want to be there. Realizing that it's just a natural part of adolescent development doesn't help alleviate the tension around a campfire with one or more resentful teens making jokes about how much fun it's supposed to be.

I learned of a couple who saved to buy a camper to fulfill their dream of being able to spend many weekends at the lake. They were able to afford it just as their oldest daughter hit eighth grade and wanted nothing to do with her family on the weekend. They didn't feel secure in leaving her at home alone, so they insisted she accompany them. It didn't work because their daughter greatly resented missing Friday night games and the opportunity to be part of school weekend activities.

The conflict finally became too much for the parents. With two other children right behind the eighth grader, they saw little hope for solution, so they sold the camper. It didn't help when, about five years later, their high school and college youth asked peevishly why their parents had sold the camper when they could all use it to go to a lake for sailing and fishing. (Child abuse under these circumstances might be understandable.)

The good family fosters the attitude that members should agreeably participate in a certain number of family activities, but it varies these activities from sports to family visits, with perhaps a church dinner or school field day thrown in. It allows for individual activities to take precedence when they are special, but it doesn't allow routine activities to interfere.

If there's a general rule in these families regarding family-shared leisure, it's that the individual is expected to participate if it would otherwise prevent the family from participating (as in the family with the camper), but that it's unfair to expect this routinely. As in so many other areas of parenting, this calls for a fine balance, and parents are often unsure how much to ask.

Healthy families don't force everyone to enjoy or take part in the same activity. In an earlier chapter, I mentioned the family who spends time in the mountains but who once there allows each member to pursue his or her own interests, from fishing to suntanning to rock throwing. This unity-and-diversity is often achieved in families who want a shared family time but who are open to individual interests.

Once again, balance and flexibility seem to be the keys in achieving shared activity within the family. A teen remarked, "I like to do things with my friends and I like to do things with my family, but I don't like to combine the two. I am two different persons, one with my friends and one with my family." This same girl later remarked during a group discussion, "The best thing I like about getting away with my family is that I don't have to worry about my hair. I don't know anyone else around, so I feel free. If I want to swim, I just shake my wet hair a little, go to dinner, and say, 'To heck with it.' My family doesn't care what my hair looks like."

This girl voiced a feeling common among adolescents—they like being with their family more than they like their friends seeing them with their family. They like sharing family informality, being away from friends, who hold them accountable for their family's appearance and behavior. "Getting them out of town unseen is the secret," said a father of three early teens. "Once we're there, they have a ball."

2. The family prioritizes its activities.

In one of my 1979 "Talks with Parents" columns, I listed some eighty activities on which families spend time and invited my readers to photocopy the list and ask their families to individually prioritize the items on the list by selecting the twenty items they considered the most enjoyable activities, and the twenty items they least enjoyed.[19] (I didn't include items like dental appointments because they aren't optional, at least not considered so by adults).

A significant number of parents from among my four million readers wrote to me about their surprise in discovering that their children put *the highest value on the least organized activities,* choosing in their top twenty such items as going fishing, fixing the car with their dad, hiking, picnicking, sleeping outside in the tent, window shopping, and so on. My parent-readers were also greatly surprised by the low value their children put on such highly organized activities as youth leagues and scouting.

Why, then, do kids join these organized activities in such large numbers? Because the pressure that children feel from both parents and peers to join these groups is often overwhelming. True, lots of kids join because they love the sport or the activity, but I would guess that as many join to wear the uniform or because of tempting recruiting techniques or because their friends and family expect them to do so.

Consider this item offered as a recruiting gimmick by a scout-master:

Would you like to:
Canoe through rapids?
Work with ropes, saws, axes?
Build a 20-foot-high signal tower?
Pitch and live in a tent?
Spend a week at Stokes Camp?
Learn about how trees grow?
Swim a mile?
Sit with friends around a campfire?
Find your way by the stars?
Camp out in the snow?
Lead other boys?
Earn colorful badges?
March in a parade?
Fish in a 100-acre lake?
Become an Eagle Scout?
Use a compass and map?
Are you a boy 11, 12, 13?
Are you a man over 18?
Did you show this test to friends?
Did you answer "yes" to most of these questions?
If so, come to the Elizabeth Ave. School on Friday,
   April 27, between 7:30 and 8:30 P.M. We'll tell
   you all about Boy Scout Troop 95. Bring a couple
   of friends. You need us and we need you.

Look at the promises implicit in this come-on and consider the kind of pressure sure to be placed on the parents of eleven- or twelve-year-old boys who read this ad. The ad is every bit as blatant as the ads on Saturday morning cartoon time that begin, "Ask your parents for . . . ." And the youth magazines are full of this kind of gimmick to get boys and their parents involved.

In a way, this scouting ad can be considered a bait-and-switch ad because once the boys come and join, they get monthly den and pack meetings (which parents often have to force them to attend) and ongoing badge projects that become boring and burdensome and often interfere with their riding their bikes with friends to the local watering hole to fish. Then pressure is put upon the family to get these badges done so that the boys can get their awards at the next pack meeting and the den leader will be considered successful. To be fair, I offer the same kind of come-on, only in a more honest vein. I would like to see this ad run directly below the other.

Would you like to:
Go to a den meeting
    every Wednesday afternoon
    at someone's home
    and work on a project
    instead of playing football
    in the leaves?
Study your Wolf Book
    and write an essay on fire safety
    in your home
    instead of watching the Muppets?
Go to a Pack Meeting
    the first Friday evening
    of every month with your mother
    because your dad is going
    to your brother's high school
    junior varsity basketball game?

Is this an unfair indictment of scouting-type organizations? I don't believe so. If kids genuinely want to spend the kind of time required in the kind of activity that scouting offers (and some do), then by all means they should join a scout group. But every boy or girl considering scouts should be made aware *in advance* that these meetings, projects, and activities are not all camp-outs but posters, essays, and homework as well; and that these new activities will of necessity eliminate some old ones, which are often family or play activities. Kids also should be aware that scouting is their responsibility, not their parents' or family's responsibility.

I call upon the leadership of organizations such as scouts to be cognizant of their responsibility to the total family in their recruiting and programming techniques. To make families feel guilty for not supporting their child's scouting activity after the child is attracted by an ad like that is terribly unfair and irresponsible.

Pressure to join youth league and other activities is especially terrific in some communities. In a column I wrote as a follow-up to my original column about family activities, I discussed this pressure. Often it's indirect. We don't ask, "Do you want to play ball this summer?" We ask, "Which team do you think you'll make?" We don't point out what the child might miss by joining an organization. Instead, we say, "Just think—you'll get to go on an overnight camping trip." We don't ask ourselves why these activities for kids are important to us as parents. We just presume that good parents sign their children up for everything. Often the children would prefer being less scheduled. Maybe they don't even enjoy the sport or activity. Many express an adult-type longing to do things like explore and tinker, but even children as young as eleven are too calendared into activities to find the extra time.

After my second column having to do with kids' activities, a mother shared with me her reaction to both columns. "I didn't agree with your columns at first," she wrote. "I figured your antagonism toward youth league was personal, due maybe to a bad experience. But I thought I would ask my daughters just to be sure. They said, 'You mean we don't have to play baseball this summer?' I was astonished. I had no idea that they weren't enjoying it the past three years or that we were putting so much pressure on them to belong."

Hers isn't an isolated reaction but a familiar discovery made by parents who have spent a good share of their children's lifetime driving, waiting, and watching only to find that their children are plain sick of an activity by the time they reach high school. In fact, many high school coaches do not allow their own children to participate in youth league play. "They get the uniform, the team, the practices, the fans, and all of that way too early," a high school football coach told me. "I can't tell you how many good players we lose because they just aren't interested anymore." Even Hal McRae, outfielder for the Kansas City Royals, states flatly, "My kid will not play youth-league sports." These professionals can hardly be considered over-reactionary after all the years of experience they have had.

Prioritizing means that we look at the activity and ask some crucial questions. If I were considering taking a class, I would ask these questions:

- *Why do I want this activity?* Is it because someone else thinks I should, or do I really want to spend my extra time this way?
- *What activity will it replace?* Twiddling thumbs, playing ball with my kids, visiting my mother, or watching TV reruns?
- *How will it affect our family life?* If I take this course, will it mean I won't see the kids before their bedtime? Or, on the positive side, will it give me a breather so that my children and I will be more content with one another when I return? Does it take away a special family time?
- *Is it worth it?* How I've answered the previous questions will help me answer this final, bottom-line question. I know my final decision must be ultimately based on the amount of time that I think is essential to the well-being of our family and the cost of a particular activity to our collective family time.

Another general rule shared by many healthy families is that no child needs more than one activity at a time that requires practice. If the child's in competitive swimming, he or she doesn't need marching band. If the child's got a part-time job, he or she can't fit in basketball.

When parents allow children to sign up for more than they or the family can handle, they're teaching their children to have unrealistic expectations about themselves. Children need to learn at an early age to make choices.

A mother at a family stress seminar told the other parents how she'd helped her son learn to make realistic plans for himself. She told about the day when her over-scheduled son accused her of being careless in getting home in time to get him to a practice. "You're late for my practice," he said.

She responded, "No, *you're* late for your practice. If you expect me to get you there, it's got to be on my time schedule. Otherwise, walk or quit."

Some of the listening parents were very uncomfortable with her response to her son because they hadn't yet reached the point of prioritizing that this mother had.

Another effective rule commonly held in healthy families is that the activity belongs to the children, not to the parents. This deals with the pressure on parents to watch their children perform. This notion affects everyone—the child, the parents, and the coaches. From the beginning of our three children's various interests in activities, we established the idea that the purpose of their participation is for their playing pleasure, not our spectatorship. If they are not going to be happy playing if we're not watching, then that sport is not for them. (I remember hours of happy softball as a child without ever expecting my parents to come and watch. We just gathered all the kids around, chose up sides, and played, sometimes for hours. We didn't need or even want our parents watching us.)

We don't expect our children to come and watch us at our activities as part of their sonhood or daughterhood, and they shouldn't expect us to do so as part of our parenthood. It isn't that we don't like to watch, or that we don't watch occasionally — we do. What's important is examining why the child wants to take part.

It isn't healthy for a child to play primarily for parental approval. If that's the case, then he or she needs more time alone with his or her parents or some kind of professional help. I have seen parents reduced to bundles of guilt when two or three of their children have Saturday games scheduled simultaneously, and they must choose which one to attend. Add to this Saturday chores, visitation rights, and the multitude of catch-up chores piled on mothers who work outside the home, and the tyranny of youth leagues can become overwhelming.

On my thirteen-year-old's soccer newsletter sent to parents every fall, I found this line: "Sunday games will not be scheduled earlier than noon." Sunday games? What kind of guilt must this instill in a child whose family normally shares Sunday leisure-time activities or visits grandparents? I reflect back to when this particular league began a dozen years ago with a stated philosophy that all games would be played by noon on Saturday and in September and October only. Each year, the league has expanded its number of games and the subsequent number of Sundays and Wednesdays on which they are played. With added play-offs and tournaments, it's not unusual to find dozens of families affected by a conflict between a winning soccer team and Thanksgiving weekend. When a few years ago our own son was scheduled for a championship game the day after Thanksgiving, we put our foot down and said no. Several other parents did likewise, but there was a subtle pressure put on these boys to change their parents' minds and the family holiday plans to fit the needs of the schedule.

An editor friend of mine claims that children are the real victims in this pressure for parental spectatorship and involvement. "The kids are made to feel guilty by the coaches if their parents aren't active or at least there watching," he said. "At the same time, they're made to feel guilty if parents are missing something else by being there to watch them play. The kids can't win."

Noted sports psychologist Dr. Thomas Tutko questions the amount of pressure put on kids by parents who watch them play. "How would a mechanic feel if he were suddenly shown a totally new type of engine, given a box of tools, and told to repair the engine while a gallery consisting of his neighbors, friends, and opponents from a competing garage cheered or booed, depending on how he fared with the engine?"

Eulogized are those parents who are willing to be coaches or scouting leaders. Criticized are parents who aren't involved. A father made the wry observation that he agreed to be on the scouting board for the sake of his son but that it worked conversely. "It took me away from my home and my son two more evenings a month," he said. Perhaps the question we need to address is this, Do we really want more activities for our children if it means less parental time at home, or are we being told we *should* want more if we consider ourselves good parents?

It's interesting when parental hostility toward the usurpers of family time erupts. Listen to these parental comments published in an article on the morality of Little-League type sports in the magazine *U.S. Catholic*.[20]

First comment: "Time is a gift from God. We dash around looking for time, and organized sports consume so much of it that children are getting up at 2 A.M. to get ice time for hockey practice! How can children experience love, Christ's love, through parents and siblings if they are on a roller-coaster ride?"

Another: "At one game, two team managers had a fist fight, bloodying noses, and falling down a hill at the field. My son finished that season, but now plays ball in the street with his friends without tension or anxiety."

Another: "Thank you. I've been wanting to see this in print for years. I'm a teacher and I do enjoy sports—but we always want too much, too soon, too perfectly. Let's let our children be children when they're little, so they don't revert to childhood in college."

Another: "Middle-class Americans love to spend money on costumes for the kids so they can look like mini-adults—tiny baseball players, tiny ballerinas, tiny tennis players. Who needs it? If the adults want to play ball, let them form their own team! Meanwhile, let the kids be kids. Some of us may hate to find it out, but they'll have a very good time without us."

A final comment: "As a parent of a six-year-old boy, I thought it was my duty to get him involved in sports. Now I will think twice."

Since our culture so accepts the idea that families should be a support unit for the organized activities of children, I expected my survey respondents to reflect this by placing a higher value on volunteerism than they actually did. Overall, the trait "volunteers freely for school/church type activities" placed only number twenty-five out of fifty-six possible traits. Voluntary organization personnel gave it a predictably higher value than that, and family counselors gave it a significantly lower value. Another trait—"is heavily involved in little-league type activities"—landed near the bottom of the list in all but the voluntary organizations' tally. Apparently, the professionals in the four other areas surveyed view this kind of volunteerism as more costly to family health than it is beneficial.

But children aren't the only ones who need to prioritize their activities. For parents, volunteerism can become absolutely deadly. When I wrote an article on family stress, I interviewed an angry husband who said, "My wife doesn't work, but I wish she did. She's always at some committee meeting or on the damn phone. We'd see more of her if she worked." He echoed the situation found in a lot of families—parents so deeply involved in volunteer activities that their own families suffer from it.

Lions Club, booster groups, Jaycees, bowling leagues, courses and workshops, Marriage Encounter—all of these are valuable activities, but they must be kept in check or the family will suffer. In a *Denver Post* article on a particular youth league coach, I read these words from the coach: "I've always enjoyed sports and I guess there's an ego-thing involved: molding teams into winners. Some people are workaholics. I guess I'm a coach-aholic. Coaching has been an important part of my life and a real satisfaction. I don't think all the coaching was the main cause of my divorce, but it probably was a contributing factor."[21]

Some women give housekeeping, particularly cleaning, priority over other family activities. They are always too busy at home to take time to relax with their families.

Other women are finding a solution to the family-time problem: The house comes last. A divorced mother of two active boys wrote, "I used to give priority only to cooking meals and washing and sorting clothes. Now if it needs to be ironed, I don't buy it. . . ." She, like so many of her peers, embodies the concept of time control that says there are some chores that don't *deserve* doing well. If a spotless home and gourmet meals aren't that important to the family, why give up precious family-relationship time to do them? If the family would rather have tomato soup and mom than cordon bleu and that frenzied woman in the kitchen, we'd better listen. Our family's telling us something about priorities. And they should have a say-so.

Some women, however, find it impossible to allow things to go undone in their homes. A thirty-year-old mother said wistfully, "I wish I could leave some dirty dishes on the counter or some soiled clothes in the hamper, but I just can't. As long as there's something that needs doing in my house, I just can't relax with my family. It seems wrong to do so." She mirrors that moral label the traditional family put on housekeeping. Housework is not a choice, it's a moral obligation. Today, healthier parents are choosing relationships with their children over shiny floors, even though many of them are paying for it with guilty consciences.

What housework is to women, work is to men. The Liontoses, in their interviews on "Couple Life," asked a number of men the question, "If you had to rank how much time, effort, or energy you put into your work versus your marriage, how would you rank them?" The answers are somewhat depressing. The following two responses are representative.

"That's an awful question! Because when it comes down to it, I think I probably put more effort into my work than I do my marriage. And I justify it—I have a very smooth rationale. It's got to do with the Almighty Buck. It's called, 'Well, our marriage will go better if we have more money to soothe over the wounds at the end of the month.' So, therefore, I can justify putting more energy into it."

Another replied, "That's just it—work is easier for me. It takes less effort for me to do a 'good day's work' than it does for me to do a 'good day's husband.' "[22]

Our children tell us in many ways that they would rather have us and a simple life than absentee parents and a color TV in every room. Why aren't we hearing them? Is it because our jobs really are more important in our lives than they are? Do we justify our focus on the job rather than on the family by spending money on excessive family goods? Are we part of the "I'm-doing-it-all-for-you" syndrome?

I've found that in many of the families who complain loudly about children's schedules and necessary parent absenteeism, there's a certain lemming-like drive to be overscheduled. When we look into it, we often find that these families use their busy-ness to avoid having real relationships with one another. Instead, as soon as one activity closes, they add another. Such families seem fearful about having any unstructured leisure time together, although they frequently rue the lack of it. They simply don't want a stretch of two or three evenings in which there's no excuse for not being able to sit together and learn to know one another. So mother signs up for a night class in machine embroidery, father takes on another business project or joins a bowling league, and the kids watch television.

Not a pleasant family picture, but it doesn't have to be that way. Families can control their time together to a much greater extent if they want to. Healthy families want to. They are very good at prioritizing. They can say no. They listen to everyone's interests and goals and try to respect as many of them as they can, but they make sure that a certain amount of family together-time gets top priority.

3. The family prizes opportunities to spend time alone with individual members.

Just as the healthy family spends some of its collective time together, it also allows its members to spend time in activities that involve just one other family member. Husbands and wives particularly need such time. The couples in healthy families tend to pay attention to their relationship exclusive of the children. They go out together, they try to get away together, they enjoy some mutual activities and interests.

"We love our kids but not all the time," said the husband of a couple who goes out every Saturday night. If they aren't invited to a party, they go to a movie or out for dinner. "It doesn't matter where, as long as it's just the two of us," he said.

Contrast that with the successful salesman interviewed in the Lion-toses' project, who admitted that he secretly worries about the lack of couple time he and his wife have. "Getting time together—peaceful quality time—has always been a problem. I don't think work dominates my life. But I seem to be spending more time with it over the last year. . . ."[23]

Men who are forced to take on overtime work or change shifts find themselves in a no-win situation in some families. They don't like be-ing away at night or having to hold two jobs to furnish the family with necessities, but they then find themselves mollifying family members who complain that they are never around. In families like this, counselors often advise the other spouse to find a job and free the overworked spouse to spend more time with the family. Again, balance.

Parents in good families make it a point to occasionally take time with each child alone. This time can be spent pursuing an ongoing in-terest, such as fishing, or it can be used for a planned monthly or year-ly activity, such as a day at the races or a retreat together. One dad so prized having some time alone with his son that he participated in what seems on the surface like an outrageous commute. He said, "For my son to play wide receiver for Millburn's Panthers, it became necessary to drive 100 miles a week after we moved from the AYL area to North-west Denver. Round-trip to a pair of practices plus the Saturday game. It was worth it."

The difference between a father/son relationship like this one and the hazardous little coalitions in families that I spoke of earlier rests on the motivation involved. Here, the father and son enjoyed an activity together, one that involved a lot of car-talk time, one that was activity-centered. They weren't, at least to our knowledge, using this activity to escape from the rest of the family.

Writer Susan Fogg tells about the father who was watching the Super Bowl with one of his buddies when his newborn daughter started to cry in her room nearby. The father went in to check on her, promising that he'd be back in a minute. After about ten minutes, his curious buddy came to check on him and found him so engrossed in cooing and clucking with his baby that he had forgotten about the football game. "Yes, that's a true story," insists Fogg, "shocking as it may seem to a legion of gridiron widows. And social scientists believe it illustrates a new understanding of the importance of fathers in their children's lives."

Fathers *are* beginning to spend more play time with their children, in what personnel at the National Institute on Child Health and Human Development call "the rediscovery of the father." Fogg quotes experts who hold that fathers are as adept as mothers are at reading and responding to baby's cues. "Infants love novelty, and the relative infrequency of a father's appearance gives him an attraction missing in a mother who is on 24-hour call," says Fogg. "This phenomenon is familiar to many a bone-weary mother who spends a day coaxing her newborn into a happy mood, only to see the father reap the rewards in smiles and coos when he comes home from work."

According to Dr. Frank Pederson, also of the National Institute, the father, by just being there, even for brief periods, encourages "an expansion of the infant's environment and promotes an awareness that interesting and responsive people exist outside the tight, symbiotic unit with the mother." Pederson claims that infants anticipate the difference between the styles of mothers and fathers and alter their behavior to get the most out of each parent. Their doing so may help build both their intellectual capacities and their skill in handling social relationships outside the family. "Indeed, infants who are securely attached to their fathers show less fear of strangers than those who are unsure of their fathers," he said.[24]

Members of healthy families tend to find excuses to be alone with another member occasionally. Two children who are bonded by a love of music might attend a rock concert together. But one of those children might also be bonded to yet another sibling because of a common interest the two of them have in something else, perhaps roller-skating. A mother and daughter might choose sewing or collecting antiques or horseback riding as their shared interest.

I frequently ask parents to list how their various children are bonded in sibling relationships. If there's no bonding, then parents might want to make opportunities for them. Parents particularly need to look into individual opportunities to spend time with each child. The pleasure that this produces usually turns such experiences into musts rather than shoulds, into something to which the parent looks forward instead of a responsibility.

A few years ago, when my ten-year-old son was disappointed in not being able to take part in an anticipated function during his spring vacation, I offered to take him on a day that he would plan, within a limited budget. He was allowed to make the decisions about what we'd do. We began our day early by going to the wax museum, not one of my favorite places, but he was enthralled with the scenarios of guillotines, battles, and such. Because the wax museum isn't high on my list, we had never gone there before, and I'd never realized until that day how he had been longing to go.

Next we went on a free tour to the Mint and saw how our nation's money is made. Then off to McDonald's for the obligatory ten-year-old gourmet fare. After lunch, we took a free downtown shuttle bus to a tourist area, which we rarely visit because we aren't tourists, but which he wanted to see and "to spend as much time there without anybody telling me to hurry as I want to." Which is what we did.

We spent two hours at a kite shop! Now, what can I tell you? The enthusiasm I had to whip up for looking at a couple of hundred different kite designs was heroic . . . and catching.

Before long, I really began to enjoy kites. My son finally ended up buying one from some of his carefully hoarded savings, and when we exited into the rapidly darkening day, he turned to me magnanimously and said, "Now, what would *you* like to do, Mom?" We had a cup of tea and went home.

The very next day he began planning what has come to be called Our Day, as in "We can do that on Our Day, Mom." Our Day has become an annual ritual, and we both love it. It gives us sharing time and private experiences and jokes.

These experiences need not be costly. We don't even have to leave home in order to have them. My husband and one of our sons like to make pewter soldiers out of old molds. Another son doesn't care about that at all, but he and his dad do enjoy working on the car together.

Reading together is becoming a lost family art; yet, it is one of the most pleasurable of activities shared between parent and child. Parent advisor Louise Shanahan writes, "A social worker observed that in several years of working in a children's clinic, she had not met one mother who read to her children. One wonders in how many families there is time for sharing books, music, conversation, dreams, yearnings, confidences, all those intangible manifestations of love that are cultivated through patience."

One of my survey respondents, a social psychologist, asked me to stress in this book two errors that parents make in regard to having leisure time activity with individual children. The first is that parents think such activity is a luxury when, in fact, it's really a necessity to spend time alone with each child. The second error parents can make is that they give too much time to one individual child in the pursuit of some interest and little or no time to the other children. He mentioned particularly the cases of families who have a child with a skill so extraordinary that it leads them to pre-Olympic activity or something on that level of excellence. "I have been seeing many children who are victims in this kind of family," he said. "The most dramatic case is a family in which one son is an exceptional gymnast, possibly bound for the Olympics. The rest of the family coalesces around this boy. There's no parent time for the girl I am seeing as a client. It's catastrophic in that she has desperate needs herself but feels guilty if she asks for attention in a family that is so tied up in one child."

While this case may be an exaggerated instance, there are a good number of families who focus on one outstanding athlete or scholar rather than try to achieve a balance of relationships. Good families know the importance of balance.

4. The family controls television usage.

Earlier, in the chapter on communication, I spoke of the hazards to the healthy family of overuse of television. Hence, here I will be brief, commenting only on television as a usurper of family time.

One thing is clear about television: It has changed the living patterns of many families. It has had a particularly profound influence on family weekend leisure. Televised professional sports have replaced family activities in thousands of homes on those two days traditionally set aside for family shared time, Saturday and Sunday.

Some people argue that television football can bring the family together, and that may be true—but only if *all members agree* on the primacy and regularity of this activity. If any member feels forced to go along with it because Dad or Mom or one of the kids is addicted and will be resentful at missing a game, then that member has not had a real choice in the matter. "When my husband misses a game to go out with us on Sunday afternoon, he either pouts or spends his time trying to find out the score. It isn't worth it," said one wife.

The strong family manages to get control of its use of television. It isn't dependent upon it, and it uses it selectively. In many healthy families, there are some rules on the amount of time TV can be viewed—often something like only one or two hours permitted on a week night—and definite rules regarding the quality of programs allowed. Certain programs simply aren't allowed. A number of families go through the TV offerings once a week and cross out forbidden programs. According to their testimony, these families never bring sets with them on vacations or picnics. Rarely do they allow themselves to miss a social function because of a televised game or program. In other words, television only fills in the spaces in their family life; it doesn't form the framework of it.

5. *The family plans how to use its time.*

Earlier I quoted an interviewee who referred to the amount of time he was able to spend with his family as leftover time. The good family doesn't depend on this elusive promise of future time. "When the kids were younger," said a career mother, "we used to say, 'When we get time, we'll do this or that.' The result was we never got time. When I went to work, we deliberately set aside weekly time for family activity, and we all enjoy it. The irony is that we're spending more time together now that I'm working than we did before."

Her case isn't unique. Divorced fathers tell of the same paradox. "Before I never had time for my kids," said a dad of two boys. "Now that I have visitation only one day a week, I'm jealous of it, and we're doing the kinds of things I was too busy to do before."

Sometimes single parents *do* focus more on the amount of pleasurable time spent with their children because they see it as a responsibility, whereas dual parents presume that the kids don't need it as much because they are an intact family. Yet, according to my respondents, they do.

Healthy families often manage their leisure-time scheduling by employing a somewhat highly developed calendar system, in contrast to those families who simply wait for spare time to emerge. Some even keep both a long-range and a short-range calendar. On the long-range one, they pencil in well in advance such annual events as auto shows, rodeos, plays, fishing trips, bowling conventions, and Super Bowl games. Members study this calendar to watch for opportunities and to correct omissions. Are there too many activities planned for parents only? Can they afford all of these events? If not, which ones should stay and which go? Should they avoid inviting houseguests at a particular time because the family as a unit will be enjoying an activity then?

They keep a close eye on their short-range weekly calendar as well. What are they doing that's fun this week? How can they switch responsibilities or work so that they can all go to their child's game or parade? "During the week we clip notices of free things like craft fairs, a gun show, open houses, and things like that," a parent told me. "Then during the week we decide which one we'll pick to do during the weekend. It works out real well. If something like one of the kids' babysitting jobs comes up, the rest of us still go."

These scheduling techniques are hardly new. Families often indicate that they're borrowed scheduling tools from their working places. But the thing that seems to set these families aside from other families is that time control is an important value to them, important enough to put some effort into it as a family. The payoff is more time for enjoying one another, and that is integral to all three traits of the healthy family that we've just been discussing: a sense of play and humor, a balance of interaction among members, and shared leisure time.

In summary, the healthy family who shares leisure time activities has these hallmarks:
1. The family keeps its collective leisure time in balance.
2. The family prioritizes its activities.
3. The family prizes opportunities to spend time alone with individual members.
4. The family controls television usage.
5. The family plans how to use its time.

8
Fostering Responsibility

Trait 6: The healthy family exhibits a sense of shared responsibility.

> Becoming responsible adults is no longer a matter of whether children hang up their pajamas or put dirty towels in the hamper, but whether they care about themselves and others—and whether they see everyday chores as related to how we treat this planet.
>
> —Eda LeShan

A few years ago, one of my weekly columns for parents—about responsibility in the home—turned out to be rather controversial. Here is a portion of it:

Rearing Responsible Children

I don't suppose this is the day I should be writing this. I just discovered my son's clean gym clothing in his room, which means that, this being Monday morning, he will not be able to participate in his physical education class and will lose a point or something.

Yet maybe this is a good day to write this because I am not hopping in the car to take his gym suit to him. It's his responsibility to bring it home dirty on Friday afternoon and to return it clean on Monday morning, not mine. . . .

I know mothers who take the responsibility upon themselves of getting their children to school on time, getting their children's library books back when due, getting their children's big homework projects in on time, making sure their Cub Scouts pay their dues, and generally taking upon themselves the little responsibilities of their children which are there for the purpose of forcing maturity.

These mothers are wrecks. They are always frenzied. They can't get anything accomplished in their own lives because they are so busy living the lives of their various children.

One of my own children once wrote "Dust me" on top of the TV set and it was a signal that he was old enough to take on the responsibility for dusting the living room after that. Another time, one of ours in junior high became angry over a dental appointment I had scheduled at an inconvenient time. Since then, he schedules his own appointments. It's now his responsibility to make sure I'm available to drive him, not mine to make sure he keeps the day clear.

Sure, there are times we all slip up. When I'm rushed, I expect a little extra consideration from my family and when they have particularly busy schedules, we all help out. But the day-to-day responsibilities must be their own or they will never grow up into responsible adults. Our real responsibility as parents is to offer them the opportunity to grow in responsibility, not assume their responsibilities because they are our children.

> "Talks with Parents"
> © Alt Publishing Co., 1977[1]

As I mentioned, this column provoked a lot of response, both positive and negative. The positive generally came from teachers and schools, twenty-seven of whom requested permission to reprint and send the column home to parents. "Keep emphasizing to parents that they aren't doing their children a service by constantly serving them," wrote a principal. "This tends to paralyze a young person's perception of his own capabilities."

"Either you raise your children full-time for twenty years," wrote a parent counselor, "or else you end up raising them part-time forever." He wasn't talking about the full-time mother at home here, but the reverse. He was referring to the gradual process of exposing children to the pleasure and self-respect that come from developing a sense of responsibility.

But while the volume of supportive mail surprised me, so did the pathos of the angry letters I received. Many took issue with me over the role of motherhood, particularly my assertion that Mom did not exist to serve while the others existed to be served. This assertion apparently threatened many young women who see their self-worth in self-sacrifice. Here is a sampling of the letters I received:

"If a mother doesn't want to do little things for her family, she shouldn't have children in the first place. That's what being a mother is all about. I enjoy those little 'drudgeries,' as you would call them. What is so difficult about picking up the socks of those you love?"

"I'm glad *my* husband doesn't feel he has to help with dishes after working all day."

"I take issue with you over your statement that mothers shouldn't be responsible for chores that lead to family harmony. That's what we're trained for. If a mother doesn't pour oil on troubled waters, who will?"

And the most classic response of all: "It's women like you who ruin the image of motherhood for women like me. I like to think of myself as a magic carpet on which my family treads."

Well, that woman's family probably will. But the real tragedy lies in the damage that it inflicts upon the children who are doing the treading. This mother has the right to self-sacrifice, but she doesn't have the right to deny her children a sense of self-respect through assuming responsibility for themselves, which is their right.

So many obvious attitudes about self emerged from these responses that I felt an overwhelming sense of sadness toward these women. Their roles and identities were blurred, threatened. To them, their value as mothers and persons was proportionate to the quantity of service they could perform for their husbands and children. They felt that if they did less, they would have less value to their family; hence, the love they received was based not on who they were but what they could do for others in their family. Over and over, the phrase "loving mother" was used by these women in connection with some unpleasant task that long ago should have become the natural responsibility of a spouse or child.

So pervasive is this attitude, though, that we see the results of it everywhere. Irresponsible children grow into irresponsible adults—unless they bump into teachers, bosses, sergeants, or spouses along the way who expect them to be responsible. Then their growth into responsible persons is much more painful. Some of these adults never do become responsible for their own lives. They constantly look around for Mom in the form of others: a spouse, the federal government, a mentor, a friend—anyone they can dump on (to use a slang phrase coined precisely for the irresponsible people in our society).

Obviously recognizing what irresponsibility can cost in terms of a person's self-image and ultimate self-actualization, my survey respondents gave the characteristic of shared responsibility in the family a high place on their list of healthy-family traits. Their ranking it sixth indicates how important shared responsibility is to a family's health. It tells us also that the unhealthier the family, the less likely we are to find responsible children and adults.

As I mentioned in the last chapter, family stress is becoming epidemic. Dr. Joseph Procaccini, a specialist in parent burnout, states that stress comes from having to continually meet the needs of people requesting help, a process which sometimes seems endless. The person who has to provide the help feels drained because there's no more to give. According to Dr. Procaccini, parents are prime candidates for this kind of burnout. They share these common feelings:

— that they are not able to be good parents;
— that their children are demanding more than they can give;
— that they dislike their children, that they are burdensome;
— guilt, which leads to defensiveness, which in turn leads to a whole group of other problems;
— that home life is just one more hassle;
— physical exhaustion;
— and last, but certainly not least to this particular chapter, that their children are running them.[2]

One of my survey respondents attached a letter to his response in which he wrote, in part:

"I am convinced that a healthy family is established on the relationship of the adult members of that family to each other and to adult society. Parents, in my view, can allow themselves to be imprisoned by their children. They, at times, surrender their home, their privacy, and their leisure to the whims and caprices of their children. I am thinking in particular of adolescent children. Permit me to illustrate: A husband and wife had to cancel at the last minute some plans to spend a weekend with adult friends. Their principal reason was that they had 'grounded' their fifteen-year-old child. It seems to me that they allowed this child to punish them, rather than taking time to work out suitable discipline which would still have allowed them their needed leisure with adults."

Responsible children do not run their parents. They're too busy running themselves.

Responsibility, according to psychologist Eda LeShan, never evolves from being angrily coerced but rather from feeling respected and discovering how much people need each other. When I was a teacher of high school students — this was before I had children of my own—I recall my initial astonishment when I would praise a particular child to parents and they would react with surprise. Two familiar responses from such parents were "I wish she would behave like that at home," and "I can't get him to do that in the family." It was then that I began to recognize the real impact of expectations on a person's behavior and achievement. As a future teacher, I had studied educational psychology and child development, both of which emphasized the need to nurture a child from dependency to independency by way of gradual assumption of responsibility. But those texts and courses didn't prepare me for the number of parents who either are not aware of the need or refuse even to accept that it is a need.

Educators live with the paradox of the child who isn't permitted to be responsible at home but who literally begs for crumbs of responsibility in school as compensation. Something within that child, a self-esteem begging to get out, is asking for challenges, for opportunities to prove capabilities that are not being tapped at home. When a teacher recognizes this cry for growth and independence in a child and answers it by giving challenging assignments and setting high standards for the youngster, the child in turn often reacts with great enthusiasm, working hard in order to prove that he or she is competent.

Ironically, parents who refuse to permit their children to be responsible at home by taking little responsibilities off of them and then putting them down for irresponsibility are frequently ones who complain about the difficulty of their children's school's expectations. A classic example of this is physical education. Gym teachers find that those students most in need of good physical exercise, for example, are also those most likely to bring notes from parents asking that they be excused because it is too strenuous.

Healthy families tend to support their children without removing obstacles from their lives that foster growth. Here, as in most of the healthy-family traits, there's always a question of balance. How much responsibility is too much? Too little? Should parents devise opportunities that foster their children's independence if they think their children are not being given enough of them? What is a responsible spouse? A responsible parent? A responsible child? What are the hallmarks of a family that has a good attitude toward shared responsibility? I perceive six of them.

1. Parents understand the relationship between responsibility and self-esteem.

Eda LeShan states flatly that when a child feels a sense of accomplishment, the roots of responsibility are growing strong. "A belief in one's own capacity to make a contribution is essential," she said. "If there is one idea we all desperately need to believe in, it's that each individual counts and can make a difference."[3]

Almost all of the parents in the healthy families I interviewed, whether single- or dual-parented, said that the primary value in a child's developing a good sense of responsibility was that it benefited the *child*. Parents in not-so-healthy families talked about how a child's sense of responsibility was a benefit for the *family*.

"It's good for children to be responsible" was a key refrain I heard over and over. When I asked about shared responsibility, these parents admitted, "Yes, of course it helps the family when everyone shares in the chores, but . . ." and they added a comment to the effect that "even if we didn't need the help, the children need to be made to feel like contributing members of the family unit." Mothers spoke about situations in which it would be easier for them to bake the cake than take the time to teach the child to do it, or easier to repair the rip in the pocket than unjam the sewing machine. Fathers spoke about the misuse of tools and the cost of ruined materials when a child decides to "help" repair something. But both mothers and fathers stressed the need to nurture this growth. "My son was ten feet high when he finished that bird house," said a father. "He worked on it three days. It was crooked as hell and expensive. But it was his."

Many children today are furnishing a necessary part of their family's income, making these children a truly essential part of the family. With so many families, especially single-parent ones, operating economically on a survival level, we're finding more teens whose part-time jobs go for rent and groceries, not gas and pizza. These children, of necessity, grow up fast—as did their counterparts in the immigration cultures in our nation.

Families with good relationships tend to demand more of their children. Members of these families are more willing than those in others to accept responsibility. They share not only in household chores but also help out in areas like conserving energy and saving money. Dishes aren't Mom's job and finances Dad's. Both are everyone's responsibility. One of the most familiar complaints made by women who've gone back to work is that they are expected to continue performing all their household duties, even though they are working outside the home for as many hours as do others in the family.

Many parents point to increased responsibility on the part of children as a result of their mother's taking on an outside job. "I just never realized my children could do laundry and a lot of other things because I was always there to do them," said a mother. Another who was listening nodded and said, "I never asked enough of my family before. I felt guilty for not working so I took on everyone else's work to prove I was invaluable."

Some women in the work world, however, feel forced, as a condition of their working, to continue to perform home duties in the same way they did prior to working. I call this the "family-lets-me-work syndrome," an arrangement in which a family reluctantly agrees to a woman's decision to work but only as long as she promises to furnish the same services she did when she wasn't working. It's a pressure-loaded and non-supportive kind of family "agreement."

In an article on latchkey kids and responsibility, author Elisabeth Kieffer points out that the habits of recent generations are hard to break and that today, when it comes to chores, there is often a gap between the ideal and the actual. "It's Mom who usually fills the gap," she says, and quotes a mother who said, "'I still try to do most everything I did before I started working. In other words, I'm trying to carry two full-time jobs and I know it's a mistake. It's not good for me or the children.' "

She notes that Eleanor Berman shared a different experience in her book, *The Cooperating Family*: "When I started working, I learned my children were capable of far more responsibility than I had ever given them. And, rather than minding, they seemed to feel good about it. We all seem to like each other more now."[4]

There is a direct linkage between a person's sense of competence and contribution and his or her expectations of others. It's not just happenstance that responsible children end up in one family and irresponsible children in another. Competent parents by their very modeling expect children to be competent. This expectation fuels a desire on the part of children to be responsible. It's a little like a ping-pong game in which the ball bounces from parent to child—from expectation to fulfillment, from challenge to responsibility, from accomplishment to pride, from immaturity to maturity. All the while the young person is developing and becoming more independent, preparing for that time when he or she can leave the umbrella of parental responsibility and strike out as a responsible adult.

Probably one of the most unfair paradoxical aspects of this connection between responsibility and self-esteem in the family is that those parents who understand it are generally those who are already living it in their own relationship. In other words, those parents who understand it already have it while those who most need it don't understand it. A husband who treats his wife as a responsible human being contributes to her sense of self-esteem, which she then models for her children. A husband who denies his wife responsibility by refusing to allow her to make decisions, spend money, or have an opinion of her own damages her self-esteem, and damaged in this way, she isn't secure enough in herself to be a model of responsibility for her children. A woman like this is likely to rear daughters as insecure as she is and sons who are apt later on to deny their wives co-responsibility in the family.

The same danger is obvious in the reverse situation. If a woman thinks her husband is a failure because he doesn't bring in enough money or hasn't been promoted to the degree to which she would like to become accustomed, she encourages feelings of self-doubt and failure in him, which he then models to his sons. He is not likely to be able to help his sons be responsible persons if he himself feels he has failed in responsibility to his wife and family.

Men who suddenly lose their jobs at forty or fifty are often experiencing failure for the first time, and it dramatically shakes their confidence in themselves. Depression, alcohol, divorce, and suicide are the possible results. I recall a talk-show interview in which a top executive whose job was suddenly abolished due to a belt-tightening move in his corporation said, "I suddenly was nobody. I lost all my self-confidence. I couldn't hold a job. The fact that it was a good job that I had held successfully for twenty years didn't matter. I was a failure. That's what our society calls it."

He went on to say that the situation affected the total family. "My wife finally stopped trying to lift my blue moods—she said I was indulging myself. My kids started avoiding me. That's when one of our boys first became attracted to drugs, we learned later. Before that I could say to my boys, 'Hey, your grades aren't up to par,' but what can a man say to his sons about responsibility when he's lost his own job?"

He added poignantly that now he better understood those classes of society in which there's high unemployment and low self-esteem. "I used to think these men were lazy and irresponsible. Now I realize they are filled with self-doubts." His frank words give authenticity to the close relationship between responsibility and self-esteem in our culture.

2. The family understands that responsibility means more than doing chores.

When some parents begin to discuss family responsibility, they talk only of things such as dishes, lawns, and rooms. Others add homework and part-time jobs. All of these are part of growing responsibly, of course, but the strong family adds another dimension: Members are sensitive to the feelings of others as well. They display overt concern when one member thinks he or she is being treated unfairly. They respond to others' personal moods, wordlessly saying "I'll take some responsibility for making you happier, for making our home a better place." In these families, if a person is feeling down due to lack of a prom date or loss of job or a failed test, another in the family is likely to supply some loving strokes.

Sometimes these attempts are amusing, as in this story one mother told. She said that when her eldest son went away to college, she felt sad and somewhat adrift for a while. Sensing her feelings, her twelve-year-old son stuck close to her for a couple of days. "He nearly drove me mad," she confessed. "Everywhere I went, he followed. When I sat to read the paper, he just sat next to me, doing nothing. He was doing his best to make up for Chuck's absence, but I wanted to tell him to go out and play."

Another parent, a father, told about a time when he got a speeding ticket and was feeling angry about it. His six-year-old girl went into the kitchen and prepared a little tray with a glass of water, two aspirin, and a vase with dandelions in it. It was her way of accepting responsibility for soothing his feelings.

In many families just who owns the homework is debatable. Judi Bailey, writing in *Marriage and Family Living,* points out that parents can sometimes find themselves becoming the family's "Homework

Machine." She says, "These parents believe that it is up to them to motivate, nag, and at times, complete part of the homework for the child. It's risky for a parent to assume too much responsibility for the child's schoolwork. One of the dangers is that the pressure exerted by the parent can produce strained relationships, causing both parent and child to become tense. . . . As kids react to Mom's and Dad's involvement in schoolwork, the conflict over homework gains in complexity. Not doing homework can become an outlet for rebellion or source of attention."[5]

In some families one parent, usually the mother, is made solely responsible for family happiness and harmony. Family counselors often talk about this. "Mothers tend to become the repository for everyone's guilt and mood," said one. "Some mothers accept this because it gives them status and, as unpleasant as it may be, it's a status that is otherwise missing. Other mothers become the family's peacemaker simply because their mothers served in this role."

This family counselor mentioned as an example a mother who kept lists everywhere to insure absolute fairness. The lists ranged from the one on the refrigerator door, documenting who was the last to do dishes, to the one in the glove compartment of the car, stating who sat next to the windows last. By taking charge herself, this mother denied her children the opportunity to get along together on their own.

The counselor sketched the kind of life that mothers like this one live. "They feel guilty all the time. If two siblings are squabbling, the mother doesn't make them responsible for healing the quarrel but steps between them and argues with them individually. It becomes her responsibility. After a while, children begin to assume that she's responsible for their anger, their behavior, their guilt, and their bad moods. They imply that she's at fault somehow for their poor performance on a test, maybe because she didn't get them up in time to study or maybe for no reason at all. She becomes the family scapegoat—she gets dumped on by everyone."

Speaking at the White House Conference on Families, Tamara Hareven of Harvard said, "Today's family is more oriented to child rearing and domesticity—a retreat from the outside world. This makes the woman the custodian of the domestic world and to some extent traps her. And it puts a lot of pressure on the family because they all expect their source of emotional happiness and intimacy to be the family. That's a lot of pressure."[6] I add that the pressure is primarily upon the woman who is trapped in this role.

Parents in healthy families don't permit this to happen. They seem to foster an atmosphere that says clearly to one another and to their children, "We are all responsible for a reasonably harmonious household. If you don't know how to be reasonably harmonious, we will help you. If you don't wish to be, kindly remove yourself from the family circle until you are ready to assume some practical responsibility for our collective mood." These families aren't harsh, but they *are* firm. They don't allow one child to whine away everyone's good mood. They don't permit constant bickering at meals. They believe that siblings learn compromise and reconciliation by working out their differences—but not necessarily in the midst of the family.

I know a family that designated two sections of their backyard—with a generous space in between—to be "cooling off" territory. The sections were called East Turf and West Turf. When the family's children were young and got into normal but heated disputes over who owned the Big Wheel or whose turn it was to bring in the sled, they were sent to cool off on those two turfs. Neither child was allowed to leave until the shouting and recriminations were over. They didn't have to apologize and reconcile, just remove themselves from one another and the family physically during their warring period. The children are all in college today or beyond, but their parents told me that last Thanksgiving when the family gathered, there was a terrifically heated political argument around the table. The argument began to escalate even further, and finally a twenty-six-year-old daughter turned to her equally argumentative sibling and said, "You get East Turf and I get West Turf." Not only did the resultant laughter break the tensions, but this daughter was reminding them all of a valuable family lesson: They were each still responsible for peace and love in the family.

3. The family realizes that responsibility doesn't necessarily mean orderliness and perfection.

To some parents, the responsible child is one whose room is always neat and clean, whose homework is always neat and prompt, and whose mood is always accommodating and acquiescent. These parents don't grasp that failure is a necessary, real part of learning to be responsible. They don't understand that it's in the trying and failing, and trying again and not failing quite so badly, that children learn to be responsible.

In good families, a responsible child is identified as a person who keeps *trying*: to overcome a character flaw; to do better in school; to make new friends; to get along in the family; to become independent enough to be able to leave home someday and get along in the world without siblings and parents.

Psychologist Eda LeShan says, "One of the most serious mistakes we make with children is to equate success and achievement with a sense of responsibility. We need to remember that people with money and power don't always use them responsibly."[7] An educator once noted that children can be good for very bad reasons and bad for very good reasons.

Whenever I run into parents who tell me that they have one responsible and one irresponsible child, I ask them what makes them designate their children in such a way. Invariably they mention a neat room and a messy room as evidence, even though orderliness of one's room or desk is a minor part of personal responsibility. (Some psychologists says it probably has *nothing* to do with it because compulsively neat people can be irresponsible in many things.)

A child's neatness can stem from a desperate need to please his or her parents: A daughter, for instance, may keep her room tidy in order to hear her parents say "Oh, look at Janie's room. She's such a good girl . . . it's always so neat and clean." Janie's insecurity, not her sense of responsibility for her possessions, can be what drives her to keep her room abnormally clean. (To help Janie become a genuinely responsible person, she and her parents may need to focus on why she feels anxious to please adults all the time, why she doubts her parents' love, or why she can't trust herself to throw her clothes on the floor of the closet once in a while.)

Janie's brother Freddie, on the other hand, is labeled irresponsible by his parents because they're barely able to make their way across his room for the clutter. To Freddie, that's no problem. He knows where his things are, and he's perfectly content with the clutter. His room makes him feel comfortable, and he's definitely not comfortable in sister Janie's tidy, sterile environment. Freddie may reluctantly rearrange the mess and call it clean when pressured to do so by his parents, but he doesn't do it to win their approval. He's more secure in their love than Janie, but he's labeled less responsible. He knows his parents love him even though they harangue him about a messy room. "Freddie is the classic boy of thirteen," said a pediatrician when he and I discussed this. "As he gets older, it will become more important to him to know where his things are, so he'll put them in the same place twice. He'll clear out the collections that boys his age accumulate: rocks, bottles, baseball cards, matchbooks, and comics. And his parents will be happy that he's finally becoming responsible," he chuckled.

Ellen Peck makes a distinction between the nurturing parent and the nonnurturing one. "The *giving* or *nurturing* parent is not always the one who is invariably 'doing things for' other family members. (In fact, it can be the *nonnurturing* parent who always ties the children's shoes and picks up the children's toys—and the more truly *nurturing* parent who helps children learn to perform these and other simple tasks for themselves.)"[8]

To be fair, part of this focus on neatness stems from parental responsibility to keep a "neat and tidy home," one of the admonishments to the good Christian housewife of an earlier age, who was taught that cleanliness was next to godliness. In order to live up to these standards, she couldn't, as a responsible mother, allow a messy room.

But a child's room isn't a mother's responsibility. It's her child's. Certain health and safety standards must be observed, of course, but the constant harping and defensiveness that the dirty-room focus engenders often stymies personal growth rather than fostering it. One of the healthiest couples I interviewed hold that the best answer to the messy room is to close the door.

Clutter around the house is another matter. Family members shouldn't be expected to live in the midst of other members' junk. How do healthy families deal with this? In interviews, I found novel, yet effective, techniques that families use to make the members responsible for general neatness in the living areas of their homes and yards.

In some families, if children consistently leave their books and baseball mitts lying around, these items are retrieved and hidden. After a few long searches, the children become adept at putting them away themselves. One family has a huge family junk box, a wooden crate, which was brought into the family as a potential toy receptacle but was never used for that purpose. Into that box is dumped

unceremoniously everything that has to be picked up for another. If
the item so dumped is small, like car keys, the owner has to empty
everything else out of the box to retrieve them. The presence of the box
is a good deterrent to members leaving things around for others to
move. Several families use the system of assigning a child to each
room, making a room's keeper responsible for its general tidiness.
Others assign children a day to keep a certain room picked up. One
mother quipped that it was convenient having five children because
that number was sufficient to keep the family room and patio tidy on
weekdays.

In *Kiss Sleeping Beauty Good-bye,* author Madonna Kolbenschlag
points out why division of family labor is going to be vital to family
relationships in the future. She says, "By the next century—with the
pioneers of 1970 already at the front of the column—society will have
moved from (a) one demanding job for the wife and one for the husband, through (b) two demanding jobs for the wife and two for the
husband. The symmetry will be complete. Instead of two jobs there
will be four." And she adds, "Strains will be inescapable. There will inevitably be more divorces because people will be seeing a more multi-
faceted adjustment to each other, with the two outside jobs clicking
with the two inside ones; and because the task will be harder, there will
be more failures."[9]

Dr. Eda LeShan confesses that she once thought teaching responsibility meant simply making children do chores but that the past years
have changed her thinking and expanded dramatically the dimensions
of responsibility in her eyes. "I now realize that teaching children
responsibility involves sharing some of our deepest, most important
values; it is about human survival itself," she writes.[10]

4. The family gears responsibility to capability.

Families can make a lot of mistakes in their attempt to foster
responsibility. I guess we could say that responsible parents, just like
responsible children, keep trying and failing, too, thus becoming ever
more responsible themselves. One of the most familiar of parental
faults in this regard is asking children to achieve results beyond their
capabilities.

I remember the time I gave my young daughter my large desk
drawer to clean and tidy up. She wanted to do it—children often

do—so I let her. However, her attention span at that time was about seven minutes, and it was a two-hour job. The job ended up being a cause of conflict. She wanted to run off and play soon after she'd dumped everything in a pile on the patio: rubber bands, paper clips, gummed labels, and so on. I ended up sorting everything into little piles and doing the drawer myself even though I hadn't set any time aside for that particular chore that day. I was angry, and she felt a failure. It was a valuable lesson to me: to keep the responsibilities within the capability range of children.

Some parents give their eldest child responsibility for the behavior and care of the younger children, resulting all too often in impaired relationships between this sibling and the others. "Why did you let him do it?" becomes the parental scold. "He won't do anything I say," becomes the oldest child's refrain. A stark result of this too heavy responsibility is evidenced by the disproportionate number of oldest girls in large families who do not marry. They have already reared one family. They don't want another.

Often parents give an adolescent too much freedom and then expect him or her to handle it responsibly. I will talk more about this in a later chapter, but here I want to emphasize how essential it is that we as parents learn to evaluate how much freedom our children individually can handle. Responsibility isn't a commodity that you either have or don't have. Acquiring a sense of responsibility is a developmental task, and children are on all different rungs of the developmental ladder. It's not unusual to find one child in a family more responsible than another was at the same age, just as one may walk earlier than another. It doesn't mean that as adults one will be more caring and the other less, merely that they are operating on different timeclocks.

And that brings me to the most costly error parents make in their efforts to foster responsibility. Parents often don't grant proper recognition to children when they do act responsibly. Many parents make demands of their children, but they don't praise them or even acknowledge in any way that their children have acted responsibly in some matter.

5. Responsibility is paired with recognition.

Healthy parents demand the utmost responsibility from their children, *coupled with the utmost recognition of it on their part*. They praise, they thank, they commend. They acknowledge, and they proclaim in quiet ways their pride in their children's maturing judgments and behaviors.

"When a bunch of my son's friends were found vandalizing, I told my son I was proud of him that he wasn't in the group," commented one father. "He hesitated and then admitted that he had been with the group but had withdrawn when their vandalism started. This made him temporarily friendless, and he was feeling pretty bad about that, but I would never have known about his responsible judgment if I hadn't commended him first."

"My parents scolded me a lot when I was little," said a nineteen-year-old cadet at a military academy, "but I didn't mind because they always praised me when I accomplished something." He smiled. "I always remember the time I begged my dad to let me put the fertilizer on the lawn. Finally he let me, and I walked back and forth with the spreader, feeling so grown up. He said he was sure glad I was old enough to be able to do the job because it helped him so much. And I felt great. A week later, though, when the fertilizer took hold, the grass grew in stripes—dark green where I'd hit and pale green where I'd missed. I noticed it when I came home after school, and I felt awful—like, there it was for all the world to see—I wasn't big enough to fertilize the lawn."

He paused before he ended his story. "But when my dad came home, he didn't scold or even mention the stripes. He pointed to the dark green grass and said, 'Boy, look at how that fertilizer took hold.' Then he said, 'Do you suppose you could put a little more on the other spots? Some soil needs more fertilizer than other soil does.'"

A wise father. He knew he didn't need to damage an already suffering self-image by pointing out failure. Rather, he pointed out achievement and doled out a little more face-saving responsibility.

Attitudes toward work begin to emerge and develop before the child even starts school, according to Dr. Harold Munson of the University of Rochester. "Schools can do a lot," he says, "but it's harder to take the kid with misdirected attitudes and redirect his goals. Parents have to start with their children at an early age. Most don't expect much until their children are seven- or eight-year-olds. Start as soon as the child can handle a task. Be explicit. Make your standards for the job clear and make sure it's done right until the child can do it independently."

Munson points out that learning how to work has been dumped on schools. "As a result, it leaves the parents with less control of their children's attitudes and values." He suggests that parents and teachers join forces in a concerted effort to teach children the work ethic or face the end result that got him started in researching children and work in the first place: employers who told him their young employees had skills but lacked positive work attitudes and values—persistence, dependability, pride in their work, a sense of responsibility.[11]

A pessimist, it is said, looks at a glass of water and asks why it's half empty while an optimist looks at it and asks why it's half full. In the same way, parents can focus on what their children can't do or on what they can do. Healthy parents tend to focus on their children's achievements, and then they give proper recognition for those successes. "Yes, you can drive to the mountains. You took care of the car the last time you used it." "Thanks for cleaning up the kitchen. I couldn't have done a better job myself." "Where did you learn to handle little children like that?" "I can't believe this is your first pie." "I'm so pleased when you show respect for others like that." "Gee, I'm glad you don't behave the way they do." "You did a super job on this essay." "Who washed the car without being asked?" "I look forward to your coming home from school—you always cheer me up." "I think you're responsible enough to handle it." "I was right. I knew you could do it." "You paid for the gas with your own money?"

These simple comments are all effective ways of granting recognition to children who have achieved something or acted responsibly. And these comments aren't fictional. They were told to me by children in the healthy families I interviewed, who characterized the comments as ones particularly remembered and prized from their parents.

6. The family expects members to live with the consequences of irresponsibility.

Parents in competent families tend to allow their children and themselves to experience the cost of irresponsibility more easily than parents in other families. If a library book is lost through carelessness, they insist their children make restitution out of their own allowances. If children offend others because of their behavior, they, not the parents, do the apologizing. If a major homework paper isn't turned in on time or there is a tardy at school, the students face the consequences in the form of a lower grade or after-school penalty; they don't expect their parents to come up with an excuse to soften the teacher's reaction. If a newspaper delivery is late, the carrier, not the parents, has to explain to customers.

Guilt is often an underlying factor in a parent's inability to force a child to face the consequences of irresponsibility. "Most good parents somehow have been led to believe that they should be able to control every aspect of their children's development," says Ida Mae D., spokeswoman for Families Anonymous, Inc. (FA), of Torrance, California. This group originated a self-help program for parents of drug-using children that's similar in nature to the program of Alcoholics Anonymous. Author D. tells a story about a mother who refused to accept that her daughter used drugs.

"One mother who arrived at her first meeting completely distraught over the drastic personality changes of her fifteen-year-old daughter complained, 'There is too much talk of drugs here.' She told the familiar story of a young girl, once a straight 'A' student with strong feelings of family, who turned into a rebellious, unkempt, foul-mouthed teenager. . . . Longtime FA members recognized the story pattern, but rather than point out the obvious, they extended the warmth and understanding of the FA program and encouraged the woman to keep coming back. . . . As she tried to follow the principles of FA and to use new techniques of response and reaction, better avenues of communication developed with her daughter. Within a few months, the girl realized her mother had found a new source of inner strength; she admitted occasional use of drugs. Later, having learned that her mother was tough in her determination to allow the daughter to face the consequences of her own actions and accept full responsibility for them, the girl admitted her long-term use of drugs since age 10 years. She then voluntarily entered a residential care center for rehabilitation."[12]

Families Anonymous cite numerous cases of children who begin to take responsibility for their own lives after they are cut off from the security of parents who protect them from the consequences of their misdeeds. By shifting the focus of participants from their children's problems to their own lives—and stressing the powerlessness of a parent over a child's behavior—FA members often find that their children are the ultimate beneficiaries. (For any interested reader, here's the group's address: Families Anonymous, Inc., P.O. Box 344, Torrance, California 90501.)

It is easier for parents to force their children to be responsible than it is to force their children to accept the consequences of irresponsibility. Easier, but surely not better. Let me share a personal story with you. When our children were younger, we used to hatch chicken eggs in a homemade incubator every spring. It was a family tradition—my husband and our three children would drive to the hatchery and purchase three fertilized eggs, which the hatchery folk would then mark with the initials of each child. At home, we would place a piece of glass on top of the box and a light bulb and thermometer inside. Crucial to the hatching process was keeping the eggs warm, so the children were cautioned against taking their eggs out of the box for any reason.

One year, however, our youngest kept taking little friends to the box and getting his egg out and letting them hold it. We warned him a number of times and finally stopped. It was, after all, his egg to hatch. The day came when the other two eggs began to move and we watched the exciting prospect of birth. But our youngest child's egg never hatched. He was devastated. The other two had wriggling little chicks to watch grow, but he had to live with the consequences of his irresponsibility.

It was one of the hardest things my husband and I had to do as parents—withstanding the temptation to buy him a baby chick. A couple of times we even started for the hatchery, but we didn't carry it through. We empathized with his pain, and the other two promised he could play with their chicks when they got old enough, but the message came through to him quite clearly: This was the consequence of his own irresponsibility. The following year, he didn't let anyone even touch the glass, much less the egg, and he "gave birth" to a lovely little chicken. But even today he still talks about the day his chicken didn't hatch.

The stillborn chickens at age five become the auto accidents, the abortions, and the divorces later on—these all often the consequences of irresponsible behavior. If we remove from our children the unpleasantness and disappointment occasioned by their own lack of judgment and control, they miss valuable lessons that will affect their adult lives. We all see around us countless examples of irresponsible adults—those who are self-indulgent in food, alcohol, and other dependencies; those who use credit irresponsibly and put themselves in hock for years to come; those who refuse to be responsible for their errors at work; those who exhibit a disregard for others' selves and property; those who are too apathetic to study issues and vote intelligently, or don't even bother to vote at all; those who foul our environment; and those who cannot commit themselves to a person, belief, or family.

How many of these adults were allowed to grow up without accepting the consequences of irresponsibility by loving parents who removed unpleasantness from them, we can only guess. We do know that many live out their lives blaming other people and circumstances for their own lack of responsible behavior.

Not so in the healthy family. These families tend to insist that members take full responsibility for their actions and doing that means living with the consequences of irresponsibility. As one mother said, "That way, it usually happens only once." The hallmarks of a family that exhibits a strong sense of shared responsibility are as follows:

1. Parents understand the relationship between responsibility and self-esteem.
2. The family understands that responsibility means more than doing chores.
3. The family realizes that responsibility doesn't necessarily mean orderliness and perfection.
4. The family gears responsibility to capability.
5. Responsibility is paired with recognition.
6. The family expects members to live with the consequences of irresponsibility.

9
Teaching Morals

Trait 7: The healthy family teaches a sense of right and wrong.

Too many of today's children have straight teeth and crooked morals.   —High School Principal

When I studied the results of the first surveys that trickled in, I was surprised to see the high value my respondents had given to the trait "teaches a sense of right and wrong." They placed it seventh on a list of fifty-six possible characteristics of the healthy family. My surprise didn't stem from personal disagreement—in fact, I was pleased to see it receive such a strong emphasis by those who work with families—but rather from my awareness of a general cultural attitude today that suggests the reverse: that development of the self takes precedence over developing one's morality. In other words, the idea that "doing your own thing" is healthier than looking at your own behavior.

There's little question but that we're living in the midst of a rather self-centered period in our culture. Few of the available self-help books are devoted to finding one's potential by serving others, or even by responding to others' feelings and welfare. Most of the self-help books suggest finding one's core and meaning through jogging, vegetarianism, screaming primally, meditating, awareness groups, and sex therapy. This focus led a perplexed British publisher who visited our country to return home and report, "Americans seem to be finding God this year in running."

This kind of preoccupation with self is very sad, according to Dr. Robert Coles, teacher, research psychiatrist, Pulitzer prize-winning author from Harvard, and respected authority on morality and the family. In an interview with *U.S. Catholic*'s Edward Wakin, Dr. Coles said, "I personally feel that this kind of self-centeredness is connected with the sin of pride. From the Bible on, preoccupation with self has been held as one of the sad temptations of the human being. We want our children to struggle against this by trying to extend themselves to others, by being concerned not only with their own needs but with the external reality of other people and their needs."

Yet, Dr. Coles doesn't agree with those who condemn American children and families to the moral rubbish pile. "I just don't believe that American children and American youth are quite as self-centered as they appear or as some reports indicate they are. There are a lot of families in this country that are basically intact, subscribing to values that come out of the Judeo-Christian tradition, still strong on old-fashioned notions of honesty and integrity. They are still around us."[1]

Apparently my respondents agree with Dr. Coles; they must have encountered enough healthy families possessing this trait to place the trait high on their list.

It's a bit difficult to discuss the establishment of the sense of right and wrong or the development of a family's moral base apart from religious faith, but I will attempt to do so in this chapter. Although survey respondents chose "has a shared religious core" as tenth on their list (I discuss that trait in a later chapter), it's important to recognize that many families without a church membership or a central denominational core can and do teach their children right from wrong. Their teaching may not spring from a specific doctrinal belief but rather from a basic philosophy that holds that the moral person values the people and the world around him or her and treats both in a respectful way, a universal Golden Rule concept of morality. This philosophy provides families with a value system from which arises certain rules and accepted behaviors. These rules and behaviors, while varying from family to family, aid families in their attempts to live morally.

There are some people, particularly active church members and leaders, who disagree with the idea that families can be both moral and not associated with any particular religion, but most of the professionals I interviewed disagreed with that stance. "It is presumptuous of churchmen to claim ownership of moral behavior," said an Anglican theologian. "Who is to say that churches didn't assume behaviors already operating among moral peoples and put their own label on them, then implying that in order to possess them, one must belong to their church? All one needs to do is study what we call primitive peoples and tribes who have never heard of Judeo-Christian principles but who have a strong sense of right and wrong operating within themselves to realize that no one has a patent on morality."

Dr. Coles holds that children have a basic moral sense that begins to emerge and develop as early as age three and suggests that we don't emphasize sufficiently a child's struggle to make sense of the world and to evolve some kind of moral judgment on how the world works. "Within the child there is a developing moral sense," he says. "I happen to think it is God-given, that there is a craving for a moral order. I would say the child has a need for 'moral articulation' of what the world is all about, what it means, and what this life is about. This desire to figure out the world, to make sense of it, and in some way find meaning in life is built into each of us. . . . These questions are connected to one's nature as a human being."[2]

To be sure, it is helpful to have a moral community, religion teachers, and curricula to help children and families bring out and develop this moral articulation, but a moral sense is already there—it doesn't have to be planted by a particular church or doctrine. I stress this because of a growing tendency on the part of people in our society to want to offset self-centeredness and the worship of human potential by allying themselves with a group who refer to themselves as a moral majority. These groups not only imply but openly preach that to be moral, families must have a particular political and religious orientation. To be moral, they must embrace creationism over Darwinism, patriotism over conscience, censorship over free speech, and on and on. All of these demands confuse families who are trying to instill a value system consistent with their religious belief *and* operable within the context of their culture.

A good example of the confusion this mentality instills can be seen in this letter I received from a reader of my weekly column, "Talks with Parents."

I am writing in regard to some things I have read recently on humanism. The information fired me up and I became concerned about what my children are being exposed to in their school. In a nearby area parents are fighting values clarification and the showing of a film, "The Lottery." These people are being labeled as the Moral Majority but I share their viewpoint and I don't think it's because I'm a fanatic. Am I overreacting to what I read or do you think there should be some real concern?

I replied:

I think many share your dilemma. How serious is the value-laden curricula our children are being taught? All I can do is give my personal perspective. I feel the Moral Majority people are dangerous. They grasp on a normal fear and blow it out of proportion. They are often contradictory, i.e., they decry values clarification in one breath and ask for less atheistic, more moral education in the next.

I, too, share your feelings on some of these fears, especially the influence of television and some of the images our children are receiving. I opt for more censorship there—but it is going to be *my* censorship, not theirs. I am not going to be made to feel that I have to agree with all their positions on war, censorship, family, and women just because they call themselves the Moral Majority.

I believe many of us are moral and I believe we are in the majority, but I don't believe in the Moral Majority. Why not? Because they operate out of fear and despair, and we, as Christians, operate on hope and the Resurrection. We are people of hope, not despair. We look for the good in people, not the evil that the Moral Majority pronounces upon those who disagree with their stands politically, educationally, socially, or religiously.

I taught "The Lottery" as literature years ago when I was teaching sophomores, long before there was either values clarification or the Moral Majority. It wasn't considered a plot back then but a piece of literature that teaches some good moral lessons, particularly the age-old temptation of peoples to find a scapegoat for their problems and shortcomings. Is that an unacceptable value? If so, then what we are all about as Christians needs some reexamination.

I dont mean to sermonize, but I get angry when a group like the Moral Majority destroys parental confidence and faith. Use your good parental sense. If you're modeling good morals and faith at home, if your children are learning values from you, you don't have to be a watchdog over every book, class, teacher, film, activity, or idea which your children experience. Like you, they will learn to weigh and choose their values. The best way for them to learn to do this is by exposing them to a variety of ideas and values while they are living with you, so that they can come home and discuss them with you.

Far more dangerous is controlling everything they do, read, and study for 18 years and then letting them out into an uncontrolled society without any experience in choosing and discarding values. The Moral Majority would have us to do that. They would censor everything with which they disagree, even down to some very good literature.

Good luck. Don't worry and don't think you are overreacting. We all think that at times. It is better than apathy. ("Talks with Parents," © Alt Publishing Co., 1981³)

Values are personal. They may differ from culture to culture and family to family, but the healthy family operates from a clear set of values that emanates from a moral core. This core and its resultant values permits the family to teach a sense of right and wrong. Here are some hallmarks of the family that teaches a sense of right and wrong.

1. Husband and wife share a consensus of important values.

Probably one of the most destructive forces in a marriage is that of significantly different value systems held by two partners. Consider, for example, the conflict built into a marriage in which one spouse puts a low value on commitment and marital fidelity and the other puts a high value on both. Even though marriages between persons with such drastically different moral bases occur more often in literature than in real life, they still occur more often than they should, considering that people usually are free to choose their mates. Generally, it's just a matter of time before such marriages break down. (In earlier cultures, people with divergent value systems were bound together for life by religious and cultural mores, a point worth remembering when we despair over our divorce rates.)

Although infidelity is an obvious area of marital conflict, there are hundreds of more hidden ones that can be just as destructive in a life-long relationship. The various premarriage inventories, tests given engaged couples to discover real and potential value conflicts, contain many questions designed to ferret out probable danger areas in the future marriage.

Here is an exercise that I sometimes use with already-marrieds to encourage them to look beyond the argument of the moment to the

depth of the value being attacked.
1. It's okay to drive over 55 m.p.h. (or 65 or 75) even if that's the posted speed limit.
2. It's wrong to spank children.
3. Grown children should bring their elderly home to live with them.
4. It's okay to take ash trays from restaurants because they expect it.
5. Padding the expense account is a reasonable response to unreasonable taxes.
6. Separate vacations are morally wrong.
7. Prioritize those most deserving of our respect: Hispanics, retarded, unwed mothers, priests, elderly, oil executives, felons, bishops, farmers, homosexuals, Mormons, Appalachians, women, Arabs, bus drivers, whites, students, police, rich, unemployed, protestors, blacks, politicians, vandals, dropouts, bank presidents, actors, Native Americans, welfare recipients, prostitutes, alcoholics, conscientious objectors, child abusers, men, environmentalists.

One time I worked in a seminar which was put together by a couple deeply into Marriage Encounter. This couple felt that their level of communication was about as high as could be achieved. And it was—as long as they talked about their marriage and family. However, when an exercise similar to the one above was presented, they discovered a strong conflict existed between them in their attitudes toward war and peace. One felt deeply that the conscientious objector was a coward and traitor while the other felt equally strongly that those who had fled the country to avoid fighting in Viet Nam because they questioned the morality of that conflict should be respected. This subject mattered a great deal to them because they had three draft-age sons and at the time the Iranian hostage situation was paramount in the news.

Sadly, and paradoxically, this couple dealt with their conflict that day by refusing to discuss it. They became cool toward one another, and their highly technical communication skills broke down. Communication can be used to disclose and deal with value conflicts, or it can be used to avoid them. By focusing on developing the technical skills in communication rather than on the content and depth of their communication, this couple had managed to evade a lot of the deep problems that they sensed spelled trouble for their marriage.

Parents in healthy families aren't afraid to talk values. They work toward a consensus so that they can pass on a unified sense of right and wrong to their children. On important values like fidelity, equality, respect, responsibility, and trust, they work to agree. For example, thousands of men are striving hard today to overcome an old cultural conditioning that told them that women were less worthy and less equal. They are trying to rid themselves of a deeply embedded value. Often this can be a trying time for couples because today's women are becoming less patient.

But healthy couples who disagree seem to be able to do so in a way that tells children that people can disagree on some values and still care about and respect one another. Their children don't expect a unified parenthood on everything—and even if couples do try to hide value conflicts from their children, they're rarely successful. Couples who comfortably accept and admit value differences so that their children can witness their struggle to live with moral conflicts rather than submerge them model a valuable lesson in the home.

In an article on rearing children today, Dr. Charles E. Schaefer, child psychologist, interviewed a great number of parents he thought successful in order to hear their reflections on parenting based on their personal experiences. A number of them stressed strongly the need for parents to state clearly their own moral values and discuss them with their children. Here are four comments from them:

"Children should be made aware of proper values—behavioral, financial, and so forth. When they stray, parents should communicate in a manner which encourages the child to listen—do not be permissive or rigid but firm, so the children know exactly where you stand."

"Teach children to respect people, to be honest, and to treat others as they themselves would like to be treated."

"All children have to be taught right from wrong, to be honest, and to treat others as they themselves would like to be treated."

"Teach them the value of *truthfulness*. Time and again I recall telling the children that if they told us the truth about a situation, we would do all in our power to help them, for in knowing the real facts we could deal with any misstatements by others. If, however, they lied, we would be unable to be of much help because we couldn't depend on them."[4]

2. The parents teach clear and specific guidelines about right and wrong.

Although there is wide disagreement among healthy families on what constitutes moral behavior, children within individual families are taught that specific behaviors are either moral or immoral. When these children from healthy families are asked why they behave in a certain way, they inevitably reply "Because it's wrong to do otherwise" or "Because we should."

The idea that behaviors are acceptable simply because everyone else is behaving that way is less apparent in the good family, unless, of course, the behaviors under question are called for by a specific religious community. For example, to the Mormon child, it is wrong to drink caffeine in any form. To the Jehovah Witness, it is wrong to salute the flag at school. To the Seventh Day Adventist child, immunizations and blood transfusions are immoral.

We can contrast these children, who have definite ideas about what's moral, with the great numbers of American children today who don't have any idea of what's moral. The children aren't really immoral; they are amoral. They don't know what's right from what's wrong. These are the students who believe it's okay to cheat as long as they don't get caught. They see nothing wrong with vandalism, graffiti-writing, littering, or even lifting other people's property if it isn't properly secured. A college student in Colorado, questioned for stealing another student's bike, explained, "But it wasn't locked." He gave no indication of remorse or even wrongdoing. To him, the improper behavior was on the part of the victim for failing to prevent his thievery.

Dr. Coles is saddened by the contrast between American and non-American children in moral education. He said, "Until I left the country and started working abroad, I don't think I realized how hard it is for a lot of American children to get moral notions about this life.... What do they really believe in, if anything, or if anything apart from themselves and their futures, their social and economic futures?"[5]

Earlier a colleague of his, Dr. Karl Menninger, made the same observation in his book, *Whatever Became of Sin?*. The paradox here is that people trained in psychology are emphasizing the need for a moral structure to individual lives at the same time many of the religiously trained are turning to psychology for answers. Dr. Elizabeth Kübler-Ross, who has given so many insights on death and dying, observes humorlessly that of those working with the terminally ill, the chaplains sound like psychiatrists and the psychiatrists like chaplains.

Psychiatry is often forced to fill the vacuum created by lack of moral belief and moral education in our culture. Dr. Coles believes that the

American public has a prolonged and overly strenuous love affair with psychiatry. "We've been turned to with too great enthusiasm, maybe even some gullibility," he says. "Not that we aren't quite willing to be secular gods and pontificate. That's one of the great tragedies of psychiatry in American life. We've moved into a moral vacuum. We hand out too much advice, and it's accepted all too willingly by those who have lost faith in other authorities."[6]

But what happens when American parents bring their children to therapists who suggest moral nurturing in the form of a religious community or a movement dedicated to a cause? "They get very angry," said one child psychologist. "They don't come to us for religion or morals. They come—often—for justification for *not* having a basic moral or religious structure. We get a lot of comments like 'We don't want to saddle our children with a lot of dos and don'ts,' and then they ask us to do so."

3. Children are held responsible for their own moral behavior.

Parents in strong families don't find scapegoats for their own immorality or for their children's but rather they teach the idea each individual is answerable for his or her behavior. They don't subscribe to the attitude that what happened to us as children absolves us from immoral behavior as adults. On a younger level, this means that what has happened in first grade is not an excuse for misbehavior in second.

Excusing and absolving is particularly pervasive whenever there's been a divorce or serious illness. The single parent, often feeling guilty because of the divorce, rationalizes the child's behavior into mere fallout from the divorce rather than simply improper and immoral behavior. Very quickly such children are aware of this rationalization and latch onto it; they decide they don't have to behave like other children because their parents are divorced. Divorced parents, who share these feelings and experiences in support groups, are often quite distraught over the results. They have discovered that in their attempt to be good and loving parents to children suffering the pain of divorce, they are instead creating little bullies or liars or vandals. Here is a sampling of stories these parents shared in one support group:

"My children were very angry with us over our divorce, so I didn't demand respectful behavior from them at first. Before long, they were treating all adults with disrespect. I found out I hadn't done them any favor. They were floundering around because of our breakup, and then I removed the wrongness of talking back and using bad words from them and they really floundered."

"When my son came home with an eight-track tape I knew he couldn't afford, I knew he must have taken it, but I felt so guilty for not having money to buy him those things after the divorce, I didn't say anything. . . ."

"I found that my teenager was telling outrageous stories about my behavior to her father, and I was terribly hurt and angry and disappointed. When I faced her with it, she said, 'Well, you like to hear bad stories about Daddy. What's the difference?' She had become a regular fiction-writer."

Any time of stress within a family can trigger a lessening of parental attention to morality in little things, but healthy families find they can be understanding in times of stress without removing individual responsibility for moral behavior by designating a variety of scapegoats.

4. The family realizes that intent is crucial in judging behavior.

Probably one of the most repeated stories told about educator Jean Piaget's attempts to teach children to be moral is that of the child and the jam jar. "Who was naughtier," he asked some children, "the child who climbed up to the cupboard to sneak some jam and broke the jam jar or the child who was helping his mother set the table and accidentally broke four glasses?" Children at a young age will almost always choose the latter as naughtier because four glasses were broken rather than one.

It's our job as parents to lead our children into a higher level of morality by teaching them the difference between good and bad motives. A Montessori specialist told me that unfortunately parents often equate badness with the amount of damage done. "Parents react more strongly when something valuable is destroyed or mislaid or lost," she said, "even though it may have been accidental on the part of the child. At the same time, they may not react at all when the child intentionally destroys something of little value to them."

Intention has always been a basic part of evil and sin. To be sinful, a person has to know that his or her actions are wrong and, even knowing that, deliberately undertake them. A classic family situation useful in teaching children this concept occurs when the children want to punish the family cat for killing a bird. If the cat doesn't know it's wrong, should it be punished? Is it wrong for the cat to kill a bird, or is it natural? If youngsters don't know behaviors are wrong, or evil, how can they be guilty of misbehaving? In regard to obvious crimes like homicide, children don't have to be taught this, but they do need to be taught in such areas as character assassination, racism, cheating, destruction of property, disrespect for others' rights, and willingness to let another be punished for their own misbehavior.

As a part of moral training, healthy families look at the motives and particular circumstances involved in a situation. They empathize when the situation calls for it and punish when the situation calls for it. They know, too, that merely teaching right and wrong isn't enough. As Harvard's Dr. Lawrence Kohlberg, originator of a theory that humans advance through six stages of moral development, indicates, parents must realize that children don't always understand *why* something is right or wrong, even though they can repeat the lesson verbatim.

I recall the year when our daughter was about three and I heard her call her grandfather by his first name, Frank. I took her aside and scolded her gently, adding that it was disrespectful to do so and that we wouldn't permit that behavior. She nodded sincerely, her little forehead furrowed in repentance. But about a week later, when we were reading together and it was one of those moments intimate enough for her to feel safe to risk, she asked, "Mom, what does Frank mean?" She had internalized the lesson that it was wrong, but she had not grasped why. When I had said it was disrespectful, she presumed it was a naughty word.

5. Parents help children to live morally.

In a workshop in which parents were discussing the issue of teens and morality, there was a difference of opinion about how parents should support their adolescents in their efforts to withstand peer pressure. One mother said that she gave her daughter blanket permission to say "My mother won't let me" anytime her daughter felt pressured to do something against her value system. Many parents disagreed with this approach, stressing that the youth has to develop some responses himself or herself, not always use Mom as the heavy.

Later I asked the parents from the healthy families I interviewed about this situation, and most of them agreed with the mother. "Why not let the kids use us?" asked a father. "After all, we are the ones who taught them right from wrong. What's wrong with their saying, 'My dad don't let me,' when they know I'd be disappointed in their behavior if they did."

Children today can't be expected to be moral without help. When a parent is aware that a child is sexually active and yet ignores it, the parent is as irresponsible as the child may be immoral. If the child knows that the parents know about his or her sexual activity, at the same time making no attempt to point out the immorality of either the promiscuity or its consequences on others' lives, the child will assume either that the behavior is okay or that the parents' moral code is shaky.

I know a charming southern couple in their seventies who refused to allow a cherished granddaughter to stay in the same bedroom as her male roommate when they came to visit, even though her grandparents were well aware that they lived together. "I'm too old to undo the buckle on my Bible belt now," said the grandmother. This kind of standing on one's principles and morals says a lot to young people. It says that we care enough about them to take uncomfortable stands. It says that we have lived a long time and not found our values wanting. It says that in spite of the fact that our loved ones may not operate on the same value and moral system, our faith in our own isn't shaken. It doesn't depend on their approval but is solid on its own.

When parents ignore early drug usage or any of the other common situations in which morality is involved, they are avoiding a basic parental responsibility. More, they are disclosing a lack of moral structure in themselves. "How can I tell my children what is moral or immoral when I'm unsure?" is a frequent, unspoken dilemma.

My survey respondents suggest that the healthier the family the more developed is their sense of right and wrong. This doesn't necessarily mean that all other people will agree with a particular family on what is moral or immoral, only that every strong family has a moral base of some kind.

Stanley Hauerwas writes that it isn't enough to welcome children into our families and society; we must also be willing to initiate them into what we think is true and good about human existence. "For example, I think we should not admire religious or non-religious parents who fail to educate their children in the parents' convictions. It is a false and bad-faith position to think we can or should raise our children to 'make up their own minds when they grow up,'" he says. "Children are not without values today; instead, we as parents lack the courage to examine our own lives in a manner that we know what we pass on is truthful and duty-paid.

Only by recovering this kind of moral confidence will parents deserve to reclaim their claim from the 'experts.' In moral matters there are no 'experts'; and therefore all parents are charged with forming their children's lives according to what they know best."[7]

Dr. Coles, to whom I am so indebted on this topic of morals in the family, says that flagrant moral hypocrisy is as dangerous to children as hating or lying. "It's a kind of duplicity. Parents underestimate what children pick up," he writes. "Lord knows, I've spent twenty years documenting the way children at times pick out hypocrisy in parents. Many parents preach one line at home on Sundays and live another line during the week. Children find out the disparity between what is said and what is done. I agree that this can be disenchanting and can set the stage for rebelliousness and anger."[8]

Parents who care about their family's sense of morality will steer children toward good moral environments and away from suspicious ones. They pay attention to their children's friends and actively foster certain relationships and stifle others. They encourage their children to come to them when there's a moral dilemma in their lives.

One mother said that their daughter came to her with the "problem" that she was the only virgin in her crowd. Instead of either dismissing it as a nonproblem or laughing, the mother showed understanding toward her daughter's feelings. Her daughter was feeling out of the group, unpopular, and guilty. She asked her mother's help in coming up with a reason she could give the group for her reluctance to become sexually active, something she could say that wouldn't seem judgmental. But after several long introspective discussions with her mother, the girl realized that she already knew what she must do—find a group of friends whose morals were more consistent with her own. Otherwise, she would always be feeling either guilty or left out.

Why didn't her daughter want to leave the group? Because it was the popular group and leaving it abruptly would be socially tough in a small high school. Her wise mother suggested that she ease her way out of contact with the group at night—by working at her job evenings or by claiming she was grounded at night because of grades—while remaining a member of the group during the school day. This scheme took the pressure off the girl during the dating and boy-time away from school, and gradually the girl was able to move out of the group without incurring bad feelings.

But, most important, the girl's mother gave her two valuable gifts: an understanding of the relationship between friends and morals and help in moving toward friends with values more like her own. Many parents won't help a child to deal with troublesome moral situations; they think the adolescent should be old enough and strong enough to move away from the group on his or her own. These parents have short memories. They forget the terrific power of peer pressure. Healthy parents tend to step in and become the bad guys, the ones who say no, the ones who find healthier environments, and the ones who are willing to become viable moral-support systems for their children.

Let's summarize, then, the hallmarks of the family that has developed a sense of right and wrong.

1. Husband and wife share a consensus of important values.
2. The parents teach clear and specific guidelines about right and wrong.
3. Children are held responsible for their own moral behavior.
4. The family realizes that intent is crucial in judging behavior.
5. Parents help children to live morally.

10
Enjoying Traditions

Trait 8: The healthy family has a strong sense of family in which rituals and traditions abound.

> The family is our refuge and springboard; nourished on it, we can advance to new horizons. In every conceivable manner, the family is link to our past, bridge to our future.   —Alex Haley

A strong sense of family was chosen by my survey respondents as eighth most evident in healthy families today. A sense of family means much more than the begats in the family Bible or the names on the homestead papers. A family's clanship embraces its legends, its characters, its history, its focal places and persons, its hospitality, its network, its deceased, its elderly, its babies, its traditions, and its rituals. The family who owns a rich sense of kinship is able to withstand stresses and disappointments that destroy other families. It's able to do so because its members have the support that comes from knowing they are not alone, either in the neighborhood or in history. It is in this kind of family that individuals are loved not for what they have or do but for who they are—members of the family.

Stanley Hauerwas emphasized the nature of this acceptance and support when he said, "By far the most inescapable fact about families, regardless of their different forms and customs, is that we do not choose to be part of them. We do not choose our relatives; they are simply given. Of course we can like some better than others but even those we do not like are extricably ours. To be part of a family is to understand what it means to be 'stuck with' a history and a people."[1]

Columnist Ellen Goodman puts it more succinctly: "We don't have to achieve to be accepted by our families. We just have to be. Our membership is not based on credentials but on birth."

Why is it that the young in some families grow up, leave home for college or work a thousand miles away, and, for all practical purposes, sever any emotional ties with their family of origin, while the young of another family, similar in most respects to the first, retain strong emotional ties to their family? In the first, a family is regarded as a place to leave, a discarded nest to be returned to only at obligatory times like holidays, illnesses, and death, while in the second the family is considered to be a lifelong base of love and support.

Duty-to-family, not belonging-to-family, is the overriding feature of that first family. Grown children are not likely to turn to this family for sustenance and help but rather to friends and community. Relationships in this family are not necessarily uncaring, but the mood or personality of the family without kinship is distinctly different from one with it. It tends to be more private, less intrusive, less personal. It is also less comfortable. Visits to one another's homes resemble visits to friends, not family. Clanship is not fully developed, and there's little sense of the family's importance as a link in the long chain of family history.

Alex Haley, author of *Roots,* attributes the popularity of his autobiographical saga to an emotional tug on readers and viewers who are longing for a sense of historical family. Ever since his book and the resulting TV series appeared, Haley has written and lectured extensively on the need for families to look more closely at their sense of family. He recommends that families honor their "griots," those legendkeepers of early and modern Africa who enabled him to make that final link between his African heritage and American slave history. He encourages families to search their lineage so that their children are made more aware of their ancestors. He speaks of the richness of family reunions, which serve as a glue to cement generations together. "Reunions are the conveyor belts of our individual histories," he says. "They reaffirm the thread of continuity, establish pride in self and kin, and transmit a family's awareness of itself, from the youngest to the oldest."[2]

Hasley's thoughts are not original, of course, but they do give testimony to professional observations of family behavior by counselors and therapists. These professionals who work with families know the importance of a sense of belonging to an individual. They work with many adults who are spending a lifetime searching for a sense of family in some of the most unexpected places: work, chemicals, cults, movements, the military, or even multiple marriages.

Kinship and interdependency are linked, but because freedom and belonging, two of the most powerful of human emotions, are directly oppositional, the tension that the establishment of a strong sense of family requires is often painful. Some families demand too strong a family allegiance and the sense of family becomes so oppressive that members are driven to escape, whether it's to another geographical area or to another ideology. Either way, the members remove themselves from the tension of being expected for dinner every Sunday or apologizing for a political candidate not to the greater family's liking.

Other families simply abdicate clanship in favor of individual freedom and privacy. They make no attempt to foster traditions, rituals, or even family history because these might impinge upon individual freedom in daily life. This family is oppressive in a different way—it has no feeling of family. It resembles a dormitory where members come together occasionally to eat and converse but do not feel a bondedness with one another.

A sense of family is one of the more abstract of the healthy-family traits, but it also is one of the most foundational. It gives the family a frame. It places it in context historically, linking the past with the future in such a way that members feel part of a larger ethnic, religious, or world family. Joseph B. Tamney explains this sense of continuity, of being unified, as being "at one" with humanity. "Children are extensions of our bodies so that through them we transcend our own physicality. Union with children thus gives both a feeling of high physical solidarity and a sense of participation in the wider universe."[3]

Certain groups of people, particularly those in ethnic groups and in rural America, have a phrase that describes this bondedness: "We're family," or "We're kin." In the two words of these phrases are found multiple meanings. "We're family" says that we belong to one another, no matter now different our life-styles are, how many generations separate us, or how we appear to get along to outsiders. It implies that we can be called upon in need, that we will be supportive, and that even though we may not always approve of behavior, we will not judge a member worthy or unworthy as a condition of our support.

A speaker at a major conference on families said that the real definition of the family is determined by the individual. "Family is the group that the person *labels* as his family," he said. "It's where he senses his belongingness." He went on to explain that in a blood family where there is an absence of a common bond, the child will turn to a peer group, the gang, the team, the cult, the platoon, or the foster family in order to have a sense of belonging. It is in this nonblood family that such a person finds acceptance, traditions, and a sense of family.

While listening to this speaker, I thought of how evident this kind of
kinship was in both the Manson and Jonestown groups—who named
themselves families—both of which were made up of individuals seeking a stronger sense of family than they had experienced before.

That's why a sense of family is so foundational. That's why over
half of those professionals surveyed gave it a high priority on their list
of healthy traits. What are the signs, or hallmarks, of a family that
possesses this trait? Here are some of them.

1. The family treasures its legends and characters.

Everyone in the family knows the story about how immigration officials misspelled the original family name, thereby starting a new
family name. Or how Uncle Leo tricked Aunt Ellen into marrying
him. Or how they didn't find Aunt Maggie's false teeth in the oatmeal
box until long after the funeral. Or any of a number of stories that
gather fictional momentum as they pass from generation to generation. These stories are told and retold at family gatherings, much to
the disgust of some who are tired of hearing them or some who married into the family and don't quite believe them. These stories are important to the sense of family.

Why? Because they tell the story. They gather up the past for present family members, who know they must preserve and pass them on
to future generations. Stanley Hauerwas explains, "We even enjoy telling stories about our less than admirable kin because such stories help
us know what being 'stuck with' such a history entails. Unfortunately,
we have tended today to understand such storytelling primarily as
entertainment (which it surely is) rather than representing the moral
affirmation of what it means to be part of a family."[4] That moral affirmation is a vital part of the functioning family. It supports the family
as a viable and valuable unit of society.

Stories aren't icing; they're basic ingredients in any group that
claims to be family. Alex Haley reminds us that heritage is not just a
roll call of our ancestors. He says, "Rather it is the *feeling* inbred in a
family, what the forebears did, how they lived and coped, and what
they left behind. The passports that brought great-grandparents to this
country, the old letters from the attic trunk, the yellowed diaries—they
give a flavor of those from whom we have sprung. In every reunion the
old ones should have a chance to speak briefly about their past and

also to voice their hopes for the family's future."[5]

After working with large numbers of families, I'm convinced that every family has a character or two that isn't introduced to an intended spouse until well after the wedding. This character might be the one who drinks, or acts differently from the rest of the family, or is embarrassingly outspoken. In our family, we had a couple of bachelor relatives who farmed. When they wanted chicken for dinner, they merely reached out from their rocking chair and grabbed one standing on the porch railing. While they may not have furnished our family with an exemplary housekeeping style, they did furnish our family with something more important — legendary characters. As each of us brought a fiance to meet the family, the first question asked was, "When are you going to take him (or her) to meet The Boys?" By the time couples were well-married, the nonfamily spouses were so curious about The Boys that they were eager to meet this legendary part of our family fabric. That The Boys weren't nearly so colorful in reality as in tale told wasn't important. In an otherwise routine family, they were characters, and they were *ours*.

We should make the most of the legends and characters in our families. Instead of hiding them so that our particular family resembles every other family, why not treasure them and make them part of our family's uniqueness? The Hawaiians commonly get together and share family tales as a means of entertainment. When I was conducting workshops there, my husband and I were fortunate enough to stay with local families. One evening, a family came home late and explained that they had gotten together with other friends and families that evening to "talk story." Intrigued, I pressed for more information and found that talking story is a very common social activity among the Hawaiians. Talking story means sharing past tales, family or otherwise. We all need to talk story. As part of the family story, we need to pass on glimpses of what the grownups were like when they were young. Once when I was giving a seminar for parents of young children, a woman of an age to be a grandmother aroused curiosity when she signed up for the session. "I'm here as a resource person for my grandchildren," she explained. Not only was she an excellent resource person for her grandchildren but for us as well. She was able to put parenting into perspective with such quick observations as "Don't worry about it so much. Have you ever known a twenty-one-year-old walking around in diapers?"

But we are all resource persons for the next generations. We know far more about our family than do the family sociologists and specialists. They know families in general; we know ours in particular. They know statistics; we know stories. Our task is to pass on these stories. John Shea, storytelling theologian, gives us profound advice for passing on the faith: "Gather the people. Tell the story. Break the bread." The same things should be done in the intimate family unit. We need to gather our people, tell our stories, and share our bread in order to insure the passing on of our legends and our meaning.

Grandparents can serve as great resource persons in telling their grandchildren what their grandchildren's parents were like as children. In her article, "The Importance of Grandparents," Lillian Africano paints a lovely picture of family resourcing in this way. "With my mother . . . my children have a different kind of relationship. Though her brand of grandmothering was never ordinary, it was, when the children were small, fairly conventional. She gave them the kind of unhurried, unharried time that I could rarely manage. During weekend visits, when I'd be enjoying an extra hour or two of precious sleep, Mama would cook the children wonderfully elaborate breakfasts and entertain them with tales of my childhood indiscretions. ('Your mother was such a fussy eater I was afraid she would starve.')"[6]

This kind of grandparent and grandchild sharing—telling tales on parents so to speak—is very good for children, who have difficulty believing their parents were children, with all the weaknesses, fears, faults, and escapades that being a child implies. "Tell us again about the time Mom got in trouble" and "You mean Dad flunked English?" opens up a whole new world to the child. It places parents on the continuum of family history—as children of an earlier age, as parents of today, and as grandparents of tomorrow, sharing tales with their children's children about their childhood.

2. The family has a person and/or a place that serves as locus.

In her book *Families,* Jane Howard refers to this focal person as the family switchboard operator.[7] This is the person (or occasionally persons) who keeps track of everyone else and answers the questions put them by other members of the family. This is the person to whom one goes first when constructing a family tree.

This role is often assumed by a patriarch or matriarch, who also serves as chief of hospitality on holidays and other days of special family significance. Serving in this role is not usually considered a burden but a privilege in families, and although families don't actually vote on a locus, there does seem to be a tacit general consensus on person and place. When the reigning locus becomes unable to serve in this position, there's usually an already acknowledged successor in the wings.

One couple tells about how they had worried unnecessarily because their mother, who had served in this role in the family for years, was becoming too weak to remain in the matriarchal locus spot. "We were afraid she'd fall apart if she wasn't at the center of things, especially holiday life in the clan," they said. They were astonished to learn that she was just waiting to be relieved of the responsibility so that she could sit back like the others and enjoy watching a niece assume her role. This happened, and she became, in a sense, *locus emeritus* in the family.

Many families have a special place to which they return, usually the old family home, ranch, or farm. As long as the parents or even one parent remains there, it's the natural gathering spot for families, even though the grandchildren and spouses swell the family up to the walls of the house. Other brothers and sisters nearby may have larger homes, but everyone is more comfortable gathering at their childhood home because it is theirs.

Once parents have moved away from the original home or have died, another home is usually designated by the family. Some families move from home to home for special occasions, but most still have one home where everyone goes first for information and meeting. Our increasingly mobile culture is doing away with such homes, and healthy families cite this as a great loss. "We don't have a place to call home anymore," said a fifty-year-old couple who grew up in Milwaukee but lived in St. Louis. Their retired parents had sold the family home and moved to Florida and their doing so shook the roots of the family, which was spread all over the country. "I suppose we will go to Florida, but it just won't seem like home," the couple said.

3. The family makes a conscious effort to gather as a people.
Weddings, bar mitzvahs, and funerals are usually command

gatherings for all families, but those with a strong sense of clanship gather even when they don't have to. They deliberately plan reunions. They really want to get together when even a distant relative comes to town. They enjoy family gatherings, such as fiftieth wedding anniversaries, first communions, and graduations. Cousins know their cousins as people, not as mere names on a Christmas card.

In the considerable work I've done with military families, I have found that some are absolutely ingenious at establishing this sense of belonging to a larger family even when they are living an ocean away from their families. "You can either feel left out and sorry for yourself, or you can be an invisible part of your family gatherings," a young couple told me. How? This couple has a family heritage wall that goes with them wherever they move. On it go school pictures of the cousins, photos of each family at holiday time, clippings, letters from cousins, and other mementos of families back home. Each week they tape record a letter to each set of grandparents and ask them to tape one back, including on it voices and comments from other cousins and grandchildren. They ask for tapes of each holiday dinner, as silly as they might be. They send home photocopies of children's report cards and samples of their artwork. They make a conscious effort to write letters themselves to their brothers and sisters back home. In short, they work at it—so that when they get back home, they aren't strangers, and their relatives aren't unknown to their children.

We borrowed some of the techniques my military interviewees told about when a year ago our eldest went off to college a thousand miles from home. Sunday night dinner has always been our special family time (one of my sons explained to a friend that it's the night "that Mom cooks new") in which we relax together, review the week, look at the upcoming week, pray a little together, and linger awhile.

The most enjoyable kind of sharing we do with our absent daughter, Teresa, is our taping of our entire Sunday evening meal for her. Predictably, she hears us pray, and then for five or so minutes she hears mostly the clinking of silver against china. Finally, hunger abated, we begin to converse and share with one another. Yes, at first it was awkward for us, but now we talk to her as if she's there. A great deal of humor emerges in our descriptions of the food, our past week, and so on.

Initially we would shut off the tape recorder before we engaged in what has become a family habit—ending the long Sunday evening meal by getting out our individual calendars and scrutinizing them to see how much time we will have to share during the week ahead. One Sunday we forgot to turn off the tape recorder before we did that, and Teresa told us later that she had greatly enjoyed hearing about our upcoming week. "You don't write all those things in letters, but I like to hear about who has a soccer practice or dentist appointment. I don't know why, but it makes me feel more like I'm there."

Details intensify relationships. The homely and certainly far-from-exciting calendar-sharing that Teresa referred to assured her that family life was continuing on its mundane but predictable way. And that was what she most needed, not a wordy description of some big party we attended.

Strong families enjoy being together. As the man said, "You don't have to make an appointment for a visit." Some families are naturally hospitable and usually the ones with a sense of family fit into this category of openness toward others, especially family members. Its members feel comfortable in dropping in when passing by. Or a relative from out of town feels natural in calling and telling this family he is coming. He or she doesn't wait for an invitation.

Problems frequently arise when two people with different senses of kinship marry. If one is used to informal drop-in hospitality and the other is not, great tension can arise. One who grows up with loud, noisy family gatherings called for no reason at all may find a reserved by-invitation family atmosphere frigid and uncaring. At the same time, a partner who is used to that style of hospitality frequently feels overwhelmed by the more uncontrolled, informal style of celebrating. Generally, couples can work it out if they try, but it can be a real tension in an otherwise strong marriage.

Hospitable families are also the first ones to open up their homes to people outside the family—friends of relatives, visiting college students, foreign exchange students, temporarily homeless teens, foster children, and others. How much a family opens itself up in this way seems directly related to how strong a family sense it has. The healthy families that I interviewed always seemed to have an extra person around, and that person felt very comfortable. "We have more mavericks than anybody else in the block," said the father in such a family, and it was easy to see why. The family was open, friendly and sharing, making temporary members immediately feel comfortable in their midst.

4. The family views itself as a link between the past and the future.

People with a strong sense of family don't think family ends with death. Deceased relatives are discussed so that children who didn't know them feel as if they did. Ancestors become persons with human traits and foibles. Visits to the cemetery are common in such families. Also common are looking at pictures and old Bibles with the handwriting of great-great-grandparents and passing on memorabilia that once belonged to a deceased relative.

I know a widower who, upon his wife's death, presented each grandchild, niece, nephew, grand-niece, and grand-nephew with a piece of her jewelry. Even a three-year-old grandson was given one of grandmother's necklaces to pass on to his wife and daughter some day.

Another parent shared with me that she made decorator pillows out of her deceased mother's wedding dress for each of the grandchildren. A single woman told me how she'd been spending her retirement years painstakingly ferreting out the family lineage to present as a legacy to her nieces and nephews, a far greater treasure than any slim savings she might some day pass on to them.

Death is not focused on unhealthily in these families, but neither is it hidden. It's regarded as a part of life. This kind of natural acceptance of passing on in death helps us to understand our individual roles in history, especially in our family history. We didn't spring by ourselves into this moment of history, and we won't leave without a trace of being here.

Unhealthy families tend to miss the significance of being linked in family time. They often clearly deemphasize the need to pass on the story of ancestors, to listen to the elderly, and to keep in touch with roots because they think to do so is morbid. "Who wants to talk about dead relatives?" a mother said during a seminar. Her attitude is very common in a culture in which discussion of death is more a taboo than discussion of sexual intimacy.

Alex Haley writes that in every village of Africa there is what is known as the "cycle of the village." The cycle consists of three groups of people: those you can see; the ancestors who have passed on; and those waiting to be born. "In almost every reunion of any size," Haley says, "some of the family who were at the last gathering will be absent, having gone on to spend their time in eternity. Some—the new babies—will be present who were not at the previous reunion. These transitions remind us that we are here but the blink of an eye. When you think about that, every instinct tells you to reach out and hold your family—for as long as you have the privilege."[8]

5. The family honors its elders and welcomes its babies.

In some families, productive members are treasured over those who are too old to work. In others, retired loved ones are honored for who they are and what they have done. They are made to feel important, as indispensable a part of the family as if they were still active in work, home, and outside organizations. It's a joy to watch these families at a reunion. "Need a sweater, Grandma?" asks a thirteen-year-old boy (yes, *thirteen*), without any prodding from a parent. Children listen to the elders' stories even when the stories are rambling or pointless. Somehow there's a family feeling that these elders are of value and shouldn't be denied community just because they can't hear or can't "take the noise." Being overly solicitous is not a feature of this family either. There's concern and respect, yes, but not a focus on a person simply because he or she is elderly.

And just as these families welcome the elderly in their midst, so do they welcome the young. Again, in some families, young children are mercly tolerated at gatherings but not welcomed. There's an undercurrent of exasperation when they cry, spill lemonade, beg, get tired, whine. The adults in these families have a distinct attitude of endurance, an attitude that says, "We'll put up with you because you're family, but we'll be awfully glad when you've gone home." It's assumed that children will not attend any weddings and other formal family functions.

In families who are eager to accept all their members, the adults tend to share naturally in the care of the very young. If a young mother is busy with one of her children, a relative will pick up the baby and tend it. Older children automatically choose games that children of many ages can play. We shared an evening with a family like this once. "Kick the Can" was played for three hours by dozens of cousins ranging in age from three through sixteen—and they all protested when the game had to end because of darkness. This shared play today provides emotional solidarity among children who will be tomorrow's adults in the family. If they never play or share together as children, their relationship as adults is not likely to be very fully developed.

The healthy family welcomes and accepts all ages into its circle. It values its elderly and its toddlers as highly as its adults and school-aged children.

6. The family cherishes its traditions and rituals.

"The great value of traditions," says Dr. James Dobson, "is that they give a family a sense of identity, of belongingness. And everybody needs this in this harried day in which we live. That we're not just a cluster of people living together in a house, but we're a family that's conscious of its uniqueness, of its personality, of its character, and its heritage. And the special relationship within the family of love and companionship makes us a unit that has an identity, that has, as I say, a personality."[9]

Families who treasure their traditions and rituals seem automatically to have a sense of family. Traditions are the underpinning in such families, regarded as necessities not frills. If there's a conflict between a tradition and a responsibility, the tradition usually wins. These are the families who explain that they can't come to a meeting because there's a family birthday, or they refuse an opportunity for overtime on the job because they always meet for a picnic and volleyball games with another family on the first weekend of August, or they allow their children to stay home from school because it's St. Joseph's Day and the Italians like to celebrate on that day.

Ritualizing is extremely important in families. It's not coincidental that the most emotional conflict occurring between many young couples during their initial year of marriage arises not from money, in-laws, or chore division but from issues surrounding the celebration of Christmas: whether gifts should be opened on Christmas Eve or Christmas morning; whether the tree should be real or artificial; which parents should be invited at what time; and other fundamental issues. And fundamental they are, although they may seem silly to those uninvolved. Each partner is emotionally invested in passing on Christmas traditions, his or her own traditions. (This common experience is probably the best possible example of the idea that individuals do not marry, rather families do.) The couple, by a gradual selection and adaptation process, begins to develop its own set of Christmas traditions and rituals, which then mark them as a unique family and which they ultimately will pass on to their own children.

"I think I slip into rituals in December," writes *Boston Globe* writer Christina Robb, "because I need to spend some time in this archaic, storybook way. I need to revive my childhood experience of a good time that is really a time out from regular time. I need rituals as much as I need money or food or praise or even love, though I need to perform the rituals with people I love."

And then she describes the emptiness of those without traditions and rituals: "If I miss this tuneup, things can get pretty awful, and I think this is why the holidays are such a curse to people who are in so much pain that they can't manage to get themselves up for any rituals."[10]

Families don't have to have a great backlog of traditions in order to pass them along. To children, once is a tradition, and many a parent after some simple family observance is dumbfounded to hear the children describe it by saying "We always do it that way." This is a pretty good key to the depth and value placed on that experience by the children. It tells parents that the children want to repeat the experience as a family and indicates that they would welcome more such experiences, as original as those experiences might be. It's probably one of the best signals children send parents on the need for more traditions and rituals in the home.

My friend social psychologist Claire Bernreuter deplores the move away from family celebrations in our society. "The need for establishing traditions and rituals in one's own family is most often neglected," she wrote. "I feel most families live boring lives!" Not a very complimentary observation, maybe, but the author speaks from both professional and personal experience. Widowed with a two-year-old daughter several years ago, she felt a strong need to found traditions in their tiny family. "Even with just my daughter and me," she says, "we established rich events within our life-style, and we loved them and looked forward to living them together. And if a single parent with an only child can become such a ritualizing family, no one need live without such rich experiences to take into adulthood."

Encouraging words indeed. Bernreuter's professional background shows when she adds, "Hope is what we need so badly, and hope is based in the memory. Rituals do much to feed that hope through memory. And hope is the travel virtue—it gets us from yesterday into today and gives us the courage to face tomorrow." Rituals and traditions are much more than words. They give those who participate in them an opportunity to say nonverbally, "I love you. I like being with you. I want to reenact what's important in life with you because you are important to me."

An amusing part of the family celebration picture is that families tend to reenact rituals and traditions *even if they don't like them*. I have found families who faithfully dish up lutefisk or oysters on Christmas Eve although not one member can stand to eat them. "Hot milk again," sighed a relative when he glimpsed the oyster stew one Christmas Eve. But when his wife tried to change the menu the following year, he was aghast. Christmas Eve without oyster stew? It would be breaking the eleventh commandment.

Any change from an established tradition usually causes us to feel somewhat jolted. Traditions, after all, give us a sense of stability, and when traditions change because of a move, a job change, a marriage change, or other reasons, we need to take some vestige of the old and make it part of a new tradition. A family that always went through the ritual of getting their boat and seashore equipment into shape on Memorial Day weekend had to move because of a job transfer to the mountains, hundreds of miles from the nearest body of water. The wise parents, sensing the loss on the part of the family of its annual rites-of-summer weekend, decided to invest instead in hiking and camping as an activity. The family spent their first Memorial Day weekend studying tents, hiking gear, and camping paraphernalia. Together they roamed the mountaineering departments of sport stores. They eventually bought some equipment and spent the rest of the weekend together waterproofing, labeling, and learning to operate gear. They managed to follow a Memorial Day weekend ritual similar to their previous one, although the sport was different.

Families who move adjust more easily to new environments if they carry lots of family traditions with them. Professionals who counsel children of mobile families, usually those children who do not adjust well to new schools or surroundings, point out the difficulties children can have if traditions are not emphasized. "Often parents are so absorbed in the move—selling a house, buying another, becoming acclimated to a new area, facing a new work situation—that family traditions just can't be a high priority," said a family counselor. "But often they are the highest priorities. The family is being uprooted and its roots are imbedded in tradititions . . . or should be."

Family traditions are those dozens, even hundreds, of little rituals unique to each family. Here is a part of a list of traditions drawn up by one family at a seminar in which each family was given five minutes to think of and write down their family traditions and rituals.

— Youngest child always blows out the candles.
— Dad gives kids "dutch rubs" on the crown of their heads when he says goodnight.
— When a child is twelve, he or she becomes responsible for washing the car.
— Wednesday is leftover night.
— Waffles every Sunday morning.
— Mom hides the family valentines.
— We dye Easter eggs on Good Friday night.
— We have a taking-down-the-tree party on January 1.
— Once a year we go family ice skating—no friends allowed.
— We celebrate our cat's birthday.
— Together we clean out the basement the first day of summer vacation. (We always end with hot dogs cooked outside.)
— We leave notes on the refrigerator.
— We pretend to avoid Mom's goodnight kiss.
— Dad and the boys go fishing on Memorial Day weekend. Mom and the girls go shopping and out to lunch. Each girl gets one day to pick where lunch will be.
— Each child gets to talk alone to Grandma on long distance without anybody else listening.
— We make our own Mother's and Father's Day cards.
— We visit Aunt Ellen in the nursing home after church on holidays.

Likewise, I encourage readers, together with their families, to make a list of traditions and rituals. I suspect parents might be surprised at some of the rituals mentioned by children that haven't been considered rituals by the parents themselves. The list-making itself is a good tradition to reenact annually, maybe in the car on vacation or on New Year's Eve or whenever the family chooses.

Teens can go through a period in which they pull away from traditions and rituals. Parents should expect this to happen and not force too many on them but keep open the welcome to participate. Unfortunately, in some families the parents' attitude, particularly the father's, nonverbally tells the teen that he or she might be getting too old for kids' rituals. Often the teens in these families really do want to continue to be part of these rituals. But a natural pulling-up-roots stage of development prevents their comfortably participating, and any indication from their parents that it's time to stop participating is all they need to cut out what could still be enjoyable for them. Outside activities also interfere, and the adolescent is beginning to go through a separation process at this time that ultimately ends in the formation of a young adult, a new family, and new traditions.

Lillian Africano refers to the pain in this separation. "Though some of my warmest memories come from 'Grandfather's house,' I started to rebel, as I got older, about some of the formal rituals and the duty visits that were expected of all the family's children. This was a time when growing up seemed more important than tradition, and after I had chosen a football game or a movie over a family visit once too often, my Aunt Rose took me aside. Aunt Rose was the general of the clan, and when she said, 'Lily, I want to talk to you,' I knew I was in for it. 'You know,' she began, 'the man who takes off his clothes is going to feel cold someday.' There didn't seem to be much I could say to that, so she went on. 'Your family is like a suit of clothes. Sometimes the clothes feel tight, but you would be wrong to throw them away' . . . I suppose that in her own way Aunt Rose was right. Her little metaphor about the comfort and security of family ties comes back to me often, especially when I'm feeling the warmth of a family gathering in the company of my own children."[11]

One family I interviewed plays a game called family trivia on every important family day: birthdays, anniversaries, and such. The children love it. Parents try to stump the kids with questions such as these: What year were we married? Name your great-grandparents. Who is Uncle Dan, and how is he related to us? How many second cousins do you have? This game is great for family reunions. At your next one, put a bunch of teens in front of the group and see how they do.

A church counselor encourages his families to go back to the area where parents were raised and take a family history walk. "Much detail fleshes out the parents' stories of their childhood as their memories are triggered by landmarks," he said. "They talk about the games they played and the work they did, which often leads into a sharing of feelings they had as children. Children obtain a more vivid picture and understanding of a place they have visited than they can get by merely hearing about it from their parents."

Ethnic traditions are making a comeback in our culture, and it's long overdue. In a rebirth of ethnic pride, people, instead of hiding their heritage, are beginning to search out traditions, symbols, foods, and rituals that have lain dormant in their ethnic psyches, buried there for many years, even generations, by a national-melting-pot mentality.

Young couples are inserting ethnic traditions into their wedding and baptismal ceremonies. Families are beginning to observe the national holidays of their country of origin, much the way St. Patrick's Day is celebrated by the entire nation.

Ethnic traditions are celebrated in communities as well. Claire Bernreuter recalls that in rural life people worked hard but that when the traditional times of celebration came, they celebrated hard, too. "During those times everyone felt they belonged. It was a time for renewal and being fully one's self, a time for self-expansion on the level of being," she says. "At those times, one felt pride and happiness. Surely, without memories of these times, a family today can hardly be considered healthy, because such an important dimension of life has not organically spawned as a result of group interaction in family and community."

I work with many families who feel left out when I get to this part of ritualizing because they "aren't anything." They are truly all-American—a little German, a little English, a little Dutch, a little French, and a little more of everything else. I point out to them that they have inherited the lot. They are entitled to the traditions of all their ethnic and nationality groups. Because they aren't one solid nationality, they have foolishly abdicated the many treasures that are theirs. It's fun to observe a family like this discover their many cultural customs. They try many, discarding, adapting, and adding to their family treasure troves.

Religious traditions are intricately interwoven with ethnic traditions. I remember family customs, such as the annual blessing of the fields on Holy Saturday, that remain far stronger planks in my religious foundation than any papal encyclicals. In midafternoon on Holy Saturday, we went with my dad from field to field as he blessed each with new holy water. In every field, he bent down and crumbled some earth between his fingers, a gesture as natural to a farmer as kicking the tires of a car to a teenager. It was a warm and special time for us . . . we seven children trekking alongside him as he explained what was going to be planted where and when. We stopped and said a prayer together each time he blessed a field. A powerful memory of a little event.

Jewish families have a veritable treasure of family religious customs, some of them beautifully dramatized in *Fiddler on the Roof* and present in other Jewish drama and literature. A colleague of mine who is a family specialist in a large Reformed Jewish synagogue often shows *Fiddler* to young couples and asks them to discuss the family faith traditions portrayed in the film with an eye toward implementing, adapting, and fostering them in modern family life. She disclosed to me the paradox she found: Many young couples really want to establish a traditional Jewish dimension in their family life but are hesitant to do so because they find that their parents, having themselves dropped these customs and rituals, might feel betrayed if their children initiate the customs in their own blossoming families. My colleague's challenge to them is to use this opportunity to bring the generations together through the renewal of religious meaning and heritage in the family.

And that's what experiencing faith is about in strong families. Families who have a rich legacy of faith-ritualizing and symbolism need not worry quite so much about the religious curricula provided their young children.

In healthy families, then, we can observe the ties that bind, not just hear about them. We have much to learn from families who have preserved a sense of tradition and celebrating in their homes.

The hallmarks of families who have developed a strong sense of family in which rituals and traditions abound are as follows:
1. The family treasures its legends and characters.
2. The family has a person and/or place that serves as locus.
3. The family makes a conscious effort to gather as a people.
4. The family views itself as a link between the past and the future.
5. The family honors its elders and welcomes its babies.
6. The family cherishes its traditions and rituals.

11
Sharing Religion

Trait 10: The healthy family has a shared religious core.

Train up a child in a way he should go—and walk there yourself
once in a while.

— Josh Billings

How important is an agreed-upon religious belief, a denominational
core, to the health of the family? Much more important than our
culture likes to assume, it appears. My survey respondents ranked "a
shared religious core" tenth in the list of fifty-six possible healthy family traits.

"But how many of your respondents were related to church in some
way?" asked a teacher of psychology, who was uncomfortable with
how high this trait was ranked. Although there were more church-
related respondents than family counselors or health professionals, it's
important to note that percentages of respondents selecting this trait
didn't vary significantly among the five professions. For instance, as
high a percentage of psychologists chose it as did church or school professionals.

And this finding is consistent with other studies on families. The
author of the National Study of Family Strengths points out that
there is evidence linking a strong correlation between religion and
success and happiness in all phases of individual life, not just family
life. It's easy to see that a shared religious core can provide both a
base of common values and a sense of purpose in today's family.
Although the National Study of Family Strengths doesn't indicate
that a belief in God is a prerequisite for family happiness or mean
that nonreligious families will fail to be happy, the study clearly
implies that religion can be a major source of strength for families as
for individuals.[1]

George Gallup, Jr., addressed the same ideas in a seminar which
discussed a 1979 Gallup survey of parents. The survey disclosed that 63
percent of responding parents who labeled their upbringing as "very

religious" said religion had greatly strengthened family relationships, and 62 percent felt that religion was helping their children a "great deal" in regard to problems in their lives. Gallup said, "Looking to the future, we can gain encouragement from survey findings which show that homes where religion plays a central role today are producing persons whose future homes in turn will in all likelihood be religiously oriented."[2]

Prominent psychologists such as Harvard's Dr. Robert Coles tell us that children and families today are seeking a deeper explanation to life than the behavioral sciences can give. "Many of the kids I've looked at don't have faith," said Dr. Coles. "That's the problem. They don't have religious faith or the kind of human faith that can be called natural religion as St. Augustine talks about it. They have lost everything except preoccupation with themselves, and this is enhanced every day by the way they are brought up. Child psychiatrists are brought into this because parents are endlessly concerned with what stage of growing up their children are going through. This is faith centered on one's self. It isn't faith in God, in some transcendent belief."[3]

Faith in some transcendent belief is obviously a significant characteristic in establishing a healthy family in the eyes of my survey respondents, who work closely with many families. Not only was "a shared religious core" chosen for the top fifteen, but two other traits directly related to the professed role of the institutional church were prioritized there as well: "a sense of right and wrong" and "values service to others." Taken together these three traits directly relating to religious belief are found in the top dozen of fifty-six possibles. This is impressive enough to cause us to pause and look closely at the relationship between religious belief and family health, but we have even additional reasons to do so when we add those traits which are implicit to religious ideals and which placed very high on the list: respect, trust, responsibility, and sense of family.

Which religion isn't important. What is important is that a religious core of some kind be present in today's family. Secular society and the behavioral sciences simply haven't been able to help today's families find a deep enough meaning to life to teach right from wrong, to develop trust, to teach respect for others, to foster a strong sense of family, or to value service to others. Rather, we often find the reverse:

books and seminars encouraging people to find a meaning to life in themselves or in some therapy; movies and media that scoff at morality, trust, and respect; success-oriented prophets who devalue service to others.

Dr. Coles holds that parents have given up their moral authority in this nation, surrendered it to the experts. "Unfortunately, a lot of people have lost their faith in God and in our own institutions, our history, our nation." He asks, "What do they have faith in?" and then answers his own question. "They have faith in themselves and what they cultivate in themselves. They have faith in these various newspaper columnists who give advice *ad nauseum*. They have faith in fads and in secular authority."[4]

Many of the families with whom I work do know what they believe, and most of them externalize this belief in a wider faith community, a church, a synagogue, or a group of some sort which shares the belief. I also find great religious strength in healthy families that are headed by partners who have different religious faiths. Contrary to what the church denominations teach about the divisiveness of the ecumenical marriage, I found couples in healthy families who have emphasized the positives in each faith in order to enrich family faith, not destroy it. They don't focus on the negatives or on what divides them but rather on what unites them. For example, in union of Catholic and Protestant, the Catholic partner may supply a strong sacramental sense to the marriage while the Protestant partner contributes a better understanding of Scripture.

I am not implying here that two faiths are better for a marriage or that two faiths won't harm a marriage, only that the healthier families seem to be able to use the two faiths as a source of support. I didn't study unhealthy families. Perhaps a great many are unhealthy because of two-faith marriages. I am inclined to believe, though, that problems in the faith-and-family area stem more from lack of faith in the family than from too many faiths in the family.

Unfortunately, it's become a somewhat common practice for a young couple in which each partner has a faith different from the other to decide to drop the active practice of any faith rather than reconciling and merging two faiths. Maybe the negative attitudes of many churches themselves toward the two-faith marriage is what makes couples decide to avoid a conflict by dropping both. But whatever reason there is for making such a decision, the decision is unfortunate. Religion, then, becomes the unmentionable dimension in a union in which all other areas of life are shared: sexuality, intimacy, support, work, children, and the future.

It is a great tragedy that we allowed religion to become a subject to be taught rather than a belief to be ritualized in our daily lives. Faith is rarely passed on because of nuances in doctrine and theology. It is passed on because of the difference it makes in daily life. The best way of experiencing this difference is through traditions and rituals, as I discussed in the previous chapter. Sadly, however, both family and churches have allowed this rich dimension of life to languish in favor of more classes, more learning, more Sunday school lessons, more parochial schools, and more emphasis on institutionalized faith.

Often families come to us in the family center because one or more of their adolescent children have "given up" the faith. In listening to the parents, we realize the kids never really had a faith. They had a religious education. When we politely quiz the parents about the faith customs and faith life at home, we discover they have little or none. They perform their duty—they see to it that they support the local religious education system and that their children attend classes, but they don't view themselves as primary faith models or givers.

Prominent theologian John Westerhoff, in his book *Will Our Children Have Faith?*, gives us valuable insight into what he calls the four levels of faith. He theorizes that in order for us to fully develop a meaningful faith of our own as adults, we must go through three prior levels of faith. The first is *the experiential level,* the level of childhood faith, which, alas, some adults never outgrow. At this level, children experience faith through those around them.[5]

This makes great sense and is of importance to the family that is trying to instill a sense of faith through ritual and tradition. It says simply that children cannot understand theology and doctrine at this age—we already know that but largely ignore it in our frenzy to produce more classes—but that they can understand God through faith experiences with those near and dear to them. This makes the family and the church community basic to the establishment of a person's faith. What the family does at home, the simplest of evening blessings, or a spontaneous prayer around a campfire, may be more basic to a life-long faith than memorized Bible verses or learning the Commandments at age seven. (Study after study has shown that the parents' and family faith behavior is germinal and basic to a person's eventual faith life.)

According to Westerhoff, if children live a rich faith life those first twelve years or so, they will move to a second level of faith when they begin adolescence, *the affiliative level,* in which they seek a sense of belonging. Here, again, we run into the enigma of the cults and the places like Jonestown, which speak to a deep yearning on the part of individuals to belong to a believing group, a faith-based group with its own set of personalized rituals and traditions. Once again, we must ask ourselves if those drawn to the cults are not really seeking a sense of family, complete with its traditions and value systems, which may have been missing in their own childhood families.

The third level of faith, *the searching level,* often coincides with the affiliative level, particularly among youth and young adults. The search is made with peers, the testing of the parents' belief is done in groups, and the doubting, examining, and studying of one's eventually accepted faith is best done with others.

An interesting study done in 1976 by The Boys Town Center for the Study of Youth Development in conjunction with The Catholic University of America found that the first period of serious religious questioning has moved from the college years down to ages thirteen to sixteen, one reason why there's so much tension today in homes with strong religious beliefs.[6] The family that has built a solid level of experiential faith through a network of simple customs and faith behavior is far better able to weather the faith doubts of adolescents than those whose homes are religiously sterile.

I should stress here, of course, that some adults spend their entire lives searching for a faith of their own. Others go through life owning their parents' faith—and their faith remains on the experiential level. (These are the parents whose own faith is often shaken when their elderly parents die, forcing them to become responsible for their own internalized beliefs. They no longer have to go to church or practice a faith to please their parents.) For still others, faith is a happy church community, one that meets their social needs and some of their spiritual needs but makes no demands upon them. Not really interested in spiritual growth, they remain happily on an affiliative level of faith their whole lifetime.

The final level, *the owned faith,* is the prize. It is that toward which we grope. Many healthy families admit that they still search occasionally but that they constantly are moving toward a stronger owned faith, both as individuals and as a family. I found three recurring hallmarks in the family with a shared religious core.

1. Faith in God plays a foundational role in daily family life.

Sometimes this faith is spoken and taught, sometimes not. Some families make a point of bringing God overtly into daily lives, others choose to do it simply and quietly. Whatever their style, though, healthy families have a belief in something or someone larger than themselves.

Hurting families display their lack of shared belief in interesting ways. One is by idolizing the family itself. According to theologian Stuart C. Haskins, whenever the claims of family take precedence over the claims of God, the family becomes an idol. He said, "Jesus believes that the family is like everything else in life. It is always in danger of being worshiped as a false God."

There are families among us today who idolize the family to the point that they expect the impossible from themselves. This kind of family has a built-in failure device. It believes that if it just tries hard enough and focuses hard enough on itself and its needs, it will have no problems. If a child doesn't turn out the way the parents have led themselves to believe he or she should and would, they see themselves as failures. They have set themselves up as gods in their family. It is their fault if their children are not social leaders or at the top of the academic ladder. It's even their fault if the children get sick. Dr. Haskins says, "The family is one of life's great blessings. It is good but it is not God, and we need to know that in the deepest part of our beings if family is to be what God intends it to be."[7]

A second way in which families show a lack of central belief, or religious core, lies in their constant search for a meaning to life. In an extensive survey conducted in 1980 by the Lutheran Church in America, a three-million-member denomination, only 41 percent of its laity say they have found an answer to the question of purpose of life. Another 42 percent say they believe there must be an answer, although they don't know what it is.[8] Surveys like this indicate that church membership itself doesn't automatically guarantee a religious core, and church personnel are the first to say so. "We have a number of families who join expecting us to furnish a quick faith," a pastor told me. "They may have a problem they can't handle or sense something is missing in their life, so they join a church. If we don't give them an answer within a year, they're off to another church."

The Lutheran survey takes on even more significance when coupled with a poll conducted by the Research Analysis Corporation of Boston, which discovered that schools outranked religion as the institution with the greatest influence on children. Nearly a third of those responding said organized religion had little or no impact on their children. Several pieces of incidental information coming out of this survey may be of some significance to the family faith issue. An astounding 82 percent of those polled in the greater Boston area had changed residences in the previous five years, and 42 percent expected to move in the following five years. A majority also expected that their children would have premarital sexual relations.[9]

These unrelated bits of information point to a reality in modern family life: Families are losing their rootedness in neighborhood stability, traditional standards of morality, and church dependence. They must seek for rootedness elsewhere. Those families who look within themselves to a shared religious core seem to find a strength that, supported by a church affiliation, gives stability to their individual and family lives. As Alfred North Whitehead notes, religion is tending to degenerate into a decent formula to embellish a comfortable life. This is true for many families. Healthier families look for something deeper.

"Although I cannot subscribe to many of my patients' beliefs," wrote a family physician, "it's obvious that the stronger families have a strong religious affiliation."

"Healthy families still seem to embody some of the old traits," wrote a principal of a junior high. "The kids from these families come to school, go to church, and care about others."

"There's an inescapable core of strength that religious faith gives families," added a social worker. "We notice most its absence in families that seem to have little sense of purpose and in which individuals spend their lives seeking one—but not together."

A marriage and family counselor intern wrote, "Let me focus on just one item: 'religious core.' The healthy families I know have a reverence for life and communicate that with their whole being. This is true no matter what specific religion they adhere to or even if they do not."

Couples who enter marriage without any strong belief system on the part of either partner often speak about the changes wrought on their family when together they adopt one. I interviewed a former Congregationalist and former Catholic who were attracted to and became part of Mormonism because of its emphasis on family. "We found a lot more than God," said the husband. "We found our family."

Those who experience marriage enrichment weekends often say the same thing. In an article in *Marriage and Family Living,* a Catholic couple, Robert and Diane Nicholson, share their experience of prayer several years after developing couple prayer on a Marriage Encounter weekend. "Sometimes our prayer as a couple takes the form of praise. Perhaps we see a beautiful sunset, or a breathtaking view; maybe it's the smile of one of our children or a sudden, breathcatching awareness of the beauty of sexual intimacy. At the moment that we experience the majesty of God and thank him for his ongoing creation, quietly in our hearts or verbally together, we are engaged in the prayer of praise as a couple."[10]

Is this too idealistic? I asked various family professionals whom I interviewed for this book. Their answers were mixed as to the necessity of a visible and lively faith operating in a family, but they generally agreed that in the good family there exists a core or foundation of shared belief that sustains the family and gives it hope. When a *U.S. Catholic* interviewer asked where this faith came from, Dr. Robert Coles replied, "It comes from their parents—a sense of humility and awe in the face of the world's mysteries. It comes from church and from going to church and understanding that one worships something outside one's self and one's desires. It comes from a sense of mystery in this world that is cultivated at home and in schools. It comes from experiences with teachers who have the good sense to tell students they don't have all the answers, that this is a puzzling world which we must bow down to as well as try to take over and manipulate. There are communities and families and children who are willing to get down on their knees and pray to God, who look beyond one's self."[11]

Dr. Coles' words are echoed by Dr. Stanley Hauerwas: "What, briefly, do I think religious faith has to do with all this? It is not, I think, the usual assumption that the Judeo-Christian tradition keeps people on the straight and narrow sexual path necessary to sustain marriage. On the contrary, my classes on marriage are begun with the observation that both Christianity and marriage teach us that life is not about 'happiness.' Rather, the Hebrew-Christian tradition helps sustain the virtue of hope in a world which rarely provides evidence that such hope is justified. There may be a secular analogue to such hope, but for those of us who identify with Judaism or Christianity, our continued formation of families is witness to our belief that the falseness of this world is finally bounded by a more profound truth."[12]

2. A religious core strengthens the family support system.

In an earlier chapter I discussed the healthy family as an affirming support system for its members. Readers may recall that my respondents prioritized the trait "affirms and supports" to be second in a list of over fifty healthy-family traits. While a family can surely be supportive without a shared religious core, there's some evidence that in many families a family faith serves as a source, or well-spring, for mutual support. "It gives people strength to love one another—it lets them focus on others or their parents or their brothers and sisters as well as on themselves" is the way one pastoral counselor put it.

A high school student who completed my survey explained it another way when he said, "We get along easier because we all believe in God." His statement is seconded by the earlier mentioned 1981 Gallup Youth Survey on parental love and support for today's youth. Researchers found that those youth who went to church every week, that is, whose family placed a high value on religion, had parents more likely to help with their homework, praise them for something they did, hug and kiss them, tell them they were loved, and talk with them about their activities during the day. All of these extremely affirming and supportive kinds of actions build more intimate relationships in families.

Roman Catholic Bishop Walter F. Sullivan of Richmond, in a letter to his people on marriage and family life, wrote, "Studies indicate that there is a direct relationship between the quality of marital relationships and one's attitude toward religion. Through liturgical celebrations, educational programs, and special events, parishes can constantly reinforce the family and encourage couples to grow in loving, supportive, and life-fulfilling relationships."[13]

If a church focuses on some of these ideas, it's obvious that families are going to be stronger for it. When organized religion addresses some of these terribly basic traits in a practical way, with programs of mutual support, with like-to-like ministries in which families help one another through difficult times involving drugs, alienation, and other pressures, the church as symbol of religious belief can be foundational in helping families to be healthy.

This new focus on families in today's churches helps explain a little the relationship between a shared religious core and a healthy family. Gone in most churches is the old practice of using the family as a favorite whipping boy. Rather, we're finding the local church as a major source of family support today in a society that hasn't recognized its responsibility to furnish that support.

3. *The parents feel a strong responsibility for passing on the faith, but they do so in positive and meaningful ways.*

"It doesn't matter if you don't understand your Bible," a father told his now-prominent daughter sixty years ago when she was a girl. "Them are good words and that's good enough." Today's healthier parents don't accept that kind of reasoning. They want to pass on their beliefs, but they realize the futility of merely sending their children to a church school to learn something that never gets reinforced and lived out at home.

"It was so easy for our parents and grandparents," sighed a mother in one of my seminars. "All they had to do was tell us what to believe and we believed. My children ask why and point out contradictions and refuse to go to youth group. Sometimes I think it would be better just to let them go and find a faith when they need one as an adult."

It *is* tempting for today's parents to throw in the catechism. Often it seems to them as if they can't win in their effort to furnish a shared faith. With the plethora of religious movements, cults, and human potential groups beckoning to young people and promising instant nirvana, parents find it confusing and even impossible to pass on mainline beliefs to their young people. Many give up even trying.

But good parents realize they are already sharing a religious core in daily family life whether they are teaching lessons or making a point of being religious. In her *How to Help Your Child Have a Spiritual Life,* Annette Hollander, M.D., surveyed parents on their religious attitudes and practices today. "People asked, when they heard about my research, 'What have you found?' What I found, and wished to share in this book," she said, "was reassurance that in fact we *have* been attending to our children's spiritual development even if we do not give sermons every night and a home Sunday school on weekends. As we have heard again and again, from psychologists, educators, and people remembering their own childhoods, it is not *verbal* lessons that impress children. We have already been teaching by the example of our love and respect, our compassion, our wisdom, and even our struggle with negative states when we feel all these virtues have disappeared."[14]

Parents in strong families recognize the difference between breaking convention and breaking commandments. They distinguish between sin and mischief in children. They are more concerned with the faith level of their adolescent than whether he or she is in the pew with the family on Sunday. They sense the wisdom in Evelyn Kaye's words in her book about the two-faith family, *Crosscurrents*: "The love, respect, and concern for each child as an individual, which are essentials of parenting, depend little on the intricacies of religious belief and much more on the personal character of the parents and those intangible attributes of kindness, warmth, common sense, discipline, awareness, and a ready sense of humor."[15]

What these parents try to pass on is a modicum of religious learning and a maximum of themselves as models of people formed and guided by a belief. As models, they participate in those religious traditions so cherished by children and so important to Westerhoff's first level of faith, the experiential level: religious customs, storytelling, songs, prayer, all interwoven into the daily fabric of family life in a comfortable and uncomplicated way. I have visited many families who live this way, and they are a pleasure to be around because of their lack of spiritual inhibition.

Probably the healthy family's most crucial test in this area of passing on its faith comes when a maturing child rejects that faith. The healthy family accepts deviation from the family faith. It doesn't drum out those young people who are attracted to other expressions of faith and religion. Although the parents may feel a great deal of pain when this happens, they do not blame themselves if their children don't embrace the faith they have offered.

How parents react during this crucial testing time can be decisive in the young person's eventual faith stance. Gail Sheehy, in her incisive book *Passages,* gives us some insight into what's going on inside young people at this time of pull and pulling away. In speaking of people in their twenties, she writes, "Buoyed by powerful illusions and belief in the power of the will, we commonly insist in our twenties that what we have chosen to do is the one true course in life. Our backs go up at the merest hint that we are like our parents, that two decades of parental training might be reflected in our current actions and attitudes. 'Not me,' is the motto. 'I'm different.' "[16]

Thus, there is a predictable age for religious searching, a looking into other belief systems, a trying out of Woodstock-like religious experiences. During this period, some parents—those who rigidly hold themselves responsible for their grown children's life-long faith—increase the pressure on their youth to return to the fold of family faith and instead succeed in driving them further away. The children feel constricted, guilty, and traitorous. To alleviate their discomfort, they distance themselves even further away from their original church affiliation by immersing themselves even more in a new belief or movement.

Parents who have a better understanding of young people's need to test the options and test their belief structure don't react so personally and so fearfully. They listen to their children explain the attraction of est, or Freud, or finding God through selling flowers—all the while remaining strong faith models themselves. Probably an extremely significant factor in the outcome of a young person's foray into other faiths is just that: whether or not the parents remain committed to their faith during the child's searching period.

If the parents' faith is shattered by this turn of events, the child is not likely to return to his or her natal faith. If it hasn't sustained his parents, why should it sustain anyone else? If the parents become defensive and call on guilt as a means to bring the child back into the fold, the child either returns reluctantly and angrily or is driven further away. Neither alternative is desirable.

If, however, the parents remain unshaken in their faith as each child matures, tests, and either embraces or sheds the family religious belief, the model of faith the parents supply is an invaluable gift for the lifetimes of the children.

Passing on the faith is not an easy job today, but parents in healthier families are not abandoning the attempt. They recognize the foolishness of relying solely on such old reliables as Sunday school, Bible verses, and confirmation to furnish a lifelong religious belief. They also recognize the differences among children and the different kinds of approaches needed within the family. Perhaps one father summed it up best for those striving to share a strong religious core within their family when he said, "Without it, nothing else makes much sense—all the work and the worry—what's the point if you don't believe in anything?"

The hallmarks, again, of the family with a shared religious core are as follows:

1. Faith in God plays a foundational role in daily family life.
2. A religious core strengthens the family support system.
3. The parents feel a strong responsibility for passing on the faith, but they do so in positive and meaningful ways.

12
Respecting Privacy

Trait 11: The healthy family respects the privacy of one another.

I have at last got the little room I have wanted so long, and am
very happy about it. It does me good to be alone. . . .
— Louisa May Alcott

"Some people really respect others' privacy," quipped a comedian.
"They never open their mail unless it's marked *personal*." There's little
as tempting to a parent as those areas of their children's and spouse's
lives marked personal. Yet, healthy families resist the temptation. My
professional respondents situated "the healthy family respects the
privacy of one another" eleventh in a list of fifty-six possible healthy-
family traits.

But privacy in the healthy family means more than just not snoop-
ing. It means the right to have a private being in addition to functioning as a family being. That's what family life is all about: the nurturing of a dependent infant into an adult who is his or her own person.
It also includes the merging of two adults who, simultaneously,
become a couple and remain individuals. Neither of these tasks are
accomplished with a birth or marriage ceremony; they are a family
process requiring years, tears, and love. Dr. Jerry M. Lewis in his
words on the healthy family states boldly that the family has two
main tasks: to preserve the sanity of the parents (or to help each
parent's personality grow and mature) and to produce kids who can
emotionally leave home, kids who can come to love someone else
more than they love their parents.[1]

Sounds easy, but it is in this chapter that we confront
the intimidating word "discipline." Because of the preoccupation that American parents have with discipline, most parenting
books begin with some treatment of the subject of how to discipline, how to win in child-parent relationships, how to change
one another. It's interesting to realize, however, that when other
positive traits are evident in the family, discipline becomes less an
issue. It's the family without trust that needs more discipline, the
family without respect that needs more authority, the family
without affirmation and support that needs more rules and

order. In sum, the family that is short on healthy traits is long on discipline.

In recent years, however, we have eulogized rigid families. "How well behaved their children are," we say. And we've talked about permissiveness as the parental sin. Permissive parents give rise to delinquent children—so goes the popular version. But we need to remember that permissive doesn't mean overly permissive, or indulgent. Indulgent parents shower their children with goods and confusion when their children really want rules and order in their lives. These parents give them freedom and disorder before they can handle it, and the results are predictable.

Permissive, on the other hand, means permission—permission to become themselves, to peel away the layers and find out who they really are and how they relate to one another and the world. When this sort of permission is denied children—or wives and husbands—they become robots or conformists, and they require years and years in their adult lives in order to emerge as the persons they were designed to be. Often they leave disastrous marriages and crumbled families in their wake.

Healthy families realize they must allow and even encourage family members to be who they are at a given age. They expect members to change as they move from age to age. "At four, he was a delight," said a mother. "At six, a pest; at eight, another delight; at eleven, a rock fan; at thirteen, a stranger; and at seventeen, he reentered the family circle as a full-grown delight." She spoke to a process experienced by many families—significant physiological change taking place in a number of members simultaneously.

One mother explained that all her family's members were trying to find themselves, only in different places. Another pointed out the stresses that can occur when puberty and menopause collide within the family. "My daughters and I were in transition together," she said, "and it was very, very difficult. But we respected each other's right to be difficult, and that helped."

John Capel, a counseling director for the federal government's Health and Human Services department, says, "A parent's task during the teenage years is to change from a manager to a co-worker and a friend." He insists that parents have to be willing to let go, to stand back, and to place primary responsibility on the youth for solving his or her own problems.[2] His ideas were echoed in the many comments I heard from family professionals while I was doing research for this book. They described a sense of privacy within the family as the right to be alone, to be different, to change and mature, and to leave.

This doesn't mean parents have the right to abandon responsibility, to throw in the car keys and capitulate to their children's wants. "You are the parent until the day you die," psychologist Howard Halpern warns. "But giving and nurturing has to be redefined. Parents who are giving and nurturing in terms appropriate to when their children were young, who continue that same kind of nurturing, are not doing themselves and their child any good. After the very early years, the parents' job is to help their children become separate, strong, and independent individuals."[3]

How do good parents and healthy families accomplish this? I have pinpointed five hallmarks of the family that respects the privacy of one another.

1. The family looks forward to the teen and separating years.

It is entirely acceptable in our society for us to love our toddlers and hate our teenagers. But the reverse is unacceptable. If a mother mentions at a dinner party that she loves her teenagers and can't stand her toddlers, she'll soon have a wide circle of disbelievers around her. What will most astonish everyone is her claim to love teenagers. We aren't expected to love our teens, and if we do, we certainly aren't expected to say so. I call this our just-wait-until-they're-teenagers mentality, and it's destructive to parenting because it becomes a self-fulfilling prophecy. Young couples who love their children and enjoy being parents dread the day when the first child turns thirteen because family life is sure to fall apart. That's what they've been told by older parents who, seeing them enjoy some little family pleasure, warn them "Enjoy them now—life will be miserable later on." They hear that message from their own parents, who talk a lot about how difficult young people are today. Finally, they hear it constantly from the culture, which paints adolescence in many hues, all negative: distrustful, destructive, immoral, uncaring, and disrespectful.

Families who argue against this attitude find themselves swimming against a terrific current. (I've even had parents wonder to me if their family life is normal because they haven't had teenage problems.) The all-teenagers-are-horrid myth is just that—a myth—because it isn't always true. Teens don't always destroy happy family life. They can be exceedingly pleasant to have around. Parents whose youth have left the nest often speak about the absence of enthusiasm, humor, and zest they experienced in the home after their children departed. They miss the companionship found in interacting with emerging young adults. They truly enjoyed the pleasures involved in watching the unfolding of an individual. "I was so fearful all the time, looking for trouble and reasons to distrust that I didn't stop to enjoy my teenagers," confessed a mother. "Then, when they were gone, family life seemed so boring and empty."

After listening to hundreds of parents express feelings similar to these, I'm convinced that the so-called "empty nest syndrome" is as much a loss of adolescent enthusiasm around the house as it is a parental need to be needed. The healthy family doesn't accept as truth the idea that adolescence means misery in the family circle. It looks forward to these years as the ones in which the real persons their children are begin to emerge. It feels an excitement about this emergence that's missing in other families, almost a what-have-we-here attitude that includes suspense ("What will she be like tomorrow?"), pleasure, and pride. The family watches with intense interest as each young person begins the separation process from the family to become his or her own being.

One couple, giving testimony to their reverence for this process, described their feelings about adolescence to their skeptical peers in a parenting group. They said, "It's exciting to live with teens because you never know what's going to happen next. All those things you've done and said when they were little start to show up in different forms in different children. It's like looking for the prize in the Crackerjacks box."

Parents from healthy families tend to look forward to the going-away years as part of the flow of family life, not so much a getting-rid-of-them sort of relief (although that is part of it), but more the won't-it-be-satisfying-to-know-them-as-adults kind of anticipation. "It's so good to hear from our kids and how they're doing," said a father. "It's like still being part of their lives, only we're out there with them instead of having them back here with us."

2. The family moves from a base of parental rules to one of mutually negotiated rules.

On my survey, I presented these two possible healthy-family traits: "operates from a base of parental rules" and "operates from a base of mutually negotiated rules." Survey respondents placed "mutually negotiated rules" high on their prioritized list (in fact, this trait was number sixteen on their list). However, a great number of those respondents who selected these items wrote personal comments on their surveys that indicated their discomfort in choosing one, the other, or neither of them. Almost to a person, the comments spoke about the need for a process of gradual relinquishment of parental rules (authority) and movement toward mutually negotiated rules in the family. A family counselor wrote, "Both are necessary in the healthy family. Babies can't mutually negotiate rules, and adolescents can't live with parental authority."

A school counselor wrote, "If more parents recognized the need to move from one to another, much of their fear of the high school years would vanish."

A colleague of hers from another state wrote a long essay on these two traits, part of which follows: "These two are not exclusive but related to one another. Elementary teachers embody the 'parental rule' with their many necessary regulations, for example. But junior high teachers begin allowing young adolescents the right and subsequent responsibility to establish classroom and school rules, while college teachers have few school rules, believing rightfully that students should be responsible enough to assume those themselves. When there's a breakdown in teacher/class relationship, it's usually because elementary teachers give up their parental authority and the children become confused and disorderly, or that high school teachers refuse to give up their authority and their students become resentful and disorderly."

Dr. Sally Ryan, researcher at Catholic University in Washington, D.C., recently concluded a study on children's social and moral rule systems and found a distinct difference among age groups in regard to how children deal with their parental relationships. By the time teenagers are sixteen and seventeen, according to Dr. Ryan, they were moving to another level of maturity in those relationships and talked more about understanding parents and seeing them as people, not just parents. "The developmental shift," she explained, "is from viewing the parent-child relationship as one of authority and unilateral respect to viewing it as a relationship more like friendship with peers—one involving equality and mutual respect."[4]

I've discovered from my interviews with families that this mutual respect has to be truly mutual in order to work, and that's why it breaks down in many families. It isn't mutual. Either it's a case of one parent sensing the need to bring adolescents in on the process of making decisions that control their lives while the other parent wants to remain in rigid control, or it's a case of both parents wanting to continue exercising the same kind of control they've always had while emerging young adults want to be allowed in on making decisions that touch on their daily lives. This dichotomy produces the familiar tension that brings to fruition the just-wait-until-they're-teenagers prophecy.

Many parents lack confidence in their authority to be parents. Pastoral counselor Norman Calloway teaches that any permission given should be given willingly, easily, and eagerly—not reluctantly. "Anything you are going to do for your child in the last place," he explains, "do in the first place. Added coaxing by them does not increase the importance of their request but demeans them in achieving it. All of the following are ways of saying yes: 'Sure,' 'Of course,' 'Why not?' and 'I'm for that' or, conversely, with a deep sigh, 'Well . . . all right.' "

One of the most serious mistakes parents make is to try to modify a child's behavior that doesn't really interfere with their own lives. Does a child wearing sloppy clothing, having a dirty room, or dawdling over meals have a concrete effect on a parent? Teens will be quite willing to modify behavior when they see that it interferes with someone else's life; but if the objectionable behavior has little direct effect on parents, the teenager's response is likely to be hostility and rebellion.

Those families in which members show mutual respect for one another are usually families that operate with mutually negotiated rules. Since healthy families do possess such mutual respect among members, they tend to manage mutual negotiation with a fair amount of ease. "I guess we never gave much thought to it," said one dad. "As our kids got older, we asked them what a fair curfew was, and they came up with reasonable ones. Once in a while they'd break out, but we expected that. Rules were just never a big part of our lives once they got past ten or eleven."

3. The family does not dole out respect according to age, sex, or any other criterion.

I am particularly distressed when I witness situations in which adults overlook children, acting almost as if the children didn't exist. Adult clerks in stores, for instance, sometimes "don't see" them and just automatically pass them over to serve the next adult. They talk *about* children rather than *to* them when the children are in groups. They treat them verbally and nonverbally in ways that they would never use with adults: "Get over there" instead of "Please stay in line." They automatically presume evil intentions rather than childish mischief.

Unfortunately, some families show the same kind of disrespect to their younger children; they treat the younger children as lesser citizens who have to reach puberty in order to get respect. Physical abuse is the ultimate extreme of this kind of parenting, but there are psychological abuses that can be destructive as well. When children are all lumped together and denied individuality in the family, their right to privacy is abolished. They are part of a nameless group in which if one misbehaves, all are punished or if one fails in school, everyone's homework time is increased.

In other families, girls are considered the more deserving of respect—or, more likely in our culture, boys are. One sex is taught to wait on the other, make way for them, give up their room to them, and generally accept the idea that one is more deserving of respect than the other. Again, this invades the individual's privacy, disallowing him or her the right to be a full person, proud of personal sexuality.

In still other families, those who are holding jobs are granted a right to privacy over those who aren't or can't. Or those who are compliant or religious or studious are granted privacy privileges over those who are rebellious, irreligious, or unachieving. Privacy is held out as a reward for good behavior.

Paradoxically, personal respect is also denied to individuals living in families in which a single rule is rigidly decreed for all and faithfully adhered to. "You know the rule . . ." and "Our family rule is . . ." are their bywords. They're completely inflexible in their refusal to consider individuality. What is touted as dedication to fairness is really the reverse because it destroys every individual's right to become his or her private self. I know parents who feel they must bring a gift home for every child if they buy something for one or who think they must disallow a child an opportunity to accept an invitation to go on a short vacation with another family because the others aren't going. This

kind of rigidity discloses the parents' lack of confidence in their own
authority. It invests parental power in the rule rather than in the
parents themselves.

Dr. Jerry M. Lewis found that his healthy families didn't set rigid
rules that apply to every child regardless of age. "These families treat
their children differently," he said, "according to their stage of
development. There's no old adage, 'Everybody gets treated the
same.' "[5]

Children, like adults, prefer to be treated individually rather than by
rigid rules that go by ages, and that's probably why this trait of
mutually negotiated rule-setting rated as high as it did on my survey.

4. The family respects fads, friends, confidences, room privacy, and time to be alone.

This hallmark seems so obvious that it hardly deserves any space,
but I find it lacking in enough families to justify at least a quick discussion. Once, for a group of parents, I suggested a list of ten commandments for parents of emerging teens, and one of the commandments
was this: Thou shalt listen to a new music, learn a new language, and
accept new cultural forms. The parents who were listening didn't like it
at all. They argued heatedly that parents had a right to determine
lengths of skirts, hair, and jeans. Eventually we compromised. No, I
admitted, I would not allow my daughter to go to junior high classes in
a halter top. Yes, I agreed, parents are the ultimate arbiters of good
taste. But, I stressed, there's a lot of difference between standards and
fads. Standards are guidelines to acceptable taste in clothing,
language, and behavior. Fads are fashions and behavior peculiar to an
age and era. Length of hair is a fad, not a moral issue. Saddle shoes
and poodle skirts were the fads of my era, and tee-shirts with messages
and jogging shoes are the fads of the present era.

Most tragic is the child who is forced to relive his or her parents'
childhood by dressing like the mother or father did thirty years ago.
Once in scouting we had a boy in this situation. He came dressed in
gabardine trousers and brown oxfords, and he wore a crew cut amid a
sea of jeans and sneakers. The poor boy looked so alien that it was
easy to guess how he must have been feeling.

Whenever I work with parents who want their children to dress as
they did when they were that age, I encourage them to volunteer for

the library or playground just to get a feel for how children today dress and act. A mother who absolutely refused to allow her children to use slang at home was much more amenable to it after spending time on field trips with her children's peers. "I just didn't realize that was their language," she confessed. Another couple who refused to allow a television in their home discovered, after they agreed to participate in a Great Books program at school, how left out their children must have been feeling during the many discussions at school which centered on last night's programs.

We may not always like the current fads, but denying them to our young people tells them they don't have a right to their own era. Denying them their own peer identity is a blatant invasion of privacy. They have a right to look and act like the teens of their day, within the standards of good taste, of course. Remember the mini-skirt controversies during the sixties? A grandmother told me how her daughter, now a mother of two, was recently thumbing through her old yearbook and said, "How could you let me wear skirts that short? They were obscene." The grandmother said she wanted to put her head in her arms and cry because she remembered all too well the heated arguments they had had fifteen years earlier over the length of her skirts. On the subject of peer dress, parents in healthy families realize that it's an intrusion in their adolescent's life for them to look and sound like their adolescent. And just as teens have a right to their culture, so do parents have a right to theirs. They should be able to own their own era, their own music, and their own language without apology. In good families, both parents and youngsters are permitted to be part of their respective peer groups without ridicule or nagging.

Friends are a big problem in many families, especially if the friends seem to have values contrary to the family's value system. More likely, though, it's less a question of values and more that to the parents the friends represent the loss of strict parental control over their young, who are being drawn to the peer group instead of to themselves. Instead of viewing this as natural, many parents react by finding something wrong with every friend or by intruding into the youth's friendships to the extent that they drive both their child and his or her friends from the family circle. This is surely one of the most self-destructive things that parents can do because of the pain and loss that result from it.

Healthy families allow friendships to flourish as long as they aren't destructive to their children. These parents don't pry or try to get into their children's relationships with friends, a practice particularly odious to adolescents. "I wish my mother would bug out," said a disgusted teen. "She wants to be a friend of my friends, but she doesn't know how. She acts like she's sixteen, and nobody likes it."

Sometimes parents fail to respect children's confidences. When a child is feeling down or in need and opens up himself or herself to the parents, the child is extremely vulnerable. If a parent takes advantage of this vulnerability to share the confidence with others, to bring it up for amusement, or to throw back in the young person's face later on, the parent isn't respecting the privacy in which his or her child shared the confidence. Children soon learn not to share confidences with such parents.

One particularly sensitive area of confidentiality arises when a child is involved in an incident that's very embarrassing to him or her (almost everyone has one such childhood incident). It can be a minor run-in with the law, the discovery of a girlie magazine under a mattress, some shoplifting from the family wallet, or whatever. In the healthy family, these are dealt with between parents and the individual without sharing anything about them with the siblings. A father said bluntly, "It isn't any of the others' business. If the offender wants to tell on himself, that's his decision, but parents never should."

Invading the privacy of a child's or partner's room, desk, or other personal space is reprehensible and not allowed in healthy families unless there's an exceptionally good cause such as parents having to find a friend's phone number for an emergency. "I don't even want to check out my sons' room," admitted one mother. "Ever since I found a lizard they were trying to dry and stuff as a trophy, I've stayed out." That's probably one very good reason for not prying, but there are better ones, such as respect for others' privacy. Each of us needs our own personal space where we can put and keep things that won't be disrupted or discovered by those who share our lives. In families in which this isn't respected, members are forced to hide confidential items in order to protect them. One high school girl stored her letters at her friend's home because her mother couldn't resist the temptation to read them. "There's nothing in them," complained the girl, "but they're mine."

Finally, the healthy family respects every member's need for private time. In my research for this book, I came upon some refreshing new research which suggests that solitude plays an important role in adolescent life; and if the adolescent is granted certain amounts of it, the young person is much more pleasant to have around. In a study by University of Chicago psychoiogists Reed Larson and Mihaly Csikszentmihalyi in which seventy-five volunteer students from high schools were tested in regard to the amount of time they spent alone and the effect of that private time on their moods, the researchers found that the young people spent more than a quarter of their waking hours by themselves and reported that after such time alone, they felt in better spirits when later they were with others.

During their solitude, these adolescents enjoyed heightened attention spans and powers of concentration, admitting they were better able to concentrate on their hobbies or homework when alone. They also reported that they were quite conscious of self at these times. The important finding to me, though, is their admission that *after being by themselves they returned to the company of their families or friends feeling more alert, stronger, more involved, and more cheerful.*[6] This is pretty strong support for those who believe that all of us are better off for having some spaces in our togetherness, an idea Kahlil Gibran promoted. Yet, these spaces are absent in many families, some of whom try hard to be good families but don't allow individuals their much-needed privacy. Psychologist Dr. Howard Halpern observed, "Some children live at home with parents and they get along very well as separate people. Problems occur when parents become too intrusive and the kids don't apply common courtesy."[7]

Parents, too, need time alone. "I've got to get away" can be a nearly hysterical cry for some parents, particularly single parents who must spend large amounts of unrelieved time with their children. "There's no time for me," complained one such mother. "Every minute of my day I focus on someone else's needs: my boss's, my kids', their teachers', the paper boy's . . . if only I could have just a little 'me' time."

All these areas—respect for fads, friends, confidences, room privacy, and time to be alone—come under the heading of respect for privacy. Healthy families try hard, in whatever circumstances they live, to show respect in every one of these areas. One teen put it in an interesting way when she said, "We don't have to go somewhere to be alone. We can be alone right in our own home."

5. The family lets go.

It lets go not just physically but emotionally as well. A hallmark of the good family is that it constantly focuses on these questions: How will this possible solution or this proposed rule help our children, not to be better sons or daughters, but to live happier, more fulfilled adult lives? Do we love our children enough to let them make the mistakes and do the growing they need to do in order to leave us? Many problems in families arise out of the parents' inability to let go.

Psychologist Howard Halpern, who has written two excellent books on this subject, *Cutting Loose* and *No Strings Attached*, stresses that if a child is reluctant to leave home—an increasingly common modern phenomenon—the parents have to foster the leavetaking. Dr. Halpern, a former president of The American Academy of Psychotherapists, suggests that parents first check out whether they have encouraged the situation to exist. Do they inwardly want to maintain the situation because they don't want to face their own loneliness, or because they are afraid that without the children around there is no real basis for their relationship as a couple? Halpern says that if the parents really want to correct the situation, they must serve notice that the young adult's at-home living can't go on forever. "You must reassure the child that you are not rejecting him but are helping to launch him," says Halpern. "Is there ever a time when we can stop parenting?" Halpern was asked. "There is no sudden cutoff point," he replied; "just a slow developmental process to a point when your services are not truly needed." Like others in his field, Halpern advises encouraging a child's independence at each fork in the road to adulthood rather than waiting until adulthood arrives before granting independence.[8]

The hallmarks of the family that respects the privacy of one another are as follows:

1. The family looks forward to the teen and separating years.
2. The family moves from a base of parental rules to one of mutually negotiated rules.
3. The family does not dole out respect according to age, sex, or any other criterion.
4. The family respects fads, friends, confidences, room privacy, and time to be alone.
5. The family lets go.

13
Valuing Service

Trait 12: The healthy family values service to others.

Love does not consist in gazing at each other but in looking
together in the same direction.
— Antoine De Saint-Exupéry

Ranked twelfth on the list of healthy-family traits was "values service
to others." I am encouraged not only by this trait's placement in the
top fifteen traits but also by the much lower ranking given "values high
income" and "values the work ethic." It tells me that the professionals
evidently perceive idealism and service as more conducive to health in
today's family than are our traditional cultural goals of power and acquisition. In fact, the only other value in this general category that
came even close was "values work satisfaction."

A pediatrician explained it rather thoughtfully. "Some families get
tied into competition—they try to rear children who are the biggest,
the best, the prettiest, the smartest, and all that. Others don't care
about that. They want kids who care about others and who give a little
of themselves. It makes a big difference in the families we see," he said.
"How?" I asked.

He paused, "We're seeing signs of stress in very young children today. Their parents want them to be winners. It explodes later on when
they're in college in the form of stress, drugs, maybe aimlessness for
ten years. You wouldn't believe the number of stressful families we get
in here every week." "And the others?" I probed. "Those who don't try
to win, those who care about others . . . how do you describe them?"

"Well, they're more relaxed about life, and they seem to like it more.
They live a simpler life—their kids aren't so preppy, not so many
alligator shirts and all that—but they have something else. For want of
a better phrase, I'd call it contentment." What he called "contentment"
goes under many names in the literature that describes these families:
simplicity-seeking, detached, altruistic, caring, empathetic, and even
counter-culture. In contrast to those families are those who are addicted to the pursuit of wealth. Author Philip Slater says that the cost
of this addiction to wealth lies not so much in greed but in the isolation
this pursuit generates. Goods and money can separate us from others.

When we identify ourselves according to our possessions, power, and success, we are asking others to judge us by what we have, not what we are.

Let's consider two types of families. One entertains to show off its acquisitions. The perfectly staged dinner begins with a tour of what's new in the home. The meal is a tribute to a mother's gourmet skills. The silver and linen and china (all of which match) are a tribute to the successful, breadwinning father and/or mother. Conversation swirls around the kids' honors, some of which may be displayed prominently.

Another family entertains primarily to share of itself. It likes people and likes to extend itself beyond its own walls to others. If there happens to be something new in the home, little mention is made of it. Dinner isn't for showing off but for creating a relaxed atmosphere of sharing. It might consist of soup eaten out of bowls which don't match, but that's not even noticed. What is noticed is that this family obviously enjoys sharing what it has with others.

Rosemary Haughton, noted theologian and mother of a large family, says, "Contrary to popular belief, the best marriages and the happiest families don't happen because people concentrate, first of all, on the quality of their relationships, but rather when the couple and then the family as a whole is involved in something bigger."[1] And many families today are making a real effort to go beyond themselves, to enlarge their focus to include the people around them in their communities and world. Indeed, in parent-education classes we're finding more and more families who, successful as they are in a consumer sense, want help in finding simpler values, in paring down their life-styles. This deep desire many families feel to simplify their life is quite apart from guilt for consuming so much while others are in need (though they may feel that, too). This desire speaks more to a human need for *freedom from things*.

Dr. David Thomas, noted family theologian, calls it "enlightened simplicity." He says, "What families need today, not only to survive as good Christians and Jews, but to make it in an economy which doesn't seem bent on insuring family survival, is the virtue of enlightened simplicity. It's a pioneer's virtue which values freedom—freedom that is indeed made possible by good tools, good nourishment, and transportation. But the pioneer uses these possessions to get somewhere. They are not themselves the destination. And if it becomes necessary to drop some of the goods along the way, so be it. Nothing is lost—at least, nothing that matters."[2]

Every family seems to develop its own sense of purpose. For some families in our nation—indeed most, I would say—success and pursuit of the good life is the primary purpose. As I indicated earlier, other family purposes include such things as keeping the family farm alive, supporting a particular cause or religion, promoting a future Olympic star, moving to Australia, or enjoying lots of recreation. My survey respondents, you recall, named mutual support and affirmation as the family purpose most often evident in the healthy families they experience.

Some families have service to others as their primary family purpose. However, an increasing number of families are beginning to consider service to others as an important secondary purpose. These families bear out Rosemary Haughton's words about families looking beyond themselves and their own individual family life. They don't want to be counted in the group that models what youth specialist Michael Warren calls "middle-age hedonism." They don't want to live for themselves only—to collect more goods or to buy bigger homes—because they sense that doing so isn't going to make them healthier and happier.

Paring down a life-style is difficult to do in a consumer-oriented society in which new goods are offered as a panacea to happiness. Robert Frost said, "Americans are like a rich father who wishes he knew how to give his sons the hardships that made him rich." We're like that father: We know our family life might be better off with less, but we enjoy good food, nice things, and the security and confidence that money brings.

One way in which healthy families respond to this contradiction is by extending themselves to others through offering hospitality, sharing goods, and doing a variety of caring acts. Paul Claudel, existentialist philosopher, noted, "Youth is not made for pleasure but for heroism."

A fascinating research study done by Marian Radke Yarrow, chief of the Laboratory of Developmental Psychology at the National Institute of Mental Health, found that children are not as basically hedonistic and selfish as Freud and others would have us believe. In describing the study in *Psychology Today* (June 1979), author Maya Pines writes, "Yarrow's study shows that, regardless of culture, the *capacity* for empathy and altruism exists at a remarkably early age. Many people resist the idea, she has found. 'They quote Freud and other authorities and insist it can't be true.' Some may feel guilty because, if selfishness is not the norm, they have no excuse for their own lack of altruism or that of their children."

Yarrow notes that different societies clearly produce different levels of caring and altruism. "Unfortunately, there is an expectation in our culture that young children are not able to behave altruistically," says Yarrow. "That expectation is not only wrong, but also probably harmful, since it may be self-fulfilling."[3]

I and other people who work with families frequently find this to be so. Families who presume that members can and will be caring toward others become those healthy families who value service to others. They are the ones who show up in times of community need. They are there to drive the elderly, to help families clean up after floods and fire, to offer solace and food to the grief-stricken, to help old eyes prepare income tax returns, to help families move, to spring young mothers from household child care. They are just generally aware of others' needs and welfare.

As the children from these families grow up, they tend to be quite caring and responsible persons as a result of their family experiences. They don't understand narcissism in other children. "My children just couldn't understand their cousins at all," said a mother from a caring family. "Each had his own room and toys which he wouldn't share with anyone, not even with our children, their houseguests. They were so protective and grasping. Finally, it got so embarrassing we had to take our kids to the pool to avoid the unpleasantness. 'Those poor little kids,' ours said, 'all those toys and nobody to play with.' "

This mother was speaking to a phenomenon noted by Maya Pines in the Yarrow study: "After the age of seven, children are exposed to many other influences besides their parents'. Perhaps a change in their environment, particularly an extreme change, would radically alter the children's behavior. But other things being equal, the child's willingness to give aid and sympathy—or to disregard other people's troubles—seems firmly established by the age of two or three."[4]

When I interviewed counselors, family physicians, pastoral staffs, and educators about this trait—service to others—I asked them for characteristics of families who value this trait. Here are the ones I have identified as a result of interviews and reading.

1. The family is basically empathetic and altruistic.

Sometimes the family's altruism arises from a religious base, sometimes not. Likewise, their altruism doesn't seem to have much to do with their income. Some of the most generous families, according to professionals, are lower-income families. "I believe that if any generalization is to be made," said a YMCA director, who deals directly with families in all income categories, "it would have to be in favor of the low-income families. They seem to be able to feel what it's like to be in need of something. Anyway, they're the first to help in what little way they can."

Maya Pines would say these low-income families have an ability to be involved in others' pain, and she notes that many parents are not comfortable in fostering this trait. "Obviously, many parents don't want their children to be over-burdened with altruism," she says. "It's too inconvenient and too demanding. . . . Parents generally want their children to be able to compete successfully—and how can they compete if they're altruists?"

She describes the behavior of the mothers in the study who were involved in what the researchers call bystander events, that is, who were present when other people were in need or in pain. Some rare mothers empathized with their toddlers' distress at another's suffering, but most attempted to soothe their children instead, to try to offset any discomfort that the suffering of others was inflicting on their children. Pines wrote, "What children learn from incidents in which they are innocent bystanders to other people's suffering is less clear. Far from conveying intense messages about children's responsibilities in such times, the mothers tend to ignore the suffering or—more frequently—to reassure their children and tell them not to worry about it!"[5]

Should we wonder why many children don't show any concern for others? These children have grown up in families who spend more time soothing and rationalizing away the discomfort they feel when disturbing human needs are presented to them daily via newspapers, television, and real-life experiences than they do in making any attempt to alleviate those needs. Indeed, some families even get angry at those in need because they mar their happiness by jarring their consciences. They denounce as lazy those people without housing or employment. Blaming the victim becomes a family response, while in other, healthier families an altruistic response is taught.

Jean Vanier, author of *Be Not Afraid* and a person who has spent his life working with the mentally handicapped, says, "We are afraid of the person in misery because he constitutes a danger to us. His poverty and his needs challenge our riches. So we raise the barriers to keep him from our sight."

On a child's level, serving others can be as simple as befriending the ostracized student on the playground at recess. "Some children are always alert to situations in which other classmates are hurting," said a teacher. "They help them pick up papers and crayons that have fallen in all directions. If they see a student eating alone in the lunchroom, they take their trays over and sit with him. They offset the indignity of being a poor athlete or being last chosen by saying something friendly. They're just more understanding and compassionate than other children," she said.

A school principal mentioned that caring children in the classroom are the ones who won't let a classmate be scolded or blamed unjustly. "They will speak up for him even if it means teacher disapproval," she said.

"Is this innate or learned?" I asked.

"I don't know. But I do know this . . . it runs in families."

2. The family serves others in concrete ways.

One of the major differences between the caring family and the nonresponsive family is that the latter often talks about the need for serving while the former actually serves. This difference between families (and persons) in church and volunteer groups can often be clearly seen. In those groups, there's often a certain type of adult who calls for day care centers for others, for example, or who demands to know why the church or school isn't better meeting the needs of the single parent but who later, when the project becomes a reality, isn't around to do the work.

Typical of this kind of person is a woman who was on the parish council of a church which I served as a consultant on family. She was the parish representative to the diocesan outreach program, a program designed to point out the needs of the larger community and to engage the altruism of the various churches in the area. She grasped on one need after another, haranguing others to volunteer, sometimes even badgering them into serving although they were already overcommitted. But she herself never showed up to drive for Meals on Wheels or to help clean and cook in a home in which there was illness. She always had a solid excuse and an apology. "I wish I could have been there, but . . ." became kind of a joke among other outreach members. I wondered what kind of message this woman was giving her family. Surely it had to be that talking about human needs is enough and doing something about them goes beyond expectations.

Her attitude really isn't so rare. We find it on a national level when statesmen and other national leaders cry out for altruism but look out for their own constituents' welfare first. This all-talk-and-no-action stance has become so acceptable, in fact, that in 1981 we were the only country in the United Nations to vote against an infant-formula code designed to protect babies against aggressive promoters of breast-milk substitutes in developing countries, where overdilution of formula and lack of sanitary conditions causes thousands of deaths annually from "baby bottle disease." Voting for the protective code were 181 nations, and the sole vote against it was cast by the United States. We talk a lot to other nations about the need for sanitation, better health care, and the like, even sending young Peace-Corps trained volunteers to help, but when the time came for us to serve with our vote, we weren't there. Free enterprise had won out, just as surely as tending personal interests wins in some families over any involvement in the pain of others.

Families that are committed to serving others engage in a wide variety of activities. Some join voluntary organizations, such as those dedicated to fighting leukemia, to developing youth programs, or to carrying out special community or church projects. In our community an Interfaith Task Force, which accepts no federal monies, involves thousands of families yearly. The Task Force sponsors an annual walk for funds that finds many entire families walking twenty kilometers to earn money for the food bank, which is open to all people in need. More than food is offered through this service, though. I observed a cooking class for low-income mothers, which was taught by volunteers. Across the hall was a beginning sewing class also taught by volunteers. Other volunteers collect fabric and even old sewing machines from their friends and neighbors to give to women in these families because their subsistence budgets can't provide these things. Still other volunteers help these families deal with alcoholism, child abuse, employment, housing, and the myriad of other problems familiar to low-income families.

Some families help single-parent families by offering to absorb their children into after-school car pools or by inviting them to go along on such things as fishing expeditions. Single parents often find it difficult to arrange for child care during before- and after-school hours. Who wants to babysit at 7:00 A.M.? In some neighborhoods there are families who will open their homes to the children of a mother who has to leave for work at 7:00 but whose children's school doors don't open until 8:30.

I know families who make dozens of sandwiches for Sunday lunch for the elderly who live in rundown inner city hotels and would otherwise have no lunch because all the restaurants they can afford are closed on that day. Other families help with emergency housing during blizzards, floods, occurrences of child abuse. Some families open their doors to youths who are thrown out of their own homes or to hard-to-place foster children or to babies awaiting adoption.

College students who come from caring families are likely to be the ones who help others adjust to homesickness and the myriad of new living skills called for in college life. I asked a large group of college deans if there was any noticeable difference in the adjustment of students who appeared to be empathetic persons as opposed to those who seemed more self-centered, and they were unanimous in agreement that altruistic students adjust more easily because their focus is on others, not on themselves. "Many of these students are accustomed to volunteering and serving others," one dean pointed out. "They did it at home and in their churches and high schools, so it's natural for them to keep an empathetic antenna out for students who are having difficulty adjusting. This seems to take their mind off their own homesickness and loneliness."

An Atlanta college student started a study club to help some friends with their exam preparations. She was used to getting good marks and they were not. Watching their improvement gave her a real boost, and when they did well in their tests, they experienced a new respect for themselves.

In 1981, a new kind of parenting workshop was held in St. Louis.

Fifty parents and family life leaders from various Christian denominations spent four days focusing on combating both materialism and sex-role stereotyping in the family, developing healthy racial attitudes in children, integrating social action and prayer in the family, and seeking nonviolent responses to conflict. The conference proposed the establishment of an ecumenical network of parents who would sponsor and promote parenting-for-peace-and-justice workshops. This new emphasis on helping families become more caring and giving them skills in serving others is sure to have an impact on both the families themselves and on our larger world family. (For more information contact National Parenting for Peace and Justice Network, 2913 Locust, St. Louis, Missouri 63101; $10 membership fee annually.)

3. The family seeks to simplify its life-style.

When several years ago I wrote a column on simple family living, I was astonished at the response. In it, I had mentioned Alternatives, a group which publishes materials on simplifying family life, and later the staff there told me that as a result of that column alone, they had experienced a daily increase of twenty-five to thirty-five orders for their *Alternatives Catalogue.* Alternatives describes itself as "a not-for-profit organization to help persons interested in voluntary simplicity take charge of their own lives." Its original publication, *The Alternative Celebrations Catalogue,* remains the best manual of its type for families who want to live more simply than our culture prescribes. This book is a kind of encyclopedia of ideas and actions for simpler celebrations; it contains concrete suggestions on how to change, tips on farming, self-help craft groups for making gift items, and ideas for human welfare projects. I have seen families experience new pleasures as a result of the ideas in this book and others like it. (Their address is Alternatives, 1124 Main St., Forest Park, Georgia 30050.)

"When I suggested we try making our Christmas cards, everybody just laughed," said a mother, "but we so enjoyed the quiet time together that this gave us that the very ones who laughed were the first to say, 'Can we make our valentines, too?' "

Families who begin to take charge of their own lives have great need of a support group made up of other families with whom they can gather for holidays and at other times to enjoy simple activities with one another. Here is where our institutions such as church, school, and voluntary organizations can play a valuable role. By their offering an old-fashioned family dance for which the cost is little and the interaction is high instead of offering an evening at the local dinner playhouse for which the cost is astronomical and the interaction little, they provide a real service to families trying to pare down. By sponsoring a family craft fair instead of badgering families to buy tickets for a professional ball game, they foster pleasure and community at a small cost. Families today are so often beleaguered to buy tickets for functions that steal family time from them as well as family funds. Why not substitute some group fun, such as a family hayride or skating party?

It seems as though every youth organization that exists thinks it has to sell tee-shirts with the group's logo. Instead, why not an invitation to bring an old shirt, a bag, a banner, or a pillowcase and have an evening of silkscreening the logo onto those items? It's more fun and considerably less expensive. Every group also seems to sponsor some money-raising activity to which parents must first contribute goods and then repurchase those goods under some other form. Either that, or the children go door-to-door selling. Before automatically doing those things, why not scrutinize the need for the money in the first place? Is it really necessary, or is it being raised to spend on what are really nonessentials? Can't the teams play without professional uniforms and cartons of paraphernalia unknown to earlier sandlot teams? Until parents begin to ask these questions, assumed needs and costs will continue to escalate along with the budget.

David Thomas writes, "To decide what is needed for family survival and what is superfluous is not easy. There is no pat formula which applies to each and every family. Yet, each family should examine its priorities. It should consider the manner in which it uses and values resources and possessions. Indeed, families should ask themselves: 'Does our "stuff," perhaps, *own us*?' "[6]

Healthy families don't allow that to happen. In an article on satisfied parents, Ellen Peck, after interviewing dozens of parents, wrote, "Of course, becoming a parent makes every mother and father, not just successful ones, take a fresh look at former values, goals, and activities. One difference we consistently noted, however, between satisfied and dissatisfied parents was the sense of clear family priority held by the successful mothers and fathers. These parents by no means devoted themselves *exclusively* to their children; but, when the chips were down, or when a clear conflict of interest (typically, job vs. family) occurred, they had not a moment's hesitation as to where their first allegiance was.

"As a result, the successful parents we spoke with were generally *not* at the very top of their career field—but this didn't seem to bother them, given the value they attached to their children and to their own role as parents."[7]

This is in startling contrast to the old ideal that in order to be the most successful parents possible, the parents should be at the top of their career fields so that they could give their families a better neighborhood, more goods, and the higher prestige that success and income assure. There's more in this move to pare down life-style than just Judeo-Christian teaching and guilt over failing to respond to others' needs. There's also a return to the value of seeking joy in people and in giving rather than in buying, taking, and consuming.

Healthier families seem to understand and hold this value. They aren't as concerned with status symbols as others are. Their definition of success differs significantly from families who view success in terms of possessions and power. These families often turn down promotions if they mean less time together or moving to another part of the country away from their extended families. They get more pleasure in giving things than in accumulating them. They keep Christmas and other holidays in perspective, refusing to capitulate to what television tells people they must have in order to enjoy a holiday. They live out those words of Albert Schweitzer: "Whatever you have received more than others in the way of health, in talents, in ability, in success, in a pleasant childhood, in harmonious conditions of home life—all this you must not take to yourself as a matter of course. You must pay the price for it. You must render in return an unusually great sacrifice of your life for other life."

4. The family is generously hospitable.

One way in which strong families tend to give of themselves is by sharing their homes and themselves with others. They are hospitable. They offer themselves, their tables, and their homes freely and warmly without making others feel indebted. A certain attitude comes through this family that indicates it's a joy to be hospitable. "We never think of it as giving," said a couple thoughtfully. "We just enjoy it when people spend time in our home and share with us."

Dr. Jerry M. Lewis speaks of the relationship that healthy families have with the outside world. He says that although the family styles among those families in his study differed, with some outgoing and some retiring, all the healthy families were tremendously affiliative. Upon meeting strangers, the healthy families saw the strangers as good and hopeful people while more unhealthy families saw the strangers as dangerous and oppositional. "Families who relate warmly to strangers usually promote friendliness in return," said Dr. Lewis, "thereby documenting their belief that people are friendly and good."[8]

David Thomas claims that every act of hospitality is a risk but that love of others invites us to be hospitable. "We must open the doors of our life to others, trusting that neither ourselves nor our goods will be destroyed," he said.[9] Sometimes when I travel I am housed with families that show an astounding level of hospitality. Even very small children in those families make a natural effort to be warm and hospitable. Once when a four-year-old girl learned that I had a daughter at home, she brought me a toy animal so that I wouldn't miss my daughter too much. My then fifteen-year-old daughter found that hilarious, but I found it touching.

In order to be hospitable, of course, one needs to be free enough from other problems to be open to others. If one has serious money and marital worries, it's difficult to be welcoming to others. But families who are comfortable with themselves like to have others enjoy their largesse.

5. The family keeps its volunteerism under control.

Dr. James Dobson, in his popular *Focus on the Family* series, calls overcommitment the number one marriage killer.[10] Sometimes, in an attempt to be a giving family, a parent will take on so much volunteer activity that his or her spouse and children resent it. The healthier families seem to gravitate toward a single sphere of activity, such as the handicapped or the elderly or the heart fund, but not all three, and they seem to choose an altruistic activity in which they can all share, as opposed to activities individually pursued.

Let's look at Marriage Encounter as an example of an activity that can lead to both excessive volunteerism and healthy volunteerism. Once a couple in Marriage Encounter agrees to be a leader couple, they can be asked to give great amounts of time, and many couples have found their children resentful of the time thus taken away from them. These couples discover that helping other marriages can be damaging to their own family. (Therapist Clayton Barbeau calls this losing of one's children while being engrossed in church work *the apostolic orphan syndrome.*) On the other hand, Marriage Encounter couples who become involved in a reasonable way often find their family lives enriched by their going out of themselves to serve others. Their families become more hospitable and caring.

The overcommitted-volunteer situation is particularly prevalent in church work because church work is such a respectable outlet. In addition, people who engage in it are highly praised and appreciated, so adults can sometimes more easily get their strokes from such involvement than they can at home. Many parents admit they enjoy getting away from the hassles of home where they are generally unappreciated to serve at church where they are.

Anthropologist Gregory Bateson's observation that there is always an optimum value beyond which anything is toxic is apt here. I thought of his comment when I read about the father of eight in a nearby suburb who coached softball the same summer that several of his children played on teams. The family attended more than 200 ballgames. That's over two a day. That's toxic, and he admitted it. "We got burned out on that," he said simply.

Commitment to others can become toxic if it isn't kept in check or if it's engaged in for the wrong reasons, such as escaping from priority responsibilities or assuaging guilt. But if commitment to others springs from genuine generosity and is kept under control in the family, it enriches all three: individuals, family, and the society in which we live.

The family that values service to others, then, usually bears these hallmarks:

1. The family is basically empathetic and altruistic.
2. The family serves others in concrete ways.
3. The family seeks to simplify its life-style.
4. The family is generously hospitable.
5. The family keeps its volunteerism under control.

14
Getting Help

Trait 15: The healthy family admits to and seeks help with problems.

Nobody's family can hang out the sign, "Nothing the matter here."

— Chinese proverb

It seems fitting that the final healthy-family trait we discuss has to do with finding solutions to problems in the family. It's fitting because it emphasizes the fact that healthy families aren't trouble-free families. We have the idea, probably instilled by the Waltons and the Ingalls, that good families are made up of sweet and passive and rather boring individuals who rarely have problems that can't be solved in an hour. That's about as wrong an idea as we can have. Healthy families probably have as many problems as less healthy families, but they have a different way of looking at them and solving them. "Good families deal squarely with direness," says Jane Howard in her book *Families*. The healthy family—whether single-parent or two-parent, whether rich or poor, whether urban or rural—has its share of family joys and family problems.

Nick Stinnett found the same thing in his Family Strengths Study—that healthy families confronted a wide variety of crises but that they tended to deal with these crises in similar ways. "We noticed two things," Stinnett says. "First, they had the ability to see something positive in every situation no matter how bad, and to focus on that aspect. Second, they joined together to face the crisis head-on."[1]

In this chapter, I want to discuss two hallmarks I have noticed in the family that looks at its problems with a nondefeatist attitude.

1. The family expects problems and considers them to be a normal part of family life.

Child psychologist Bruno Bettelheim tells the story of his grandmother who reared eleven children in Vienna. "One of them, I know now, was schizophrenic," he said. "I challenged her—being age four, precocious, and not very polite—what did she think of this son of hers who acted funny?"

"She said—and I translate roughly—'One out of eleven is a good batting average.' "

He added, "How come my 84-year-old grandmother with a seventh-grade education knew that not everyone can be perfect, and accepted with equanimity that one of her sons was crazy? It didn't hurt her, upset her, or shake her confidence in herself. Yet modern, well-educated parents who know all the laws of statistics cannot accept this . . . and they ruin their own life and their child's life by completely unreasonable expectations."[2]

Several years ago I was asked to write an in-depth article on why families were having fewer children today. Was it selfishness, selflessness, or neither? my editor asked. In my research, one thing became clear: Our society was operating on the myth that families in the past were all happy families. My research showed me that families of the past did, indeed, have marital tensions and schizophrenic children and a lot of other problems to boot. Why the real-life historical family became fictionalized to the contrary in recent decades is probably due to the fact that the good family of the past was taught to hide its problems.

Quite recently there's been an incredible cultural shift in regard to our expectations about family problems. The "good" family of yesterday claimed it had no problems; today's healthy family expects a variety of problems. The "good" family of the past never admitted any need for help; today's healthy family is healthy because it is able to admit to need and seek help in the early stages of a problem. In fact, it might even be said that the healthier the family today, the sooner it is likely to admit its weakness and work on it publicly, a direct turnaround from a couple of generations ago when the best families were problemless.

This legacy from the perfect family of the past has been costly to us because we feel as if we are failures if we have weaknesses and failures in our families. How did our ancestors cope with the problems we know they had? They coped in a way that modern parents can't and don't want to use. They wrote off the people owning the problem as different. Over and over in my research, I came upon the term *black sheep,* but this flock of sheep came in many forms. The spouse who was unfaithful or alcoholic was labeled "ne'er-do-well" by the community, thus sparing the family the responsibility and shame for his or her behavior. The depressed woman was "going through her time" or "in the change," and her family was thus alleviated from blaming itself for her problem. The teenage boy who wanted a slice of life bigger than his local community had to offer had "itchy feet," and if he decided to go off for a year or two to find himself, his parents weren't castigated for pushing him out. Always he was the problem, not they. Old people got "ornery," children who were heard as well as seen were dismissed as "young upstarts," and women who asked for more out of marriage than cooking and children were considered suspect. A child with an emotional or learning problem was "not quite right," and those who questioned approved mores and customs were "just plain crazy." In sum, the problems in the family of the past were attributed solely to the individual, never to the family.

Bettelheim says that in those days the family was spared the unpleasant truth "that the difficulties of children are caused by their parents. Such a truth should be carefully hidden from everybody, most of all the parents. It doesn't do them any good and it doesn't do the child any good," he says.[3]

Today's family professionals don't like to attribute problems in a family to either children or their parents but rather to the family system. Dr. Jerry M. Lewis explains that in the past he and his colleagues would treat troubled children in an institutional setting, and then when they seemed able to handle their difficulties, they would send them home, whereupon the children immediately assumed their old problems. That's when he and his staff began to study the families in order to find out what was going on inside them that was causing either the children or the adults to become less healthy individuals. Their study led Lewis to conclude that we cannot study individuals alone but have to look at them as part of a family system. In psychology, this is called *the family systems approach,* and from it, we have obtained much of what we know about both unhealthy and healthy families.[4]

"The family is a system like a spiderweb," says Dr. Charles Figley, director of the Family Research Institute at Purdue University. "When you pluck one strand, the entire web is affected."

2. The family develops problem-solving techniques.

In some of the healthy families I studied I found such problems as severely retarded children, unemployment, the working-mother dilemma, and chemical dependency. But what I heard from and about these families were references to the problems they had already solved.

Many had overcome severe drawbacks and remained healthy. They didn't have unreasonable expectations about achieving that fantasy family life where smiles and joy reign forever, but they did work hard at developing ways of dealing with problems instead of being destroyed by them.

Dr. Bruno Bettelheim states, "We expect everything to go smoothly and easily, and think that something is wrong if we run into a problem. That's the worst view a family can have."[5]

The first thing that healthy families do is to rid themselves of the erroneous idea that something is wrong if they run into difficulties. "With us, it started our first month of marriage when we went to buy a mattress," said one woman. "I wanted the softest one available, and my husband wanted to sleep on concrete. I thought, oh-oh, here goes the marriage." Then she divulged that she and her husband had been married for twenty-four years.

Other couples laugh when they hear about this kind of experience. They know that problems early in marriage provide the training ground for developing problem-solving techniques. They also know that the problems don't seem amusing at the time they're happening. I have heard story after story of the anguish families have felt over such things as a child's school behavior, some act of petty vandalism, or a move at the worst of all possible times. But when families look back at them, they are able to perceive how their handling of the given situation made them stronger (or weaker) and better able (or not) to face the next conflict.

According to Dr. Jerry M. Lewis, healthy families solve problems well. If a problem concerns the whole family, everyone gets a chance to speak. Someone in the group assesses whether there's a consensus or not, and if not, compromises are made. "Healthy families negotiate well," he said. "They recognize problems very well. Unhappy families never recognize some problems."[6]

Recognition of when a problem is a problem is a skill that strong families develop. This can be difficult for some parents. When is a child sick enough to see a professional? At what point does normal sibling rivalry become serious enough to seek help? How much spousal bickering over money is normal? How much should a woman expect in the way of communication with her husband? What to do about obvious differences in sexual expectations? Are our in-laws intruding too much? These are all potential family hazards; yet, few want to overreact.

A husband confided to me, "Sometimes when my wife and I have an argument, I try to figure out if I have to do any more than be aware of her feelings on this. Through many painful arguments of the past, I've learned that a lot of the time she doesn't want me to act on an issue but just know how she feels about it." This couple, married for twelve years, had begun to develop a method of dealing with problems—sorting out which needed specific response and which needed only awareness.

I have found that airing anxieties and worries in a group setting helps people decide whether something's a problem or not. Last year when I was asked to conduct a family stress management workshop for women who were at home full time, I began by asking each participant what she hoped to get out of the workshop. As each volunteered her hope, I wrote a phrase on the chalkboard. Soon smiles appeared as participants one after the other would say, "All of the above plus . . ." and they would add another concern to the list. Here are some of the items listed: techniques of prioritizing; what's normal stress; scheduling in the family; what to do with a husband at home; how to avoid feeling overwhelmed; wanting more quality time with spouse and children; can't relax with family; adjusting to staying home; trying to be a perfect mother; sharing child care with husband; feeling guilty all of the time for not getting things done; no time for self; how to resolve anger for being angry; and the "someday complex," as in "Someday, I'm going to . . . ." Half of my work was done by the time we compiled the list because the women began to perceive that what they regarded as personal problems were really the normal situations of women who are at home full time. *That* perception was the workshop's real value for the women, not any words that I said.

The healthy couple and family develop a skill for pegging potentially serious problems and tackling them early. "We saw some attitudes developing in our son when he was thirteen—attitudes toward work we didn't like—so we got together and decided to work on them," said a mother. "He didn't like it at the time, but he tells us now, at seventeen, that he's glad we faced it when we did because so many of his friends can't handle responsibility."

Another couple told of the pain they went through trying to

separate from their own parents after marriage. "We were both very close to our parents, and so we were delighted to move into a home equidistant from them. For the first five years, most of our problems involved one or the other set of parents. Finally, we looked at the situation and talked about what it was doing to our own relationship. We ultimately made a decision to move farther away from them. It meant more commuting for Bob and driving with the kids, but we were both ready to separate by then. Our parents thought we just wanted to live closer to the country. Now, whenever we have a problem with money or kids, we tell each other that if we got through our parent problems, we can get through anything."

A professor of psychology at the University of Texas, Dr. Blair Justice, says that effective families do not become overly concerned or stressed by unpleasant events. "They've learned to see events as annoying, inconvenient, or frustrating. They've learned to say, 'I don't like that' rather than 'I can't stand it' or 'This is awful and I can't live with it.' "[7]

Once healthy families determine that they do have a problem that needs solving, they bring out one of the many problem-solving tools they have developed over their years of being a family. Some families might talk together as a group. Others might find individual conferences work better for them.

My husband and I have found it most effective in our family to first approach a problem with the individual involved and then if the individual wants to discuss it with the larger family, that is his or her choice. For instance, let's say we think a child is exhibiting an inordinate amount of anger toward someone, something, or the whole world. My husband and I will talk it over first, exploring symptoms and guessing at causes. Then we'll talk with that person alone, inviting the child to share his or her feelings with us. Usually, but not always, this is successful. If, as is sometimes the case, the child directs some anger toward other members of the family or toward an unjust rule or expectation, we ask if he or she wants to bring it up with the entire family. About half the time, our children do want to. We tend to follow the same procedure with our adult problems. I can't recall how we started this procedure, but we reach for this tool because it seems to work for us.

Some families permit and even encourage loud shouting matches to take place, after which everyone settles down and compromises (much the way we handle things in the larger world). Other families never raise their voices. But these approaches have to do with family style, that's all. That the family uses some technique to solve its problems is what's important, not the style that accompanies the problem-solving techniques. Some families bring in grandparents and outsiders for input. Others head directly for a support group or some kind of professional help. Some see teachers, some pediatricians.

"I'd say about a third of my time is spent helping parents with nonmedical problems in the family," said a prominent Colorado pediatrician. And he tallied up a list of problems he had counseled families about during that week alone: nightmares, sibling fighting, teen depression, hyperactive behavior, admitted child abuse, and the effect of divorce.

Blair Justice claims that successful families are good problem-solvers because they come up with several options when trying to solve a problem. "They don't become locked into one way of responding, like anger, overeating, drinking, or violence," he says. "They recognize other approaches to problem-solving. They ignore, placate, assert, put up with, divert, negotiate," he says.

And, he adds, unlike maladjusted families who often depend on others to rescue them from a dilemma, the successful family possesses high initiative. "They are resourceful. They take action quickly to solve problems through trial and error methods."[8]

Here is another area in which churches, schools, and the helping professions can support families. If marriage partners come from families that didn't have tools for meeting normal family difficulties, we need to give these partners some help in the form of workshops and even private counseling on how to determine and deal with family failures and conflicts.

Children learn to solve problems by living in a family. If the family refuses to face problems or invokes silence or secrecy as a solution, a child is likely to follow that procedure in his or her personal life. Robert Amoury, a national authority on suicide, says, "Kids paint life with a heavy brush. You and I are used to failures—we've rolled with failures—kids are not that accustomed. We've had ten- and twelve-year-old children who have killed themselves because they failed arithmetic." This is a very good reason for making sure we teach children how to deal with failure, and we can learn lots from healthy families in this regard because their children do learn how to deal with it.[9]

Some problems, of course, cannot be solved within the family, and that's where support systems and professional help come in. Support system is a new phrase describing an old way in which people helped one another meet needs. I don't suppose the women who gathered around the wells to exchange conversation in biblical times called themselves a support system, but that's what they were. So are their modern counterparts: the coffee klatsch, the bowling team, or the divorce group. In recent years, I've witnessed groups of young mothers who meet to talk and receive support from one another for their daily living, groups of elderly persons, divorced persons, and parents of children with learning disabilities. Probably the earliest of modern support groups was Alcoholics Anonymous with its later offshoots for families of alcoholics, Al-Anon and Alateen. There are similar groups for abusive parents, grief-stricken parents, families of drug-addicted children, and unwed parents. Often these support groups come into being because the traditional institutions in society do not, and perhaps cannot, meet their needs in an increasingly complex society.

Healthy families aren't afraid to turn to support groups or professionals when they think they need them. They don't try to be self-supporting in all ways. They aren't afraid of stigmas and finger-pointing if they attend a group or seek some help. I find that it is much more difficult for families in small towns to seek this kind of support because of an ingrained attitude passed on from generation to generation that says good families don't need help. Today's good families believe just the opposite. They know they need help at times, and they aren't afraid or embarrassed to seek it out because their families mean more to them than their community status.

Dr. Bruno Bettelheim has given much of himself to families throughout the years, but perhaps one of his greatest gifts to us has been his assurance that good families have rough times. "A family doesn't prove itself through having a good time together," he reflects. "Your worst enemy will be willing to have a good time with you. You need your family when things are rough. Then children know what a parent is here for—to bind up the wounds, particularly the psychic ones. Realize that you can prove your worth to your mate or to your child only when things have gone wrong by sticking together and making things right. That's the best thing we can give our children, the hope and conviction that even when things get tough, we'll be able to cope."[10]

Healthy families evidence this because they experience failure, they cope, they enjoy, and they experience another failure. In their repetition of this cycle, they become healthier.

Again, the family that admits to and seeks help with problems has these hallmarks:

1. The family expects problems and considers them to be a normal part of family life.
2. The family develops problem-solving techniques.

A Final Word

No matter how many communes anybody invents, the family always creeps back.

— Margaret Mead

After eighteen months of research and writing on the healthy family, I felt reasonably secure in finishing this work and sending it off to my editor. The following day I heard of another family study in the formative stages, and the following week, yet another. I dug through my notes to find a comment by Kristin A. Moore, social scientist, who wrote, "Changes in our society are occurring so rapidly that the experts can't gather information on the family fast enough, put it on computer tape, and analyze it before things change again and the information is out of date."

Even though this is probably true, and given the fact that the structure of the family may change from generation to generation to meet new functions and adapt to cultural changes, I believe that the really enduring values of the family remain relatively constant. These values give meaning to the mystery of life and are perpetuated through regeneration.

Parents who may have experienced great heartache with their own children open their arms joyfully to grandchildren, the fruit of the very ones who have caused them such heartache. How to explain this? Rationally, we could predict that such parents would approach a newborn grandchild with fear and despair instead of joy and hope. But we know enough grandparents to realize that we're foolish to expect such a rational response. Some of the most bruised parents gaze upon a tiny grandchild with such love and hope that the joys and sorrows involved in creating and rearing a family begin to make eminent sense.

Regeneration places us in the continuum of history. It defines us as lovers, parents, and nurturers of generations to come. It gives meaning to Carl Sandburg's poetry: "A baby is God's opinion that the world should go on."

Thousands of families are making the world go on in positive and hopeful ways today. Instead of reaping our fears and censure, they deserve our gratitude and honor because as a people and as a nation, we inherit their strengths. Let others proclaim the death of the family, not I nor my colleagues who work with such families.

Healthy families are our greatest national resource. It is in them that we find our meaning, our strength, and our future. It is to them that we say thank you.

Notes

Chapter 1: Once Upon a Family
1. Ashley Montagu, "Can the Family Survive Free Love?" *Empire Magazine,* November 4, 1979.
2. Louise Cook, "Child-rearing Cost Can Top $100,000," Associated Press, *Chicago Tribune,* November 7, 1981.
3. Antoinette Bosco, "How Can Kid from Good Family Go Wrong," NC News Service, Washington, D.C., April, 1981.
4. "Nation's School Report," Capitol Publications, December 15, 1980.
5. Montagu, op. cit.
6. Patricia McCormack, "Survey of College Freshmen Reveals Raising Family Among Highest Goals," *The Denver Post,* February 4, 1981.
7. Eda LeShan, "The Family Is *NOT* Dead," *Woman's Day,* August 7, 1979.
8. Evelyn Kaye, *Crosscurrents: Children, Families, and Religion* (New York: Potter, 1980).

Chapter 2: The Search for Family Strengths
1. Dolores Curran, *Family: A Church Challenge for the '80s* (Minneapolis: Winston Press, 1980).
2. This research was conducted at the Timberlawn Psychiatric Research Foundation in Dallas, Texas, under the direction of Jerry M. Lewis, M.D. It is described in Lewis, J.M., Beavers, W.R., Gossett, J.T., and Phillips, V.A., *No Single Thread: Psychological Health in Family Systems* (New York: Brunner/Mazel, 1976), as well as in other technical publications.
3. Nick Stinnett, Barbara Chesser, and John DeFrain, *Building Family Strengths* (Lincoln, Neb.: University of Nebraska Press, 1979).
4. Kenneth Keniston and the Carnegie Council on Children, *All Our Children: The American Family Under Pressure* (New York: Harcourt Brace Jovanovich, 1977).
5. Pat Lewis, "Family Working Overtime to Survive," *Washington Star,* April 11, 1980.
6. Urie Bronfenbrenner, "Parent Education: It's Not Just for Parents," *Columbia University Teachers College Record,* May 1978.

Chapter 3: Communicating
1. David R. Mace, "Strictly Personal," *Marriage and Family Living,* September 1980.
2. Natalie Gittelson, "Women Who Feel Trapped in Lonely Marriages," *McCall's,* March 1981.
3. Bruno Manno, "Husbands and Wives: New Expectations, New Demands," *Marriage and Family Living,* June 1980.
4. Jerry M. Lewis, address delivered at The Ecumenical Center for Religion and Health, San Antonio, Texas, 1979.
5. Gittelson, op. cit.
6. Joan Anderson Wilkins, "A Four-week Program to Turn Off the Tube," *Family Circle,* April 22, 1980.
7. Ann McCarroll, "Getting to Know Children Requires Lots of Good Talk,"

Christian Science Monitor News Service. Reprinted in *The Denver Post,* June 19, 1980.
8. Paul F. Wilczak, "Listening as Ministry," *Marriage and Family Living,* March 1980.
9. Colin Dangaard, "Guilt Feelings Led to 'Kramer vs. Kramer' Success," *Rocky Mountain News,* March 20, 1979.
10. McCarroll, op. cit.
11. Ibid.
12. Jerry M. Lewis, address in San Antonio, Texas.
13. Mace, op. cit.
14. Gittelson, op. cit.
15. Stuart Covington, "The Impassive Father," *Marriage and Family Living,* June 1980.
16. Jerry M. Lewis, address in San Antonio, Texas.
17. Jayne L. Greene, "Adolescence: The Time of Life You Love to Hate," *The Sentinel,* Montgomery County, Md., March 11, 1981.
18. "Dolores Curran Talks with Parents," weekly column, Alt Publishing, Green Bay, Wisc., May 4, 1981.
19. Jerry M. Lewis, address in San Antonio, Texas.
20. "The Traditional Family Will Make a Comeback," interview with Dr. Lee Salk, *U.S. News and World Report,* June 16, 1980.
21. Kim Upton, "Food Goals Include Cheap, Fast and Good," *The Denver Post,* December 3, 1980.
22. "Culturally Speaking: A Tasty Tale," *WeightWatchers Magazine,* February 1981.
23. Ibid.

Chapter 4: Affirming and Supporting
1. David R. Mace, "Strictly Personal: Expressing Affection in Families," *Marriage and Family Living,* November 1980.
2. Dorothy Corkille Briggs, *Your Child's Self-Esteem: The Key to His Life* (New York: Doubleday, 1970).
3. Urie Bronfenbrenner, "The American Family," tape: The Harvard Seminar Series (Cambridge: Harvard University Press, 1981).
4. Fredelle Maynard, "The Holistic Explosion," *Woman's Day,* May 13, 1980.
5. Neil Solomon, "Family Doctor," *Pittsburgh Press,* April 3, 1981.
6. Michael Cavanagh, "How to Choose a Spouse Wisely," *Catholic Update* (Cincinnati: St. Anthony Messenger Press, 1980).
7. Marilyn Elias, "The Human Angle," Crown Syndicate Inc., 1980.
8. Jeannie Ramseir, "Aspen Family Happily Accepts Extraordinary Lifestyle," *The Denver Post,* April 8, 1981.
9. Joan B. Lindroth, "The Tools of Happiness," *Marriage and Family Living,* April 1981.
10. Jerry M. Lewis, address in San Antonio, Texas.
11. George Gallup, Jr., "Gallup Youth Survey," Associated Press, 1979.

12. Linda Sanford Tschirhart, "How to Make Your Children Feel Good About Themselves," *Family Circle,* November 18, 1980.
13. Don Hamachek, *Encounters with Self* (New York: Holt, Rinehart & Winston, 1978).
14. Maureen Early, "Want Your Child to Be a Winner?" *The Denver Post,* February 15, 1981.
15. Ralph Keyes, *Is There Life After High School?* (New York: Warner, 1977).

Chapter 5: Respecting Others
1. Thomas E. Legere, "The Albert Einsteins Are Seldom Well-Adjusted," *The Brooklyn Tablet,* September 1981.
2. Michael de Courcy Hinds, "Parenthood Can Be a Real Culture Shock," *The Denver Post,* May 17, 1981.
3. Sanford, op. cit.
4. Dolores Curran, *Who, Me Teach My Child Religion?* (Minneapolis: Winston Press, 1982).
5. "Dear Abby," daily column by Abigail Van Buren, *The Denver Post,* 1981.
6. "At Wit's End," daily column by Erma Bombeck, circa 1975.
7. Rudolph Dreikurs, *Children: the Challenge* (New York: Dutton, 1964).
8. Wayne W. Dyer, "Questions Women Ask Me," *Family Circle,* April 3, 1979.

Chapter 6: Trusting
1. Erik Erikson, *Childhood and Society* (New York: Norton, 1963).
2. Ibid.
3. Montagu, op. cit.
4. Erikson, op. cit.
5. Stanley Hauerwas, "The Moral Meaning of the Family," *Commonweal,* August, 1980. For a more extended treatment, see *A Community of Character* by Dr. Hauerwas, Notre Dame Press, 1981.
6. Jerry M. Lewis, address in San Antonio, Texas.
7. Hauerwas, op. cit.
8. Bombeck, op. cit.
9. Bob Thomas, "Tragedy Lurks for Children of the Stars," *Rocky Mountain News,* November 5, 1980.

Chapter 7: Sharing Time
1. Stinnett, et al, op. cit.
2. Louis T. Grant, "Fast Folk," *Harpers,* October 1979.
3. Lyn Balster Liontos and Demetri Liontos, "Couple Life," *The Denver Post,* January 18, 1981.
4. Diane Rothbard Margolis, *The Managers: Corporate Life in America* (New York: Morrow, 1979).
5. Robert S. Weiss, "The American Family," tape: The Harvard Seminar Series (Cambridge: Harvard University Press, 1981).
6. Keniston, op. cit.

7. Norman Cousins, *Anatomy of an Illness* (New York: Norton, 1979).
8. Elias, op. cit.
9. Stinnett, op. cit.
10. Roger Ricklefs, "Single-Mindedness: Firms Become Willing—or Eager—to Hire Divorced Executives," *The Wall Street Journal,* May 18, 1978.
11. Liontos, op. cit.
12. ACYF Media Tip Sheet, U.S. Department of Health, Education, and Welfare: Administration for Children, Youth, and Families, Number 26-79-J, Washington, D.C.
13. Marty Meitus, "Two Career Household Extra Drain on Energy," *Rocky Mountain News,* April 30, 1981.
14. John M. Drescher, *If I Were Starting My Family Again* (Nashville: Abingdon, 1979).
15. Jerry M. Lewis, address in San Antonio, Texas.
16. Linda Konner, "From Brotherly (and Sisterly) 'Love,'" *WeightWatchers Magazine,* May 1981.
17. Grant, op. cit.
18. ACYF, op. cit.
19. Curran, "Talks with Parents," op. cit.
20. Gary Warner, "Little-league Sports Can Be Immoral," *U.S. Catholic,* May 1981. Reprinted with permission from *U.S. Catholic,* published by Claretian Publications, 221 W. Madison, Chicago, Ill. 60606.
21. J. Sebastian Sinisi, "He Coaches Winners: With Class, Character," *The Denver Post,* November 25, 1979.
22. Liontos, op. cit.
23. Ibid.
24. Susan Fogg, "Skip TV, Dad, Baby Likes Your Attention," *The Denver Post,* March 22, 1981.

Chapter 8: Fostering Responsibility
1. Curran, op. cit.
2. Joseph Procaccini and Mark Kiefaber, *Parent Burnout: How to Rekindle the Fire* (New York: Doubleday, 1982).
3. LeShan, op. cit.
4. Elisabeth Kieffer, "The Latchkey Kids: How Are They Doing?" *Family Circle,* February 24, 1981.
5. Judi Bailey, "So Homework Is Your Problem?" *Marriage and Family Living,* September 1980.
6. Ann McFeatters, "American Family Changing, but Breakup a Myth," *Rocky Mountain News,* April 10, 1980.
7. LeShan, op. cit.
8. Ellen Peck, "How to Be a Happy Parent," *Family Circle,* September 27, 1978.
9. Madonna Kolbenschlag, *Kiss Sleeping Beauty Good-bye* (New York: Doubleday, 1979).
10. LeShan, op. cit.

11. Mark D. Frank, "Child's Work Role in Family Limited," *The Denver Post,* May 3, 1981.
12. William H. Crosby, "When Friends or Patients Ask About Problem Children," *Journal of the American Medical Association,* January 12, 1979.

Chapter 9: Teaching Morals
1. Robert Coles, "What Makes Children Grow Up Good?" An interview conducted by Edward Wakin, *U.S. Catholic,* August 1979. Reprinted with permission from *U.S. Catholic,* published by Claretian Publications, 221 W. Madison, Chicago, Ill. 60606.
2. Ibid.
3. Curran, op. cit.
4. Charles E. Schaefer, "Raising Children by Old-Fashioned Parent Sense," *Children Today,* November-December 1978.
5. Coles, op. cit.
6. Ibid.
7. Hauerwas, op. cit.
8. Coles, op. cit.

Chapter 10: Enjoying Traditions
1. Hauerwas, op. cit.
2. Alex Haley, "The Joy of Reunions," *Families,* Fall 1980.
3. Peck, op. cit.
4. Hauerwas, op. cit.
5. Haley, op. cit.
6. Lillian Africano, "The Importance of Grandparents," *Woman's Day,* November 25, 1980.
7. Jane Howard, *Families* (New York: Simon and Schuster, 1978).
8. Haley, op. cit.
9. James Dobson, "Focus on Family," tape series (Waco, Texas: Word Incorporated, 1978).
10. Christina Robb, "Hope: the Renewable Christmas Option," *The Denver Post,* December 21, 1980.
11. Africano, op. cit.

Chapter 11: Sharing Religion
1. Stinnett, op. cit.
2. George Gallup, Jr., "Emerging Trend Newsletter," Princeton, Volume 1, November 4, April 1979.
3. Coles, op. cit.
4. Ibid.
5. John Westerhoff III, *Will Our Children Have Faith?* (New York: Seabury, 1976).
6. Raymond H. Potvin, Dean R. Hoge, and Hart M. Nelsen, "Religion and

American Youth," The Boys Town Center for the Study of Youth Development and The Catholic University of America, Washington, D.C., 1976.

7. Stuart Haskins, "Worshiping the Family," privately published paper, May 11, 1980.

8. "Pastors Top Laity in Finding Answers," *The Arizona Daily Star,* Tucson, May 10, 1980.

9. Research Analysis Corporation Poll reported in *The Boston Globe,* August 11, 1980.

10. Robert and Diane Nicholson, "Praying with Your Spouse," *Marriage and Family Living,* September 1980.

11. Coles, op. cit.

12. Hauerwas, op. cit.

13. Walter F. Sullivan, "Marriage and Family Life: A Pastoral Letter by Bishop Walter F. Sullivan," Richmond, Virginia.

14. Annette Hollander, *How to Help Your Child Have a Spiritual Life: A Parent's Guide to Inner Development* (New York: A&W Publishers, 1980).

15. Kaye, op. cit.

16. Gail Sheehy, *Passages* (New York: Dutton, 1974).

Chapter 12: Respecting Privacy

1. Jerry M. Lewis, address in San Antonio, Texas.

2. ACYF Media Tip Sheet, U.S. Department of Health, Education, and Welfare: Administration for Children, Youth, and Families, Number 35-81, Washington, D.C.

3. Howard Halpern, *No Strings Attached: A Guide to a Better Relationship with Your Grown-Up Child* (New York: Simon and Schuster, 1980).

4. ACYF Media Tip Sheet, U.S. Department of Health, Education, and Welfare: Administration for Children, Youth, and Families, Number 25-79-Ma, Washington, D.C.

5. Jerry M. Lewis, address in San Antonio, Texas.

6. Dava Sobel, *Time Alone Boosts Teenagers' Spirits,* New York Times' News Service, 1980.

7. Halpern, op. cit.

8. Ibid.

Chapter 13: Valuing Service

1. Rosemary Haughton, *Origins,* Volume 5, August 28, 1975, NC Documentary Service, Washington, D.C.

2. David Thomas, "Simplicity: Frontier of the Spirit," *Marriage and Family Living,* May 1981.

3. Maya Pines, "Good Samaritans at Age Two?" *Psychology Today,* June 1979.

4. Ibid.

5. Ibid.

6. Thomas, op. cit.

7. Peck, op. cit.

8. Jerry M. Lewis, address in San Antonio, Texas.
9. Thomas, op. cit.
10. Dobson, op. cit.

Chapter 14: Getting Help
1. Stinnett, op. cit.
2. Carol Krucoff, "Need 'Space'? Don't Wed, Have Kids," *The Denver Post,* May 29, 1981.
3. Ibid.
4. Jerry M. Lewis, address in San Antonio, Texas.
5. Krucoff, op. cit.
6. Jerry M. Lewis, address in San Antonio, Texas.
7. Don Branning, "Healthy Families to Be Book Subject," *Gazette Telegraph,* Colorado Springs, December 5, 1980.
8. Ibid.
9. UPI, "'60 Minutes' Show Upsets Suicide-Prevention Forces," *Rocky Mountain News,* November 5, 1980.
10. Krucoff, op. cit.

Sources

The Alternative Celebrations Catalogue. Forest Park, Georgia: Alternatives, 1978.

The American Family: Current Perspectives. Six tapes from The Harvard Seminar Series. Cambridge: Harvard University Press, 1981.

Anthony, E.J., and Benedek, T., eds. *Parenthood: Its Psychology and Psychopathology.* Boston: Little, Brown, 1970.

Aries, P. *Centuries of Childhood: A Social History of Family Life.* New York: Knopf, 1962.

Barbeau, C. *Delivering the Male.* Minneapolis: Winston Press, 1982.

Barbeau, C. *Joy of Marriage.* Minneapolis: Winston Press, 1980.

Barbeau, C. *The Male Condition.* Six tapes. Cincinnati: St. Anthony Messenger Press, 1975.

Berman, E. *The New-Fashioned Parent: How to Make Your Family Style Work.* New York: Prentice-Hall, 1980.

Bettelheim, B. *The Uses of Enchantment.* New York: Random House, 1977.

Brazelton, T. *Toddlers and Parents.* New York: Delacourt, 1974.

Briggs, D.C. *Your Child's Self-Esteem: The Key to His Life.* New York: Doubleday, 1970.

Bronfenbrenner, U. *Two Worlds of Childhood: U.S. and U.S.S.R.* London: Allen & Unwin, 1970.

Cable, M. *The Little Darlings: A History of Child Rearing in America.* New York: Scribners, 1975.

Calhoun, J.A., et al. *The Status of Children, Youth, and Families 1979.* U.S. Department of Health and Human Services, 1980.

Clarke, J.I. *Self-Esteem: A Family Affair.* Minneapolis: Winston Press, 1978.

Coigney, V. *Children Are People Too.* New York: William Morrow, 1975.

Coles, R. *Twelve to Sixteen: Early Adolescence.* New York: Norton, 1973.

Curran, D. *Family: A Church Challenge for the '80s.* Minneapolis: Winston Press, 1980.

Curran, D. *In the Beginning There Were the Parents.* Minneapolis: Winston Press, 1978.

Curran, D. *Who, Me Teach My Child Religion?* Minneapolis: Winston Press, 1982.

DeBeauvoir, S. *The Second Sex.* New York: Bantam, 1952.

DeGidio, S. *Sharing Faith in the Family.* Mystic, Conn.: Twenty-third Publications, 1980.

Dobson, J. *Preparing for Adolescence.* New York: Bantam, 1980.

Dreikurs, R. *Challenges of Parenthood.* New York: Dutton, 1979.

Dreikurs, R., and Soltz, V. *Children: the Challenge.* New York: Dutton, 1964.

Drescher, J.M. *If I Were Starting My Family Again.* Nashville: Abingdon, 1979.

Eimers, R., and Aitchison, R. *Effective Parents/Responsible Children.* New York: McGraw-Hill, 1977.

Erikson, Erik. *Childhood and Society.* New York: Norton, 1963.

Erikson, Erik. *Identity, Youth and Crisis.* New York: Norton, 1968.

Farb, P., and Armelagos, G. *Consuming Passions: The Anthropology of Eating.* Boston: Houghton Mifflin, 1980.

Fishel, E. *Sisters: Love and Rivalry Inside the Family and Beyond.* New York: Bantam, 1980.

Ford, E.E., and Englund, S. *Permanent Love: Practical Steps to a Lasting Relationship*. Minneapolis: Winston Press, 1979.

Francoeur, R.T. "The Sexual Revolution: Will Hard Times Turn Back the Clock?" *The Futurist* XIV, No. 2, April 1980.

Friedan, B. *The Feminine Mystique*. New York: Dell, 1963.

Galinsky, E. *Between Generations: The Six Stages of Parenthood*. New York: Times Books, 1981.

Ginnott, H.G. *Between Parent and Child*. New York: Macmillan, 1965.

Goodman, E. *Close to Home*. New York: Fawcett, 1981.

Gordon, T. *Parent Effectiveness Training*. New York: Peter H. Wyden, 1971.

Greeley, A.M. *The Young Catholic Family: Religious Images and Marriage Fulfillment*. Chicago: Thomas More Press, 1980.

Green, M. *Fathering: A New Look at the Creative Art of Being a Father*. New York: McGraw-Hill, 1976.

Greiff, B.S., and Munter, P. *Tradeoffs: Executive, Family and Organizational Life*. New York: New American Library, 1980.

Halpern, H. *Cutting Loose: An Adult Guide to Coming to Terms with Your Parents*. New York: Bantam, 1978.

Halpern, H. *No Strings Attached*. New York: Simon and Schuster, 1980.

Hamachek, D. *Encounters with Self*. New York: Holt, 1978.

Handy, E.S.C., and Pukui, M.K. *The Polynesian Family System in Ka-u, Hawaii*. Rutland, Vt.: Charles E. Tuttle, 1972.

Heffner, E. *Mothering: How Women Can Enjoy a New Productive Relationship with Their Children — and a New Image of Themselves*. New York: Doubleday, 1980.

Herzog, E., and Sudia, C. *Boys in Fatherless Families*. Washington, D.C.: U.S. Department of Health, Education, and Welfare, 1970.

Hollander, A. *How to Help Your Child Have a Spiritual Life: A Parent's Guide to Inner Development*. New York: A&W Publishers, 1980.

Howard, J. *Families*. New York: Simon and Schuster, 1978.

Johnson, W. *Muddling Toward Frugality: A Blueprint for Survival in the 1980's*. Boulder, Colo.: Shambhala, 1979.

Kaye, E. *Crosscurrents: Children, Families, and Religion*. New York: Potter, 1980.

Keniston, K., and The Carnegie Council on Children. *All Our Children: The American Family Under Pressure*. New York: Harcourt, 1977.

Kennedy, E. *If You Really Knew Me Would You Still Like Me?* Niles, Ill.: Argus, 1975.

Keyes, R. *Is There Life After High School?* New York: Warner, 1977.

Kolbenschlag, M. *Kiss Sleeping Beauty Good-bye*. New York: Doubleday, 1979.

Kress, R. *Whither Womankind? The Humanity of Women*. St. Meinrad, Ind.: Abbey Press, 1975.

Lakein, *How to Get Control of Your Time and Your Life*. New York: New American Library, 1973.

Larrick, N. *A Parent's Guide to Children's Reading*. New York: Bantam, 1975.

Leichter, H. *The Family as Educator.* New York: Columbia University Teachers College Press, 1974.

LeMasters, E.E. *Parents in Modern America: A Sociological Analysis.* Homewood, Ill.: Dorsey, 1974.

Lerman, S. *Parent Awareness: Positive Parenting for the 1980's.* Minneapolis: Winston Press, 1980.

Levinson, D.J., et al. *The Seasons of a Man's Life.* New York: Ballantine, 1978.

Lewis, J.M. *How's Your Family?* New York: Brunner/Mazel, 1979.

Lewis, J.M., et al. *No Single Thread: Psychological Health in Family Systems.* New York: Brunner/Mazel, 1976.

Lewis, J.M. *To Be a Therapist: The Teaching and Learning.* New York: Brunner/Mazel, 1978.

Linder, S.B. *The Harried Leisure Class.* New York: Columbia University Press, 1970.

Listening to America's Families: The Report to President, Congress, and Families of the Nation. Washington, D.C.: The White House Conference on Families, 1980.

Macpherson, M.C. *The Family Years: A Guide to Positive Parenting.* Minneapolis: Winston Press, 1981.

Maslow, A.H. *Toward a Psychology of Being.* Princeton: Van Nostrand, 1962.

Masnick, G., and Bane, M.J. *The Nation's Families: 1960-1990.* Cambridge: Harvard University Press, 1980.

McBride, A.B. *Living with Contradictions: A Married Feminist.* New York: Harper, 1977.

McGinnis, K. and J. *Parenting for Peace and Justice.* New York: Orbis, 1981.

Montagu, A., and Matson, F. *The Human Connection.* New York: McGraw-Hill, 1979.

National Elementary Principal Magazine: The American Family. Part I, Vol. 55, No. 5, May/June 1976. Part II, No. 6, July/August 1976.

Neal, M.A. *A Socio-Theology of Letting Go.* New York: Paulist Press, 1977.

Okun, B., and Rappaport, L.J. *Working with Families: An Introduction to Family Therapy.* Boston: Duxbury, 1980.

Pappas, M. *Prime Time for Families.* Minneapolis: Winston Press, 1980.

Peck, E. *The Baby Trap.* New York: Bernard Geis, 1975.

Polk, L., and LeShan, E. *The Incredible Television Machine.* New York: Macmillan, 1977.

Rappaport, R., Rappaport, R.N., and Stelitz, Z. *Fathers, Mothers, and Society: Perspectives on Parenting.* New York: Random House, 1980.

Rhodes, S., and Wilson, J. *Surviving Family Life: The Seven Crises of Living Together.* New York: Putnam, 1981.

Robertiello, R.C. *Hold Them Very Close, Then Let Them Go.* New York: Dial, 1975.

Salk, L. *What Every Child Would Like His Parents to Know.* New York: Warner, 1973.

Satir, V. *Peoplemaking.* Palo Alto, Cal.: Science and Behavior Books, 1972.

Schaef, A.W. *Women's Reality.* Minneapolis: Winston Press, 1981.

Shorter, E. *The Making of the Modern Family*. New York: Basic Books, 1975.
Spock, B. *Bringing Up Children in a Difficult Time*. London: Bodley Head, 1974.
Stinnett, N., et al, eds. *Building Family Strengths*. Lincoln, Neb.: University of
    Nebraska Press, 1979.
Stinnett, N., et al, eds. *Family Strengths: Positive Models for Family Life*. Lincoln,
    Neb.: University of Nebraska Press, 1980.
Strassfield, S., and Green, K. *The Jewish Family Book*. New York: Bantam, 1981.
Strengthening Families Through Informal Support Systems: A Wingspread Report.
    Racine, Wis.: The Johnson Foundation, 1979.
Talbot, N., ed. *Raising Children in Modern America*. Boston: Little, Brown, 1976.
Toffler, A. *The Third Wave*. New York: William Morrow, 1980.
Westerhoff, J.H., III. *Bringing Up Children in the Christian Faith*. Minneapolis:
    Winston Press, 1980.
Westerhoff, J.H., III. *Will Our Children Have Faith?* New York: Seabury, 1976.
Yankelovich, D. *New Rules: Searching for Self-Fulfillment in a World Turned Up-
    side Down*. New York: Random House, 1981.
Yankelovich, Skelly, and White. *Raising Children in a Changing Society*. The
    General Mills American Family Report. Minneapolis: General Mills, 1977.
Zerof, H.G. *Finding Intimacy: The Art of Happiness in Living Together*. Min-
    neapolis: Winston Press, 1978.

Index

A

A.C. Nielsen Company, 39
Adolescence, 48, 72, 86, 97,
    105-16, 139, 141, 146-8, 168,
    179, 195, 197-8, 214, 227,
    232, 233-42, 261
Affirmation, 59-77, 118, 225
Africano, Lillian, 204, 214
Alcoholics Anonymous, 32, 182,
    264
Alcott, Louisa May, 231
*All Our Children: The American
    Family Under Pressure*, 23,
    123
Alternatives Catalogue, 251
Alternatives movement, 251
Altruism, 245-7
American Academy of
    Psychotherapists, 242
American Civil Liberties Union,
    89
American Council on Education,
    15
Anatomy of an Illness, 131
Arguments, family, 48, 53, 54,
    67, 175
Armelagos, George, 57, 58
Armoury, Robert, 263

B

Babysitting, 102
Bailey, Judi, 173
Balance of interaction, 26, 117-9,
    133-44
Barbeau, Clayton, 255

Bateson, Gregory, 255
Be Not Afraid, 248
Behavior, 48, 83, 92-97, 233-42
Benson, Stella, 117
Benton, Robert, 41, 136
Berman, Eleanor, 171
Bernreuter, Claire, 211, 215
Bettelheim, Bruno, 75, 257-8,
    260, 264
*Between Generations: The Six
    Stages of Parenthood*, 82
Bible, 5, 185, 226
Bombeck, Erma, 85, 113
Bonding, 99-103, 159
Bosco, Antoinette, 13
Boy Scouts, 32, 149-51
Boys Town Center for the Study
    of Youth Development, 221
Brazelton, T. Berry, 17
Briggs, Dorothy Corkille, 62
Bronfenbrenner, Urie, 12, 17, 27,
    28, 62, 67
Bureau of Labor, 137

C

Calloway, Norman, 41, 236
Capel, John, 232
Caplow, Theodore, 13
Carnegie Council on Children,
    23
Cavanaugh, Michael, 64
Center for Pastoral Ministry, 40
Chemical dependency, 69, 243
Chesser, Barbara, 18
Chores, 173, 180
Christian Science Monitor, 39

Church, 60, 77, 119, 138, 186-7, 217-30, 248-9, 255
Clanship, 199-202, 207
Claudel, Paul, 245
Coles, Robert, 17, 185, 192-3, 197, 218, 219, 224
Collier, Peter, 1
Colorado, 12
Communication, 31-58, 67, 117, 188
Competition, 243
Conflict, 32, 44
Continuing Passions: The Anthropology of Eating, 57
Cooperating Family, The, 171
Copley News Service, 84
Couple Communication, 32, 41, 188
"Couple Life," 118, 127, 136, 137, 156
Cousins, Norman, 131
Covington, Stuart, 46
Crosscurrents, 227
Csikszentmihalyi, Mihaly, 241
Curran, Dolores, 27, 84, 148, 166, 187
Cutting Loose, 242

D

"Dear Abby," 85
Death, 208
De Frain, John, 18
Denver Post, 155
Discipline, 231, 234
Disrespect, 93-97

Divorce, 82, 89, 113, 133, 155, 162, 193-4
Dobson, James, 210, 254
Dreikurs, Rudolph, 90
Drescher, John M., 139
Duhl, Leonard, 63
Dyer, Wayne W., 93

E

Education, 5, 10, 75-77
Educators, 32, 63, 138, 169, 235, 248
Einstein, Albert, 80
Empathy, 43, 246
Empty nest, 233
Encounters with the Self, 74
Enlightened simplicity, 244
Erikson, Erik, 99-101, 113
Ethnic, 215
Ewald, Kurt, 17

F

Faith, 220-5, 226-9
Families, 59, 204, 257
Families Anonymous, Inc. (FA), 182
Family: attitudes, 83, 261; calendar, 58, 122, 126, 146-63; coalitions, 139-144; disagreement, 83; economics, 4, 8, 64; functions, 4-9; hospitality, 207, 253; military, 206; mood, 71, 173, 175; personality, 82, 210; play and humor, 125-32; problems, 119,

257-65; rootedness, 223; sense of, 119, 199-216; service to others, 243-56; stories, 202-4; strengths, 16-17; stress, 120, 128; style, 83, 263; support systems, 264; systems approach, 259; table, 55-58, 68, 119; time, 117-63; traditional structure, 4, 15, 33, 35, 156; trust, 99-116, 118, 141

Family: A Church Challenge of the 80's, 17

Family Research Institute, 259

"Fast Folk," 117, 144

Fathering, 14, 41, 46, 66, 101, 133, 139, 158

Feelings, 32, 43, 47, 173, 261

Figley, Charles, 259

Fischer, Henry, 69

Focus on Families, 210, 254

Fogg, Susan, 158

Freud, Sigmund, 245

Friedan, Betty, 14

Frost, Robert, 245

Fry, William, 132

G

Galinsky, Ellen, 82

Gallup, George, Jr., 217

Gallup Poll, 38

Gallup Youth Survey, 72, 225

Gibran, Kahlil, 241

Gittleson, Natalie, 45

Goals, 59

Golden rule, 186

Goodman, Ellen, 199

Gordon, Thomas, 3

Grandparents, 102, 203-4, 209, 214, 267

Grant, Louis T., 117, 144

Guilt, 28, 94, 123, 126, 128, 135, 150, 153, 156, 168, 174, 182

H

Haley, Alex, 199-200, 202, 208

Halpern, Howard, 233, 241-2

Hamachek, Don, 74

Hareven, Tamara, 174

Harpers, 117

Harris, Patricia, 10

Harris Survey, 15

Haskins, Stuart C., 222

Hauerwas, Stanley, 103, 113, 197, 199, 202, 224

Haughton, Rosemary, 244

Hawaii, 54, 202

Hedonism, 60

"He's Losing My Faith," 84

Hinckley, John, 12

Hollander, Annette, 226

Homework, 173

Homosexuality, 88

Hoover-Ogburn Commission, 10

Hope, 71

Howard, Jane, 59, 204, 257

Humor, 125-32

I

Identity, 48

If I Were Starting My Family Again, 139
Impassivity, 46
Independence, 47, 233-6, 241-2
Individuality, 80, 84, 90
Infidelity, 100, 103
Insecurity, 99-103
Institutions, 27, 74, 124, 137, 150, 252
Interfaith Task Force, 249-50
Interruptions, 52
Intimacy, 10, 14, 32, 33, 34, 35, 60, 103-4, 110, 118, 137, 174
Is There Life After High School?, 75

J

Jourbert, Joseph, 85
Judaism, 216, 224, 253
Jungian, 87
Justice, Blair, 262, 263

K

Kaye, Evelyn, 16, 227
Keniston, Ken, 17, 23, 123
Kennicott, Carol, 33
Keyes, Ralph, 75
Kieffer, Elizabeth, 171
Kinship, 199-202, 207
Kiss Sleeping Beauty Goodbye, 178
Kohlberg, Lawrence, 195
Kolbenschlag, Madonna, 178
Kübler-Ross, Elizabeth, 192
Kramer vs. Kramer, 41

L

Language, 49
Larson, Reed, 241
Latchkey kids, 171
Legere, Thomas E., 80
Leisure time, 28, 60, 144-57
LeShan, Eda, 15, 165, 168, 170, 176, 178
Letting go, 233-4, 241-2
Lewis, Jerry M., 17, 31, 35, 43, 47, 52, 71, 91, 103, 140, 231, 238, 254, 259, 260
Lewis, Sinclair, 33
Lindroth, Joan B., 70
Liontos, Demetri, 118, 127, 136, 137, 156
Liontos, Lynn Balster, 118, 127, 136, 137, 156
Listening, 31-58
Logical consequences, 90
Love, 24, 100, 103
Lowe, Janet, 84
Lutheran Church in America, 220
Lying, 108

M

Mace, David R., 31, 44, 59
Main Street, 33
Manno, Bruno, 34
Margolis, Diane Rothbard, 119
Marriage and Family Living, 31, 34, 46, 70, 173, 224
Marriage Encounter, 32, 188, 254

Maslow, Abraham, 10
Materialism, 60
McCall's, 34, 45
McCarroll, Ann, 39, 42
Mead, Margaret, 142, 267
Meeks, John, 48
Mencken, H.L., 129
Menninger, Karl, 191
Mobility, 68, 92, 112, 212
Montagu, Ashley, 7, 14, 100
Montessori, 194
Moore, Kristin A., 267
Moral majority, 187
Morality, 185-97, 223
Mother Teresa, 133
Mothering, 65, 66, 99-103,
    165-9, 177
Munson, Harold, 180

N

National Institute of Mental
    Health, 245
National Institute on Child
    Health and Human
    Development, 159
National Parenting for Peace and
    Justice Network, 251
National Study of Family
    Strengths, 18, 31, 59, 117,
    133, 217, 257
Nicholson, Robert and Diane,
    224
No Single Thread, 35
No Strings Attached, 242
Nonverbal messages, 42

O

Offit, Avodah K., 34

P

Parent Awareness, 32
Parent Effectiveness Training, 3,
    32
Parental: coalitions, 139-44;
    consistency, 74; cop-outs, 108;
    disappointments, 82-83;
    letting go, 242; satisfaction,
    252; self-esteem, 62-63; self-
    respect, 93-95; support, 69-71
Parents Anonymous, 32
Pascoe, Jack, 63
Passages, 228
Patriotism, 74
Peck, Ellen, 177, 252
Pederson, Frank, 159
Peer group, 86
Perfectionism, 175, 258
Permissiveness, 232
Piaget, Jean, 194
Pilgrim's Progress, 5
Pines, Maya, 245-7
Play, 125-32
Power, 35
Praise, 70, 72, 180-1
Pressure, 69-71
Priestley, J.B., 79
Prioritizing, 130, 148-57
Privacy, 119, 231-42
Problem-solving, 259
Problems, 119, 135, 257-65
Procaccini, Joseph, 168

Psychiatric Institute of
  Montgomery County, 48
Psychology Today, 245

R

Racism, 88
Rapaport, Rhona, 17
Rapaport, Robert, 17
Reagan, President, 13
"Rearing Responsible
  Children," 165
Recognition, 179
Reconciliation, 52
Recreation, 124
Regeneration, 267
Relational, 10, 33
Relationships, 34, 35, 59, 117,
  118, 141-3, 156-8, 168, 178,
  200, 233-4
Religion, 4, 9, 47, 77, 83, 119,
  217-30
Research Analysis Corporation of
  Boston, 223
Respect: 79-98, 118; for others,
  88; for privacy, 233-42; self-,
  86-88; 93
Responsibility, 26, 72, 97, 106,
  119, 150, 165-84
Right and wrong, 28, 119, 185-97
Rituals, 53, 199-216
Robb, Christina, 211
Ross, Helgola G., 86, 142
Rules, 234-7
Ryan, Sally, 235

S

Saint-Exupéry, Antoine De, 243,
  256
Salk, Lee, 56
Sandburg, Carl, 267
Sanford, Linda Tschirhart, 73,
  82
Satir, Virginia, 17, 31
Schaefer, Charles E., 191
Schlafly, Phyllis, 14
School, 75, 138
Schweitzer, Albert, 253
Scouting, 32, 149-51, 154
Self-esteem, 36, 62, 63, 70, 73,
  75, 86, 94, 108, 167, 169, 172
Sensitivity, 49, 51
Service to others, 119, 243-55
Sex, 24, 104
Sexual roles, 33, 35, 156, 166,
  177-8, 237
Shanahan, Louise, 160
Shea, John, 204
Sheehy, Gail, 228
Shoplifting, 96-97, 120
Shorter, Edward, 17
Siblings, 43, 67, 71, 86, 120,
  141-3, 159, 179
Sierra Club, 84
Silence, 44
Single parents, 26, 82, 113, 119,
  146, 162, 193-4
Skelly, Florence, 57
Slater, Philip, 243
Staines, Graham, 137, 146
Status, 5, 10
Stinnett, Nick, 18, 131, 133, 257
Stollack, Gary, 66

Stress, 120, 128, 243, 261
Suicide, 69, 263
Sullivan, Walter F., 225
Superachievers, 69-70
Support systems, 59, 264
Surgeon General's Report, 38
Survey instrument, 20
Survey respondents, 19, 23
Systematic Training for Effective
    Parenting, 32

T

Table time, 55, 58, 68, 119
"Talks with Parents," 27, 148,
    166, 187
Tanney, Joseph B., 201
Tarr, Jim, 32
Television, 32, 36, 57, 108, 161-2
Thomas, David, 244, 252, 254
Timberlawn Psychiatric Center,
    17, 31
Time, 117-63, 241
Toffler, Alvin, 102
Tolstoy, Leo, 3, 56
Touching, 72
Traditions, 73, 119, 199-216
Traits of the healthy family, 23,
    25
Transactional Analysis, 32
Trust, 99-116, 118, 141
Tucker, Jim Guy, 133
Tutko, Thomas, 154

U

U.S. Catholic, 154-5, 185, 224

V

Values, 185-97, 267
Values clarification, 38
Vandalism, 97, 120, 180
Vanier, Jean, 248
Voluntary organizations, 32, 138,
    155
Volunteerism, 125, 138, 155,
    254-5

W

Wahl, Charles William, 114
Wakin, Edward, 185
Wall Street Journal, 133
War and Peace, 56
WeightWatchers, 32
Weiss, Helen, 75
Weiss, Martin, 75
Weiss, Robert T., 119
Wellness, 12, 131
Westerhoff, John, III, 220, 227
Wetzel, Jodi, 137
Whatever Became of Sin?, 192
White House Conference on
    Families, 12, 27, 38, 133, 174
Who, Me Teach My Child
    Religion?, 84
Wilczak, Paul F., 40
Wilkins, Joan Anderson, 37
Womanhood, 65, 121, 143, 171
Woman's Day, 117
Work, 126, 127, 134-8, 143, 146,
    156, 171
World War II, 121

Y

Yankelovich, Skelly and White, 57

Yarrow, Marian Radke, 245

Your Child's Self-Esteem, 62

Youth leagues, 81, 93, 138-9, 148, 151-5, 255